CHUCK

'The best of this year's blockbusters'
Glenn Moore, *Independent*

'Gascoigne the player deserves to be remembered. And *Gazza* the book deserves to be read'
Tom Watt, *Mail on Sunday*

'A rattlingly good read' John Rawling, *Guardian*

'A moving book about a tragic figure in a wonderful if tainted game' Ray Connolly, *Daily Mail*

'Hilarious, terrifying and touching' *Daily Express*

'A very honest book' *Daily Telegraph*

'One of the scariest football books ever printed'
D.J. Taylor, *New Statesman*

'[Gascoigne] deserves credit for refusing to gloss over his misdeeds' *Liverpool Echo*

'A sad, reflective, often very funny tale'
Birmingham Post

'Painfully honest, but compelling' *York Evening Press*

'Gazza writes with honesty and sincerity'
Scotland on Sunday

Paul Gascoigne was born in Gateshead in 1967. He made his professional debut for Newcastle United at 17, before moving to Tottenham Hotspur in 1988 for a record £2 million transfer. After the 1990 World Cup he became one of the greatest stars in the game, and moved to Lazio in 1992 after a career-threatening injury. In 1995 he returned to Britain to play for Rangers, then Middlesbrough, Everton and Burnley. Following a brief spell in China, with Gansu Tianma, he became player-coach of Boston United from July to October 2004.

He made his debut for England in 1988 and was a key member of the sides that reached the semi-finals of the 1990 World Cup and Euro 96. In total he won 57 caps and scored ten goals for England.

Hunter Davies, who worked with Paul Gascoigne on the writing of his autobiography, is one of the most distinguished sports writers and biographers in the country and the author of more than 30 books. *The Glory Game* is a footballing classic that is still in print almost 30 years since publication. His other football books include *Boots, Balls and Haircuts*, *The Fan*, and biographies of Dwight Yorke and Joe Kinnear. He is also the authorised biographer of the Beatles. He lives with his wife in the Lake District and in London.

GAZZA
My Story

Paul Gascoigne
with Hunter Davies

headline

First published in 2004
by HEADLINE BOOK PUBLISHING

First published in paperback in 2005
by HEADLINE BOOK PUBLISHING

11

ISBN 978-0-7472-6818-5

Typeset by Palimpsest Book Production Limited, Polmont, Stirlingshire
Text design by Ben Cracknell Studios
Career statistics supplied by Hunter Davies and Jack Rollin
Printed and bound in Great Britain by
Clays Ltd, St Ives plc

Headline's policy is to use papers that are natural,
renewable and recyclable products and made from wood grown
in sustainable forests. The logging and manufacturing processes are
expected to conform to the environmental regulations of the country of origin.

HEADLINE BOOK PUBLISHING
A division of Hodder Headline
338 Euston Road
London NW1 3BH

www.headline.co.uk
www.hodderheadline.com

www.paulgascoigne.biz

CONTENTS

ACKNOWLEDGEMENTS

Thanks and then thanks to my mam and dad who have supported me throughout my life and career, even when things were bad, and to all the others, too many to name, who have stuck by me through thick and thin. And to Hunter Davies who did my head in, asking so many questions, but has done a fantastic job. Cheers.

> This is the third thing I've won in two years. I won against alcohol and drugs. The third is the book award. This one is for life – I just hope I can make sure the other two are as well.
>
> *Paul Gascoigne on receiving his award for Sports Book of the Year at the British Book Awards, 20 April 2005*

SUMMER 2003

I've just made a chart of my life. It's six feet long and three feet wide. That's the chart, not me. I've never been three feet wide. Not yet. It's on brown paper, written in white chalk, plus coloured crayons for the major problems I've faced, such as BEER, WINE, VODKA, COCAINE, MORPHINE, PARANOID, ANXIETY.

Across the chart I've recorded all the key events, from the beginning, being born, right up to today, thirty-six years later, and I hope I've got most of the dates right. Always Fighting at School, Professional at Newcastle, Steven Dying, World Cup, Nine Twitches, Meet Sheryl, Broke Arm, Spurs, Broken Kneecap, Lazio, Rangers, IRA Threat, Fight with Sheryl, China . . . oh, loads of stuff, all the things that have happened to me, all the awful, shitty horrible things. It's called PATH TO RECOVERY.

I started working on it in China, making lists of all the memories that came into my head; memories I didn't really want to come into my head, but they're there and won't go away.

Then, in Arizona, at the clinic, I wrote it out neatly on the brown paper. It was part of the therapy, but I'd started to do it anyway, for my own sake, to confront the terrible things I've done, to stand back and look at myself, to tell the absolute truth and not avoid anything.

It wasn't a picnic, being in the clinic. It's miles from anywhere, out in the desert, and they take everything away from you. You don't have any money, any mobile phone. They don't allow you aftershave or even mouthwash. Alcoholics, when they're desperate, will drink any old shit. I'm now admitting I'm an alcoholic. I'm proud to admit it, to say I'm an alcoholic. That's what you have to do. I'm going to AA meetings. Three a week, if I can make it. And I have a counsellor I'm going to keep on seeing.

I've got an illness, I realise that now. It's not alcoholism, not really – that's more a result than a cause. What I've been suffering from all my life is a disease in my head. I'm still scared of dying, that's part of it. If I have a sore eye, I'm convinced I'm going blind. If I've got a twitch, I panic about it, and it gets worse. I get obsessed about the simplest, silliest things, just like many children do, wanting things in exact rows, right numbers, proper places. Most people grow out of it and forget it ever bothered them. If, of course, they ever grow up.

At this very moment I can feel a new twitch. God knows where it's come from. I can't stop myself pulling the flesh on my stomach every five minutes, over and over, for no reason. It's as if I fear my stomach will disappear if I don't check it's there. I tell myself it's to make sure I'm not getting fat, but obviously that's not something I need to check every five minutes. Even I don't get fat that quickly. Besides, at present I've hardly got any stomach – I'm the thinnest I've been for years. But there's no logic to these sorts of anxieties.

We were four to a room in Arizona. People came and went. All sorts of people. A few were sportsmen. One guy was a brilliant frisbee player. He was amazing. You are involved in sessions all day. I was up at 5.30 every morning and on the go till 10 at night.

I was in for thirty-three days. I'd been there before, a couple of years earlier, and I was so busy helping others that I didn't concentrate on myself enough. Now I've got all the books and I've got all the tools. I know the questions to ask myself. Was life good beforehand? No, it wasn't. Getting depressed is no fun, not with all the panic attacks. Getting drunk all the time, to escape feeling depressed, now that I did like, no question. That was good. It was a buzz. What I didn't like was afterwards. I didn't like waking up in the morning, not remembering what had happened, feeling ashamed and filthy and guilty, feeling crap. So overall, was life good? No, it fucking wasn't.

I was living a plonky life, being a plonky person, being Gazza instead of being Paul Gascoigne. I got so upset by all the Gazza stuff in the press. People say don't read the papers, but you can't help it. Then I tell myself it doesn't matter what they say, what lies they write, what lies other people give them. But they have the upper hand. They always win. They might pay you a lot of money, and I've had loads from them, but it works against you because if you sign up with one paper the others will turn you over, dig up all the dirt. Then the one that paid you turns against you as well, or runs negative stuff at the same time as the piece they've paid you for. So what do you do? It's a waste of energy worrying what they say, either way. I know that now. All I really have to worry about is waking up each day sober and staying clean.

But that produces another fear. If I stay sober, will I turn into a boring person? I was always fun when I was drinking. That's what I always thought at the time, anyway. It was all a good laugh – the only bad bit was afterwards. Now it feels really good to wake up every morning with a clear head and remember where I've been. But what if the penalty, the by-product, is to become a sensible, dreary, boring twat? We'll see.

I'm supposed to drink only one cup of coffee a day, decaffeinated, and not have any sweets. I have a handful of Jelly Babies in my pocket, just for emergencies, such as now, sitting here in Sheryl's garden, my ex-wife's, thinking back over my life. And no smoking. I was on thirty a day, now I'm down to about twenty. I'll just have one now, to settle me. When I'm sitting comfortably, then I'll begin.

I have the chart spread out in front of me, with all the main incidents, all the horrible, serious ones. I'll also try to recall as many of the fun bits as I can. There were so many hilarious times – at least, I thought they were hilarious. And my mate Jimmy thought so. But the main point, for me, is to get to grips with what started it all, how I got to be like I am; to record everything, however bad, as truthfully as possible. I hope that putting it all down on paper will distance me from these events, and allow me to move on to wherever it is I'm going. Then, with God's help, I'll get some real smiles back. Yes, I believe in God. What else is there?

I'd like to be a child again. I want to be seven, when I had a genuine smile on my face all the time, when I was always happy. Since then my smiles have too often been false, there to try to please other people.

I ended up at the clinic in Arizona because of what happened in China. I'll tell yous about China later, but on the whole, I liked it out there, playing football and doing a bit of coaching. I coached the kids on the field, but off the field I was more like an agent to them, helping them with contracts and deals and advising them on what to do.

I haven't had a drink now for, let's see, three months. Yes, I've been on the wagon before. For even longer periods. But I knew then it wouldn't last. I hope it will this time. Sheryl says I can stay here with her, if I stay sober and sensible. But I don't think I'll get another chance if I fuck this one up.

I've had no panic attacks recently, so that's good.

Jimmy hasn't been to see me, and I haven't been up to the north-east. Shel isn't keen on all that. She says it's where my problems always begin.

So I'm just taking things easy. Playing with the kids, going to the garden centre, having a quiet meal out. When we have friends or Shel's relations over for a barbecue, they are all very good. They don't drink while they're here.

I'm on various tablets, to keep me calm or cheer me up, stop me getting depressed. I did take more than I should the other day – four instead of one – wanting a quick buzz, to feel better immediately, which, of course, was stupid. And I got in a bit of a state last night watching TV. There was a programme showing some lads getting drunk round a bar, falling about, as I used to do, and I couldn't face it. It really upset me. So I went out into the garden. I told my doctor all this, and he says it's a good sign. I wasn't envying them, or wanting to be like them, so it wasn't that I was being tempted back into my old ways. I suppose I was horrified by the sight of other people behaving as I used to behave.

I honestly don't know whether I'll keep this up. I haven't done in the past, so everyone thinks it won't last this time. Shel and I still have arguments over silly things, who said what, who didn't say what. But I'd never hit her again. I've hit nobody since that episode and I won't ever do it again.

She has got a bit tougher with me. All her friends were surprised when they found out I had hit her. They always thought she was a strong person. She thought that herself.

She now realises, she says, that she did fit into the classic pattern of women in this situation – keeping it secret, feeling guilty and ashamed, as if it was her fault, and of course telling herself it was a one-off. She did everything she could to please me. She says.

Now she's got the whip hand. She's mentally tougher than she was; she stands her own ground more. She's pushing me, in a way, just to test me, to see if I'll fail again. I think the children are testing me as well. They are sure it won't last, that I'll get into a rage and be off, as has happened before. I'm not as aggressive and full of anger as I used to be, so that's good. But Shel says if it doesn't work this time, that's it. No way will she put up with any more of what I put her through in the past. I'll be out on my ear.

She wrote all that down, just to remind herself of what things were like. Every time, over the years, I've rung up and pleaded with her to let me come back or help me. She's often read her notes to keep things fresh in her mind. She's not read them lately, which is something. It shows she thinks we might have a chance. I know she loves me. I think. I hope.

Life was easier for her when I wasn't around, but she was lonely and she did miss me. She gets upset when people or newspapers say she's only after me for my money. She does love me – except when I'm being horrible. She has put up with so much from me over all these years that she doesn't want to miss out on the benefits now that I am sober and living sensibly. She has invested a lot, endured a lot, and she doesn't want someone else to enjoy the good Gazza when she's had to suffer the bad Gazza.

It's a lovely day in early summer and the kids are playing in the swimming pool. There's also a tennis court, sauna, lots of stuff. We're going to have a barbecue this evening, when Sheryl's dad comes round.

The garden's looking lovely, Shel is being nice to me, I'm being nice to her – everything is going great. Doing my chart has cleared my head a bit, brought the main events and dramas of my life into focus. So it's the perfect time now to tell you all about my brilliant career. And it has been. No question. Despite everything.

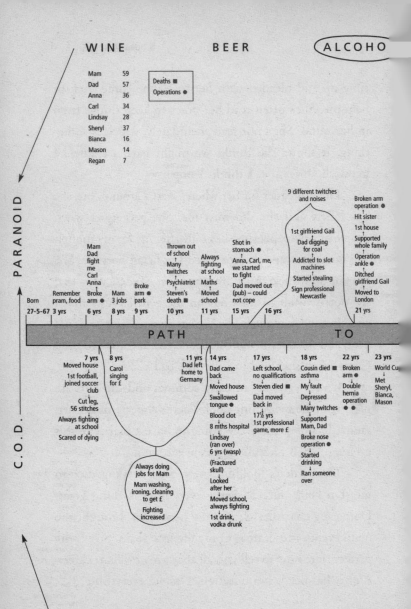

WINE   BEER   (ALCOHO

Mam	59
Dad	57
Anna	36
Carl	34
Lindsay	28
Sheryl	37
Bianca	16
Mason	14
Regan	7

Deaths ■
Operations ●

PARANOID

9 different twitches
and noises

Broken arm
operation ●
↑
Hit sister
↑
1st girlfriend Gail   1st house
↑   ↑
Dad digging   Supported
for coal   whole family
↑   ↑
Addicted to slot   Operation
machines   ankle ●
↑   ↑
Started stealing   Ditched
↑   girlfriend Gail
Sign professional   ↑
Newcastle   Moved to
             London

Mam
Dad
fight
me   Thrown out
Carl   of school   Always
Anna   ↑   fighting   Shot in
        Many   at school   stomach ●
        twitches   ↑   ↑
        ↑   Maths   Anna, Carl, me,
Remember   Psychiatrist   ↑   we started
pram, food   Broke   Mam   Broke   ↑   Moved   to fight   Dad moved out
        arm ●   3 jobs   arm ●   Steven's   school   (pub) – could
Born   park   death ■   not cope

27-5-67   3 yrs   6 yrs   8 yrs   9 yrs   10 yrs   11 yrs   15 yrs   16 yrs   21 yrs

PATH   TO

C.O.D.

7 yrs   8 yrs   11 yrs   14 yrs   17 yrs   18 yrs   22 yrs   23 yrs
Moved house   Carol   Dad left   Dad came   Left school,   Cousin died ■   Broken   World Cup
       singing   home to   back   no qualifications   ↑   arm ●   ↑
1st football,   for £   Germany   ↑   ↑   My fault   ↑   Met
joined soccer   Moved house   Steven died ■   ↑   Double   Sheryl,
club   ↑   ↑   Depressed   hernia   Bianca,
↑   Swallowed   Dad moved   ↑   operation   Mason
Cut leg,   tongue ●   back in   Many twitches   ● ●
56 stitches   ↑   17½ yrs   ↑
↑   Blood clot   1st professional   Supported
Always fighting   ↑   game, more £   Mam, Dad
at school   8 mths hospital   ↑
↑   ↑   Broke nose
Scared of dying   Lindsay   operation ●
                        (ran over)   ↑
                        6 yrs (wasp)   Started
                        ↑   drinking
                        (Fractured   ↑
Always doing   skull)   Ran someone
jobs for Mam   ↑   over
                 Looked
Mam washing,   after her
ironing, cleaning   ↑
to get £   Moved school,
                 always fighting
Fighting   ↑
increased   1st drink,
                 vodka drunk

COCAINE   MORPHINE   (DRUGS

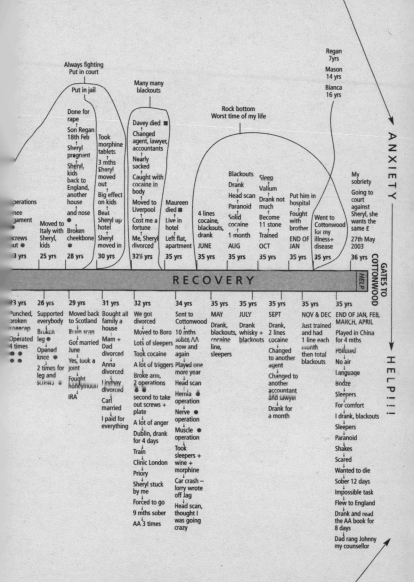

1

CHILDHOOD SCRAPES
AND SCREAMS

When I was born, on 27 May 1967, we were living at 29 Pitt Street, Gateshead. We had an upstairs room and a shared bathroom in a council-owned house. My nan lived next door. I remember the house as always being full of relations and friends. My great-grandad, Bobby Gascoigne, was still alive at the time, probably aged about ninety, and one day he came home from the pub and announced that this young lass there fancied him. After that, every time he'd been to the pub he went on about it, maintaining that this lass was always staring at him. In the end my dad went to the pub with him to see who she was, find out what her game was. Grandad Bobby took him to the corner where he always sat. And sure enough, there *was* this lass, staring at him – from a Babycham poster.

Some say our surname is French, and several of my relatives are supposed to have traced it back, but I've got no idea about its origin. All I know is that my dad, John Gascoigne, was a hod-carrier. And a good fighter. Over the years, I've seen him hit quite a few people.

My mam, Carol, was born Carol Harold. She hated her name when she was young as kids in her class at school would shout at her, 'Carol Harold, fat as a barrel.' Which she wasn't, so she says. She was one of eight sisters. Her father was a bricklayer, and my dad worked for him at one time. In her family, they think they might be related to George Stephenson, the railway man, because her dad had a watch with his name on it. It's possible, of course, but there are lots of George Stephensons on Tyneside.

When my mam left school, she worked in a hair-dressing salon, sweeping the floor for £1.50 a week. Then she got a job in a clothes factory. She met my dad at a local dance. She heard these four girls in the toilets talking about whose turn it was to go home with this lad. She couldn't believe four lasses would be fighting over the same lad, and wondered who it could be. It turned out to be John Gascoigne. Eeh, he was handsome, and funny, so me mam still says.

They got married in 1966 and that room in the council house was all they could find. It was in a part of Gateshead called Teams, down near the River Tyne, which is said to be a tough area, not far from the Dunston Staithes, where the coal barges used to be loaded. They already had one baby, my sister Anna Maria, when they moved in. My nan chose her name, after she'd been to see *The Sound of Music*.

When I came along a year later, my mam picked my name. She was a mad keen Beatles fan. All the way to the register office she was thinking, should it be John Paul, or Paul John? When she opened the office door, she was still going John Paul, Paul John – but then she stopped at Paul John and that was how I was registered. So I am named after Paul McCartney. I was born quickly, in an hour, so my mam says, at Pitt Street, whereas Anna took four hours, and was delivered in Queen Elizabeth Hospital in Gateshead. I arrived with long, black hair, which soon turned blond. My first memory is of being in my pram and being pushed along Pitt Street eating a fishcake. Exciting memory, eh. About a year after me came my brother, Carl, and then, about seven years later, our baby sister, Lindsay. All of us as kids had very blond hair.

My dad was a Roman Catholic, but he never went to church. My mam is Church of England, but her mam was Catholic. We were sent to Sunday school, so I suppose you could say I was brought up Church of England, but religion didn't play much of a part in our lives.

We moved houses quite a few times when I was young, trying to get more space. When we found a two-bedroomed flat I slept with Anna in one bedroom, and used to amuse myself by pulling the plaster off the walls and throwing it at her. We were eventually given a whole council house in Edison Gardens in Dunston, nearer the middle of Gateshead, beside Saltwell Park. It was a brilliant park, with a lake, tennis courts and a bowling green. We lived in Edison Gardens for about eight years, so that's the house I remember most from my childhood. For the first time we had a front and back garden and Carl and I had our own bedroom. We had bunk beds and used to fight all the time about who slept on top.

Anna was the talented one, great at singing and dancing, and we used to put on little shows for the neighbours, entrance 2p. She would sing and dance and I would rush in and do a striptease, which infuriated her because she took it all very seriously.

My mam remembers a gypsy coming to the door one day. She never turned gypsies away, but she had no money as my dad was out of work at the time. The gypsy asked if she had any toast. My mam went and made two slices of toast, and the gypsy said she would read her palm. Mam held out her hand and the gypsy said: 'It's full of feet. I can't see your palm for feet coming out of it.' Me mam asked what this all meant and the gypsy told her that one of her children would be famous for their feet. Naturally, Mam thought it would be Anna. It wasn't till I was about six or seven that she thought it might be me.

When my dad did have a job we felt quite well off. We never went on holiday – a day trip to Whitley Bay was the nearest we came to that – but he got himself a little car and there would be good presents for us at Christmas. I got my first football when I was about seven, and Carl and I were given a Tomahawk bike each when I was eight. Carl proved himself better than I was at doing wheelies. When money was tight there would be trouble paying the clothes club. At Christmas I did a lot of carol-singing to get money to buy sweets or cigarettes for my mam and dad. They both smoked, but I never did, not even as a teenager.

My mam was the one who mainly tried to discipline

us. She'd use a slipper on us when we'd done something really bad. Fighting with Carl once, my dad tried to stop us, but I was sent flying over the TV and smashed it. I ran out of the house, knowing I'd get a real bollocking this time. Eventually I came home and apologised.

Both the TV and our electricity supply ran on meters. You had to put 50p in the slot to get them working, and a man used to come from time to time to unlock the meters and take the money away. Carl and I watched him carefully to see how it was done, but we couldn't figure out how to get the meters open so in the end we just forced the lock on one of them. We got the slipper for that.

I remember my mam bringing home a goldfish each for me, Anna and Carl, which she'd won at the Town Moor fair. We decided to race them. We took them out of their bowl, put them on the edge of the table and each banged our own goldfish on its tail to make it move, trying to be the first to get our fish across the table. None of them made it, because of course they all died. When Mam came in and discovered what we were up to, out came the slipper again. She used to hold it in her hand like John Wayne held his pistol.

My dad never hit me, though I did see him and

Mam have violent rows. I think it was just frustration. I'm not trying to excuse him, but I can understand it. It was hard for him being out of work. He wanted to work; he was trying to be a winner.

In the summertime, Mam would send Carl and me to bed when it was still daylight. Sometimes we would climb out of the window and go off to play in the park. The first time she discovered we were missing from our bedroom she was frantic, thinking we'd been abducted or something. We'd throw the mattress out of the window and jump down on to it. Often we hurt ourselves as we fell. Every summer either Carl or I had a broken arm or leg. Usually it was me. My sisters didn't seem so injury-prone, but I was from an early age.

My first visit to the hospital was when I was about three, but I don't remember it. My mam says I was hit on the head with a brick. It wasn't my fault. She saw this kid holding a brick and told him to put it down, but he threw it at me. I had to have stitches.

Then, when I was around six, there was some sort of open day at Anna's school, with a demonstration in the school gym. After they'd done their bit, I decided to have a go as well. I ran across and climbed on to this piece of equipment before anyone could stop me – and fell off and broke my arm. That was the first trip to Casualty at the Queen Elizabeth, but certainly not the last. I ended up with a season ticket. Oh not you again, the nurses would say.

I don't think it was simply clumsiness – well, not always. It was more to do with the daredevil in me. I was always doing daft things. I was playing on some pipes one day – big concrete ones on a building site, which had been piled up against a wall – and I was sliding down the biggest one, legs open. I hadn't realised there was a big nail sticking out. That time I had to have fifty-six stitches. Butterfly stitches, they were called.

Then, in Saltwell Park, when I was seven, I fell off a tree and broke my arm. I was trying to swing from tree to tree but missed the one I was aiming for. My arm was in plaster for six weeks, but that didn't stop me going swimming in the lake in the park. I swam with my arm in the air, or tried to, but the plaster would get all soggy and I'd have to have it redone.

My first school was Brighton Junior Mixed. I got into quite a few fights there because the other kids called me names. I can't remember them all, but one of them was 'Tramp'. Because of my clothes, perhaps, or the family I came from, I don't know. So I had to defend my honour, didn't I? Not in school, or in the play-ground: I waited till the name-callers came out of school, and then I got them.

At home, I often fought with Anna as well as Carl. I knocked out one of her teeth once. The fighting Gascoignes. We'd fight over anything, even crisps. My mam would empty several packets out into a bowl, and then we'd all fight each other for our favourite flavour. But when we weren't scrapping, we were singing and dancing and loving each other. I'd say I had a very happy childhood, at least up to the age of twelve or so. If my mam and dad had an argument, I would rush across and hug both of them. I'd cry if they started rowing, or if my dad left us. I loved them both so much.

When my dad was out of work, he'd go out at night and dig in the field for coal. This didn't involve any actual digging. There was a coal depot near us at Dunston, and when the coal wagons were being shunted, a lot of coal would fall off into the field, so people would go out and pick it up in the dark. Me dad would put his salvaged coal on the fire and we'd toast bread and have beans on toast. It was my favourite meal. Some of my earliest memories are of going with my mam to bingo. One night – I must have been very young then because I was sitting on her knee – she won a tin of beans. That was brilliant. Even today I prefer beans on toast to caviar or a fillet steak.

My mam and dad fell out several times and he moved out, sometimes to a room over a pub, on his own. When I was about ten he moved to Germany, to look for work on the building sites, like the blokes in *Auf Wiedersehen, Pet.* He was away about a year and we kids fought even more in his absence. I don't think he always sent money home. My mother had three jobs at one time: she went out cleaning in the mornings, did two hours in a factory in the afternoon before coming home to give us our tea, then more cleaning in the evening. She also worked for a while in a chip shop.

We didn't starve but we didn't have much. All four of us kids would get into the bath together, then we'd put our clothes in the bath and wash them. We only had one decent set of clothes each, so me mam would have to take them to the all-night launderette to dry them, then stay up half the night ironing them for us to wear in the morning.

When I was seven, I had a weird experience. I'd been playing football in the park all afternoon and all evening. I had my new football and I kept on playing, even though it had got dark and all the other kids had gone home.

As I was walking home on my own, I looked up at the stars and thought, how long do stars go on for? Then I wondered, how long is life? How long will I live? How long will I be dead? Will it be OK when I'm dead or will I feel different? Suddenly I was scared, and I ran all the way home, screaming and crying.

I got into bed with me mam and dad, squeezed in beside them, cuddled close. I didn't tell them why I'd been screaming. I just sort of hid it in my head. In fact it didn't come out again till recently, in a conversation with a counsellor at a clinic. It was a massive relief to talk about that. Looking back, it was the first time in my life I was aware of death. I'd never actually seen anyone die. I've always been afraid of dying, for many reasons, since then, but until that counselling session, I'd never realised when it all began.

> Paul did make us laugh. I used to look forward to him coming home from school and telling us the latest joke he'd heard, or something funny that had happened.
> *Carol Gascoigne, Paul's mother*

2

STEVEN

According to me mam, I was playing football when I was nine months old. I walked at nine months, and talked at nine months, so I might have managed to push a ball around as well. From about four or five I was playing all the time, in the street and in the park, just like most of the other boys in our neighbourhood.

My dad had played when he was younger, just for a local team, a railway team, and on Sunday afternoons he used to have a knockaround in the park, after he'd been to the pub, just with his mates, other grown-ups, most of them probably half-drunk. I used to play with them, even though I was only little. He would encourage me to do tricks and I could tell he was proud of my skill.

I suppose I knew from about the age of seven, when I was given that first football, that I had a talent for the game. I was aware that I could play it better than other boys. My dad would give me tests, getting me to dribble down the pavement with my ball to the shops and back, timing me, and then making me do it again, only quicker. When I did a paper round, I used to kick a ball with me all the way, in and out of the houses.

I first got into the school football team when I was eight, even though I was younger and smaller than everyone else. At ten I won my first little trophy, and from then on, I wanted to be a professional player, though if you'd asked me at the time what I wanted to be when I grew up I would probably have said a millionaire. I remember announcing just that on the bus one day when the other lads were talking about their own ambitions.

I was awarded my cup in a penalty competition for all Gateshead primary schools, scoring 12 out of 12. I took my trophy home and kept it under the bed in case any burglars found it. I then got a place on a weekend coaching course at a country camp, where I met Keith

Spraggon. He lived not far away from me but went to a different school. He was very good at football, and we became close friends.

What I wanted was to get into the local Redheugh Boys' Club. They had a brilliant football team, and their big rivals were Wallsend Boys, who have produced many well-known Newcastle players over the years. I was too young to join the club, but I'd climb over the wall and watch them training. I pestered everyone to take me along until finally I persuaded my dad to get me in. He had to swear that I was a couple of years older than I was. At first I just acted as ballboy or helped put up the nets, but eventually I got into the team, and so did Keith Spraggon.

My first hero was Johan Cruyff. I watched him on telly over and over again, and copied his turn. I also loved Pele, like every other football fan. I was a Newcastle supporter, of course, from an early age. When we lived at Edison Gardens, we could hear the roar from the Gallowgate End at St James' Park. The player I liked best in the team was Malcolm Macdonald. He was my first local hero, I suppose.

At eleven, I left Brighton Junior Mixed for Breckenbeds Junior High. I was good at all sports, usually the best in the school. I won cups for basketball, tennis and badminton and of course played football for the school. I liked maths and was quite good at it, and I learned to play chess. I pestered my mother to buy me a set, and when she did I taught her how to play as well. I'd also play cards with her for money. I usually won, but she'd keep going till either she won her money back or I fell asleep.

Whenever I had any money, I'd spend it on sweets. Keith and I and some other boys used to go into one particular shop where we'd take the mickey out of the woman who ran it, winding her up and causing trouble. We'd try to nick the sweets and she'd chase us out. One day, when I was ten, I took Keith's little brother Steven with us, telling his mam I'd look after him. I was mucking around in the shop when Steven ran out into Derwentwater Road in front of a parked ice-cream van. He didn't see there was an oncoming car and it went right into him.

I ran out and and stood over his crumpled little body, screaming, 'Please move, please move!' His lips did seem to be moving slightly, but soon he was completely still. I was on my own with him for what seemed like ages, while someone went for his mother. I just had to sit there, watching him die, waiting for his mam and the ambulance to arrive. I can still see his mother, Maureen, running down the road. She'd rushed out of her house with no shoes or stockings on, screaming and screaming.

It was the first dead body I'd ever seen – and I felt Steven's death was my fault. I had said I would look after him and I didn't. I couldn't understand why he had died when he was so young and hadn't harmed anybody. It didn't make sense. Why had God let him die? For weeks and weeks I'd wake in the night, reliving the scene. I suppose I should have had grief counselling, if they had such a thing in those days. I've talked to psychiatrists about it since, and I still go over the accident in my mind. Just speaking of it can make me cry.

Something else awful happened about that time. My dad had returned from Germany, but he wasn't well. From the age of sixteen, he'd suffered with a lot of headaches, terrible migraines which could last for fourteen days. Then he started having seizures, which the doctors decided in the end was some form of epilepsy. He was on medication, but he still got these sort of fits, during which he would be out of it for about twenty minutes, unable to talk. He wouldn't know who he was or the names of his own children.

This happened to him once when I was alone at home with him in the room. I didn't know what the fuck was going on, and I thought he was dying. I tried to pull his tongue out of his throat because he was swallowing it. I was afraid he'd choke and die in front of me and it would be my fault for not rescuing him. Anyway, my mam appeared and said I should keep my finger in his mouth while she rang for the ambulance. He was biting my finger so hard it was killing me, so I put a spoon in his mouth instead. I kept it there till the ambulance came. He recovered that time, but not long afterwards, when he was alone in the house and just getting out of his bath, he had a brain haemorrhage and collapsed. He was rushed to hospital, where he had countless operations. They thought he was a goner, that that was it: he'd either die or, if he lived, never fully recover.

I think he was in hospital for about eight months. Before he was finally allowed to come home, they gave him lots of tests to see if his brain was working properly. They showed him photographs of people on bikes, cars in the street, and he had to tell them what he could see. When they showed him some pictures of animals, and asked him what they were, he said: 'That's an elephant fucking another elephant.' They knew then he was back to normal. 'OK, then, Mr Gascoigne, you can go home now.'

But he couldn't go back to work. From the time I was twelve, he was never able to work again. So my mam had to do even more jobs to try to make ends meet. My dad would make us our tea while she went out to work. I don't know how she managed to bring up the four of us on so little money.

It was around this time that I started displaying peculiar twitches and began making lots of noises. Just silly sounds, sort of swallowing all the time, gulping, or just shouting. I got thrown out of school for a week for making so much noise that no one else could concentrate. I liked school and hated not being able to go. I was never late and always went, even when I was ill. I even got a star once for good attendance.

Along with the twitches I developed various obsessions. I became obsessed by the number five, and had to touch certain objects five times, put the light on and off five times, or open and close a door five times. I had to have everything lined up at a certain angle, whether it was plates on a table or my clothes. I insisted on keeping the light on at night and still do. Even today I can't sleep unless there is a light on. My mother now says she thinks this was her fault. She was like that herself as a girl, and she inherited the habit from her own mam who, as a child, used to see the ghosts of nuns sitting in her bedroom unless the light was kept on. So my mam did the same with us, leaving a nightlight on so that we wouldn't be scared and she could keep an eye on the four of us and see that we were all right. Anna, Carl and Lindsay stopped all that once they had left home, but I never did.

My mam got worried by these twitches, the hyper-activity and my inability to concentrate at school, and decided to take me to the doctor. He sent me to see a psychiatrist at the Queen Elizabeth. Dad took me for my appointment, as my mam was working. This psychi-atrist made me play with a load of sand and bricks, which I thought was really stupid, so I refused to go again. My dad thought it was fucking silly as well. My mam wanted me to go back, but I dug my heels in. So all the twitches and stuff just carried on.

I hated being thirteen. Not just because it was an unlucky number; I hated being that in-between age. I was very depressed for all of that year, or so it seems to me now, looking back. I got obsessed with stealing. Anything, really. Sweets from shops – Twixes, Yorkies,

Mars bars, Marathons – or stupid things from Woolies which I'd give away. Or money from my mother's purse. Or milk bottles from people's doorsteps. The police only came to our door about me once, and that was to do with some football nets a kid had actually given me, which turned out to be stolen. I genuinely didn't know anything about it, so they let me off.

One of my money-making scams was collecting empty beer bottles and taking them back to the pub to claim the deposit. On one trip, I noticed that they put the empty bottles in a crate at the back of the pub, so I sneaked round the back and nicked them, then went to the front to hand them their own bottles and get the money. It worked for a while, till they realised what I was up to and chased me out of the pub.

I stole apples and was always being pursued by people threatening me with the police. One bloke fired an air pistol at me and I got a pellet in my stomach. I was shitting myself. When I told my mam what had happened, she gave me a clip round the ear. I stole out of slot machines, the sort you get sweets from in railway stations. I learned how to put a bit of tissue into the machine so that people couldn't get their money out and thought it was broken. I'd wait till they'd given up and gone off and then pull out the tissue and get their money.

I stole for the buzz, not because I really needed anything. It seemed exciting. While I was doing it my heart would be thumping.

There was this little shop I'd go to where when you opened the door there'd be that ding-dong that tells the shopkeeper a customer has come in. The shopkeeper would appear and look over his counter but see nobody. He'd think he'd been mistaken, or that the customer had changed his mind and gone out again, and return to his back room. But I'd be there, lying flat on the floor against the counter out of his line of vision. When he'd left I'd fill up a bag with all the sweets I could get my hands on and run out of the shop. I gave most of them away. I couldn't take them home, could I, or my mam would find out.

I stole things for years, just for fun. In fact I pinched some clothes from a shop not long ago. Just to see if I could, for the thrill of it. Obviously I didn't need them, and I had more than enough money to buy them if I had wanted them. I just found myself sneaking them out to see if I could get away with it. Which I did. I took them back later.

When I reached fourteen, things seemed to get much better. Perhaps I'd begun to get over the events of recent years, or at least to learn to live with them. But more probably it was football that kept me happy and out of trouble – or some trouble, anyway. By fourteen I was playing more serious football, in proper teams, and I found that was what I liked doing best in life. I didn't have twitches or worry about death when I was playing football.

> We played the usual children's games, but Paul always believed them. 'Stand on a crack, you'll break your back. Stand on a line, you'll break your spine.' So he would never do either. He insisted on jumping over car shadows because he thought it was bad luck to stand on the shadow of a car. He could never wait for a table to be cleared, at home or at a pub. Still can't. He has to jump up and clear everything away, even though no one else is at all bothered.
> *Anna Gascoigne, Paul's sister*

3

FOOTBALL TO
THE RESCUE

Scouts first started appearing at our back door when I was about twelve. I'd got into the Redheugh Boys' Club Under-14 team at that age and I did well. I loved playing for Redheugh. It was brilliant being with a proper club and playing on a proper pitch with real goalposts and nets, even if they had to be taken down after each game in case they got nicked.

I think David Lloyd from Middlesbrough might have been one of the first serious scouts to come and watch me. John Carruthers of Ipswich was another who arrived at our house. He'd seen me playing for Gateshead Boys when I scored a goal from twenty yards. That day I was wearing a brand-new pair of Patrick boots which my mam had worked overtime to buy. I felt I owed her something.

The first real trial I was offered was with Ipswich. They wanted both me and Keith Spraggon to come down for a few days. I'm not sure if I would have gone all that way on my own if it had just been me. We were put in digs and at the ground we met some of the stars I had seen on the telly: Terry Butcher, John Wark, Mick Mills. I asked them for their autographs and they were very kind. There was none of that pushing you away while they got into their flash cars. Not that I can remember many flash cars then. In 1980, footballers were well paid, but not that well paid.

Bobby Robson, the manager, was very kind to us as well. I liked the idea that he was a Geordie and could understand what I was saying. Not that I actually said much – I was very nervous. I felt so small alongside the grown-up players. Even Keith seemed to tower above me. Bobby Robson explained that most of us wouldn't make it, but we shouldn't get too upset about it. In spite of the kindness of Bobby and the players, I didn't take to Ipswich, and I didn't do very well. Which could explain why nothing happened there.

Keith and I rushed home to play for Redheugh in a Cup final. Before the match, while the other team were warming up in trainers, I sneaked into the dressing room and swapped round all their boots. We won the game 5–0.

My next trial was with Middlesbrough. This time we were put in a proper hotel, not a hostel or digs. I know it was a proper hotel because it had a real snooker table, which I had to be dragged away from. I bunked off during the trial and came back to support Redheugh in a big match. I managed to step on some broken glass, cut my feet badly and had to go to Queen Elizabeth yet again. So it was my own fault that I never heard from Boro, but Keith was more successful: he was offered schoolboy forms.

Southampton were next. Lawrie McMenemy was in charge at the time, but I didn't see much of him as he didn't seem to be involved with the kids. I didn't think much of the coaching and I didn't like it there, either. I came home after a few days.

Finally, in the summer of 1980, Newcastle United came along. I suppose they'd been watching me, but perhaps they weren't sure about me. When their scout finally turned up at the back door, my dad said: 'What kept you so long?' Newcastle had always been my team and I'd worn a black-and-white shirt since I was a nipper. I hardly even took it off to get it washed.

Newcastle took me on as a schoolboy. We trained at the club for two hours every Tuesday after school, and for longer in the school holidays. I still had a kickaround with my old mates, in the street or the park, and they'd want to know all the gossip about their heroes.

I got a chance to be a ballboy during one Newcastle home game, and it was brilliant throwing the ball back to the first-team stars. At St James' Park I would often see people like Peter Beardsley and Chris Waddle. I loved them so much. Newcastle were in the Second Division then, and the previous season (1979–80) they'd finished a disappointing ninth. Bill McGarry was the manager when I first joined the club, but after a month he was out and Arthur Cox took over. I admired him, hated him, loved him and was terrified of him. He made a point of watching the kids play and nothing escaped his notice. He soon knew all of us by name. I could hear his voice booming out 'Gascoigne!' in my sleep. I used to play a few tricks and scams but I got away with them. I think he turned a blind eye to many of them as he seemed to like me.

Among the first team, Kenny Wharton was friendly to me, as was Colin Suggett, but it wasn't exactly a star-studded side. They were an ageing side, on the look-out for new young stars.

I used to get the bus from Dunston to the training ground at Benwell, which cost 5p. You were allowed a maximum of £5 travelling expenses a week because of course many of the lads came by train from quite a long way away. I didn't, but I usually managed to claim the maximum. With the money I'd buy presents for my mam and dad or just spend it on silly things such as slot machines.

I'd developed a passion for one-armed bandits and spent all my money on them. I'd often put my last 5p, my bus fare home, in a machine and lose it, and have to run home. I suppose it did help to keep me fit. At one stage I was so mad about gambling on slot machines that I'd steal to fund the habit. I remember once being so desperate for money that I stole £15 from my sister Anna's purse, and went off and lost it all. Anna was heartbroken. She'd just left school and it was her first week's wages. She had wanted to be an actress, but the careers people at school advised her to try office work, so she'd become a telephonist. She'd saved the money for a night out. She was in a terrible state and I felt so guilty. It just hadn't occurred to me it meant so much to her.

I hope I've made the loss up to her since. I vowed then not to gamble again, and I haven't done – not seriously. I might have many other vices, but gambling on machines or on horses, which so many players do, has not been one of them. Well, apart from a few years later when I bought a 25p scratchcard. This was an isolated example. But, guess what, I won £2,000. When I came home with the money, me mam said: 'Where have you stolen it from?'

When I was fourteen, I moved to a bigger school, Heathfield High. Mr Hepworth, the geography teacher, was my form master there. One day he was going on about something dead boring, like the Alps, while I spent the whole lesson practising my autograph on my school bag. He came over eventually.

'What are you doing, Gascoigne?'

'I'm practising my autograph.'

'What for?'

'I need to practise it as I am going to be a famous footballer.'

'Only one in a million becomes a professional footballer,' Mr Hepworth said. 'So stop it at once.'

I told him I was going to be that one in a million.

But I still had a long way to go. I did get picked for

Newcastle Schoolboys at a much younger age than my team-mates, but I never played for the county, which is the next step up towards playing for England Schoolboys. I was asked to a trial for Durham County and I got a hat-trick, but I never heard from them again. I never found out why. I'd rush downstairs when I heard the postman at the door, but the letter never came. Was it me, or my family, or our reputation, or what? Even now, I don't know. I think one of the reasons may have been that my dad wouldn't arse-lick the powers that be, which all the other dads did. He never grovelled to teachers. He'd tell them to fuck off. There was one person involved with the county who definitely didn't like me. It did upset me at the time, not getting a chance to play for England, but I told myself they were all stupid. They preferred to pick joke players, just as long as they were all overgrown.

I must have been just over fourteen when I got drunk for the first time. A friend of mine called Sean stole a bottle of vodka from a shop and we both drank it. I came home staggering, my speech slurred, and felt terrible, so terrible I vowed never to touch alcohol again, which I didn't, not for another four years, till I was about eighteen.

But my brother Carl got caught up in something much worse – glue-sniffing. I cried for about two weeks when I found out what he was doing to himself. When I think of all the awful things our family has had to go through, I feel proud of them, that they've survived.

Carl fell in with a bad lot, got into other things as well, and was eventually sent off to a home for naughty boys. I don't know where it was – I never visited him. Somewhere on the coast. When he left, I promised to send letters to him all the time and he promised to write back. In my first letter, I said, 'Please come back soon. We miss you so much. Please, please come back.' Carl took a while to reply, so I was dead excited when I opened his first letter to me. 'Fuck off, Paul,' he wrote. 'I love it here. We get three meals a day and you can play table tennis and snooker. So fuck off . . .'

Later on, though, I could tell from his letters he was not enjoying it so much. He was being picked on and bullied by a bigger lad and didn't know what to do about it. He'd written earlier mentioning a boot room, so in my next letter I suggested he should invite this lad into the boot room and then, the moment he was in, turn off the light and hit him over the head with the biggest boot he could find. And that's what he did. He wrote back telling me he was now 'Top Boy'. He'd become the best in the school for fighting.

Carl was a good footballer himself, and played for Newcastle Youth. Many years later, I was talking to David Batty and he remembered playing against Carl, when he was with Leeds Youth. It was a match in which Carl got thumped. Some kid just smashed him and he was seriously injured. When I started playing, I looked out for that kid to pay him back.

Carl was good, but he gave up not long afterwards. That injury didn't help, but his main problem was that he was more interested in drinking, chasing girls, all the usual stuff that can distract lads at that age. Basically, he couldn't be bothered.

As a teenager, as I said, I didn't drink, not at all, and nor did I get involved in drugs. I might have done a bit of silly stealing, but that was it. I wasn't really much interested in girls, either. I got on with them OK, though when I was younger I worried about my spots and whether girls would fancy me or not. Me mam bought us some of this special soap which you were supposed to rub on your spots, leave for two minutes, and then wash off. I thought I'd give it a really good go, so I put it on my face before I went to bed and slept with the stuff on all night. When I woke up in the morning, I felt as if I'd got third-degree burns.

The spots went anyway, of their own accord, as I got older, but I still didn't bother much about girls. I preferred being with the lads, having a laugh, to chasing lasses. In any case, the main thing in my life was football. There was something inside me that told me I had to put football first. I had to stay fit and healthy and, most of all, stay determined, otherwise I knew I would never succeed.

There was great excitement in August 1982 when Kevin Keegan signed to play for Newcastle. Arthur Cox had done so well to get him. We were still in the Second Division, but he was seen as the Messiah who would get us back in the First. Sure enough, he scored the only goal of the game in his debut against QPR.

Arthur had me doing little jobs for Kevin, such as cleaning his boots, perhaps to give me an example about how a real pro behaved. I even got to break in a new pair of boots for him, even though he took at least a size smaller than I did.

I took a pair of Keegan's new boots home with me one day to show off to my mates at school. I let them all look at them on the bus, and when I got off at school, I found I was one boot short. Someone had nicked the other one, or I had lost it. I cried all the way home and made my dad go with me to the bus depot, to see if anyone had handed in the missing boot. They didn't really believe it when we said we were looking for one of Kevin Keegan's boots. It never turned up and I was dreading having to confess what had happened. I had to come clean in the end. But Kevin was brilliant. He didn't shout at me. When I told him the story he just laughed.

At school, when I was coming up for sixteen, we had to sit some CSE exams. I never paid much attention to lessons, but I don't consider I was wild at school, just a bit lively and very noisy. The nearer it came to the end, the more often I'd get thrown out of lessons, so I'd go off and practise my ball skills in the playground. I'm sure they were glad to get rid of me.

I know I could have done better if I'd been been more interested. I was still quite good at maths and I liked English. They put me in for six CSEs and I passed two, English and Environmental Studies. I should have passed maths, but my desk broke in the exam. That's my excuse, anyway. The screws were a bit loose and I made them worse by fiddling with them; eventually, the desk fell to pieces and I spent the rest of the exam time trying to put it back together. That's why I failed.

But I wasn't bothered. On my sixteenth birthday, 27 May 1983, I signed as an apprentice for Newcastle United.

> I think he's a bit like my mother. She can get easily stressed, worrying about ordinary things. Me and me dad are more laid back.
> *Anna Gascoigne*

4

JIMMY APPEARS

I wanted both my mam and my dad to be there when I signed the forms to become an apprentice – and both of them to sign the forms as well. But they weren't speaking at the time. I think my dad might have been in one of his living-away-from-home phases. Anyway, they did at least both come, even if they sat there glaring at each other. I could see that Willie McFaul, Newcastle's former goalie, who was then one of the coaches, was wondering what the fuck was going on, and I felt a bit embarrassed.

I was signed up for two years, on £25 a week. My mam was given another £30 a week to look after me, as I was living at home rather than in club digs.

Colin Suggett was the youth team coach, having finally retired from playing. He told me later that I gave him more aggravation and grief than any other player in his whole coaching life. He had me running lap after lap of the ground in training, trying to get my weight down. One very hot day, he coaxed me to do just one more lap. I was knackered already and said I couldn't do any more. 'Just one, son.' I set off. I managed to stagger round somehow. I could see my mates in the youth team, leaning on the fence sucking ice lollies. They'd done their training to Colin's satisfaction. When I completed my final lap, Colin said to me, 'You lied. You could do another one. So I want you to go round one more time.' I told him to fuck off, which of course I shouldn't have done. I got punished for that.

It was Colin Suggett who first called me 'Gazza'. My dad had been known as Gassa to his friends, and I'd sometimes been called that as well. But it was Colin who turned it into Gazza. I don't think he did it deliberately – it was just his Sunderland accent, the way he pronounced it. And I became Gazza from then on.

I had all the ball skills, shooting and dribbling, but I have to admit I wasn't very fast and I *was* a bit overweight. In the gym, we often did exercises with the first-team players, such as Chris Waddle and Peter Beardsley. I learned a lot from them, and tried to copy what they did. The senior professionals had a session where you had to trap the ball with one touch and then shoot through different-shaped targets – a circle, a square, a triangle. You didn't know which target to aim at till the coach shouted it out, so you had to be quick and accurate. I was usually the only apprentice who could do it. I always had confidence in my ability and succeeded in most of the ball exercises and tests, but things didn't always go so smoothly off the pitch.

We apprentices had to be at the training ground by 9.15 every morning. I went there on the bus from Dunston and I was never late. I couldn't wait to get there. As well as training, the apprentices had to do a lot of the shitty jobs: sweeping the dressing-room floors, cleaning the toilets and the showers, cleaning the boots for the first team. I did Wes Saunders' boots for a while and then Chris Waddle's. Chris had come to the club from non-league Tow Law. Arthur Cox had signed him for a set of second-hand floodlights, but he'd become one of the stars of the team.

Chris, so he says now, thought I was a joke, the smallest, podgiest player he'd seen in his life, but when he saw me with the ball, he realised I was in a different class. Our relationship didn't get off to a very good start, however. One day, when I gave him his boots, he said I hadn't cleaned them well enough. 'They are the tools of your trade and they have to be kept in top condition,' so he lectured me. But I was only sixteen, and lippy, so I told him to fuck off and clean them himself.

Chris gave me a dead leg and in front of everyone. Somehow I managed not to cry, but after that I didn't give him any more cheek.

Not long after I signed as an apprentice, the youth team was involved in a tournament up in Aberdeen. It was a big event, involving youth teams from Rangers and Bayern Munich, and it provided a brilliant break from normal training and cleaning people's boots. It lasted quite a few days, and in the middle of it, over the weekend, we were allowed home.

That weekend I decided to have a go on an 80cc scrambler motorbike belonging to a friend. I didn't have a licence, and couldn't really ride it, but I'd been on a smaller bike before, so I thought I knew what to do. I got as far as the first bend, going too fast, and flew off. I ended up at my regular haunt, Queen Elizabeth Hospital, having loads of stitches in my knee. I think the doctor who put them in must have been an apprentice himself, because he made a right mess of the job and my legs looked worse than they were. I went back to Aberdeen but I missed out on playing in the semi-final.

I didn't tell the club what had really happened, but when I returned to training I still had these terrible marks on my legs. Long trousers or tracksuit bottoms would have hidden them, but of course you don't wear them for training. I had the bad luck to meet Arthur Cox just as I arrived on my first day back. He immediately realised I had been in some sort of accident, so I had to tell him the truth.

'Do you really want to be a professional footballer, Gascoigne?'

'Yes, sir.' I could feel myself starting to cry.

'Then behave like one. One more stupid trick like this, and you're out. Do you understand?'

We'd all been lectured on the usual things: keep off the booze, don't smoke, don't get mixed up with the wrong sort of women, don't do anything risky which might lead to accidents. At least I didn't drink or smoke. In fact I couldn't bear to be in the same room as people smoking, perhaps because my mam and dad smoked so much. And I certainly didn't get involved with the wrong sort of women. I started going out with my first proper girlfriend when I was about sixteen. She was Gail Pringle, the daughter of Alfie Pringle, who coached Dunston Boys. I spent a lot of time at their house, and they were very good to me. I went out with Gail for about two years before we slept together, so I must have been eighteen by then. Yeah, it does seem a long time to wait, but I was too nervous at that age, and I think she was as well. When I finally took the plunge, it was a relief more than anything else.

When I was seventeen, I had to cope with another death in my life: that of Steven Wilson, who had been a friend for a long time. He'd become an apprentice at Middlesbrough at the same time as I signed forms with Newcastle. He didn't really like it there and I thought I might be able to get him into our youth squad with me, so I encouraged him to chuck it in at Boro. While he waited for an opening at Newcastle, he went to work with his uncle in the building trade. It was at work that he became the victim of a fatal building-site accident. I cried for days. I blamed myself for his death because I'd been the one who encouraged him to leave Boro. If he'd stayed there, it wouldn't have happened. I know it didn't really make sense to blame myself, but I did, and I felt terrible.

The deaths of little Steven Spraggon and then Steven Wilson were not the only ones on my conscience over the years. A long while later a cousin of mine who had bad asthma collapsed and died after suffering an asthma attack while playing football. Some doctors had said it was bad to play when you had asthma, but I told my cousin that was rubbish, it was OK to play, and he went ahead.

It seemed to me that, ever since Steven Spraggon had run into the road that day, I'd been surrounded by young people dying, and that I was partly to blame. Why had they died, and not me? Perhaps I would be next. I was cheeky and chubby and appeared happy-go-lucky to most people, but I was still plagued by those obsessions, little rituals I couldn't shake off. I still had to lay out my clothes and kit in a certain way, and I didn't sleep very well, either. Thinking about death could keep me awake all night.

I was also worried about my career. I was afraid that Newcastle would chuck me out because of my weight. Maybe they would release me at eighteen, once I'd completed my two-year apprenticeship, and I'd never become a professional. I still ate sweets all the time, and chips and hamburgers, and then I would secretly make myself sick to get rid of it all. I don't know how I found out you could do that. Perhaps I saw someone on TV who was bulimic. Someone who stuck two fingers down their throat and brought all their food up. Funnily enough, my sister Anna later got a role in a television series as a bulimic girl. Little did she realise that she needed to look no further than her own doorstep to research the part.

Anna didn't train to become an actress till she was twenty, though she'd always wanted to be one. She did various office jobs, then she gave it all up to go and do a performing arts course at North Tyneside College. She got a part in a local film, *Sheila's Stories*, and then became one of the original actresses in *Byker Grove*, the TV series set on Tyneside. She was also in a feature film called *Dream On*. Aye, she did well, when you think about it. Coming from the Gascoigne family. She later had a part in *Coronation Street*, too.

Apart from the bulimia, or attempted bulimia, the twitches got worse. Between the ages of sixteen and twenty-one I developed nine different nervous tics. I was still making those gulping noises, like the noises a pigeon makes. In the morning, I'd wake up and tell myself I wasn't going to gulp any more; I'd do something else instead, like blinking all the time. Then that in turn became a habit I couldn't stop. Or I'd keep opening my mouth, as wide as I could, or stretch my lips until they hurt. Another twitch was moving my right hip all the time, or my right shoulder, or my neck. Even when I was playing, I'd find my neck twitching from side to side. Sometimes coaches would shout at me to stop it, so I'd try for a while, or start another twitch. I was too embarrassed to tell the doctor about all this.

One compulsion, which I still have to this day, was kicking my right toe on the ground when I was running. I developed that when I was an apprentice. I did it in training, or when playing, and it got so bad that my right toenail came off, I'd been banging it so often. All that blinking over and over again could be painful as well. I would end up with my eyes hurting like hell.

I can't explain these nervous twitches. I knew I was doing them, but that knowledge didn't mean I could control them. I'd often go to my bedroom, or somewhere on my own, and twitch my neck twenty times, telling myself that would get rid of the compulsion so that I wouldn't have to do it again when I was in public. That strategy usually worked – up to a point. I'd stop doing whatever I'd been doing, but then I'd develop another twitch.

One thing I hated was being on my own. Solitude always seemed to make my problems worse. Luckily, it was around this time that I met a mate who was to become my closest and longest-standing friend. I was hardly ever alone again from then on.

Jimmy 'Five Bellies' Gardner says he remembers me from when I was about four or five, when his nan lived in Edison Gardens, near us, and that he used to play in the street with me. I have no memory of that. But his recollection might be better than mine because he's older than me. About three years older and thirty stone heavier.

My first clear memory of him is seeing him on the pitch with some Sunday league side – Whickham Sports, I think it was – when I was sixteen or so. No, he wasn't playing. He was this fat kid running on with a bucket and sponge whenever someone got injured. He's not very tall, smaller than me, but he had so many bellies. I burst out laughing every time he appeared, shouting something like, 'Go on, you fat bastard,' and he probably gave me a mouthful back. After the game, he came across and asked me: 'Are you Paul Gascoigne?' I think by then he must have known I was an apprentice with Newcastle.

Not long afterwards, he came into the Dunston Excelsior, where I was sitting with my girlfriend, Gail. When she went off to powder her nose, Jimmy sat down in her chair. 'That's my lass's seat,' I informed him. He said he just wanted to tell me that he could give me a lift to training any time I wanted. He didn't actually have a car, but he could borrow his dad's. From that moment on, we became best friends. The first day he took me to training, I asked if I could drive the car, and drove straight into a wall.

Jimmy taught me to drive in that car of his dad's. After a fashion. I was always bashing into kerbs, hitting things. One Bonfire Night, we stuck some Catherine wheels on the windscreen of Jimmy's dad's car and drove it round with them whirling away. It looked brilliant, and everyone was staring at us – till the front windscreen turned black from the smoke. When we touched it, it fell out.

Out of my wages, I eventually managed to buy an old Mini, although I hadn't passed my test and nor did I have any insurance and that. Jimmy worked in a garage at the time, so he knew a bit about old cars and gave it the once-over for me. We were out together in the Mini one day, after giving a lift to some girls we fancied (or girls Jimmy fancied), just driving round and round, messing about, when suddenly this hippy ran across the road in front of us. At least, he looked a bit like a hippy. Whoever he was, we hit him.

I was at the wheel and flew into a complete panic. I just drove on, back to Newcastle. When we got there, I dumped the car and smashed the front windscreen to make it look as if the Mini had been stolen and wrecked.

I didn't really know what I was doing. It was stupid, but I was in such a state, thinking that was it, my career was over, the club would definitely get rid of me now.

I had saved up some money which I'd put in the bank, and I told Jimmy that he could have £100 if he took the blame and said he'd been driving the car if we got caught. I was staying at Gail's house at the time. I didn't tell her, or her dad, Alfie, what had happened. They had been so good to me and I didn't want them to be angry with me. Jimmy went back to his home nearby.

In the middle of the night, I hear this banging at the door. The police have arrived. They tell Alfie they've come about an accident, but of course he doesn't know anything about it. They get me out of bed and say there's been a car accident. I tell them my car's been stolen and I haven't been in any accident. And they say, 'Don't try that, son, we know the whole story. Jimmy has told us what happened.'

What a fat bastard. He's supposed to be my best friend and he's told them everything, even that I had been driving. Or so the police said.

I asked about the kid who had been run over. Was he OK? They said he'd had something like twenty-four stitches, but was now recovering. I asked if I could visit him and they said no. I think they thought I'd try to bribe him not to let it get to court. As it was, it all came out and we had to answer the charges.

In court, when Jimmy was giving evidence, I was kicking him under the table. The bastard. I was fined £260 and got eight points on my non-existent licence and Jimmy received a £120 fine and four points. When Jimmy was asked by the judge how he would like to pay, he said he'd pay £1 a week. The judge inquired if he could make it £2, and Jimmy said, OK, he'd try. When I was asked, I said I'd pay my £260 right away.

That evening, Jimmy and I went out and got drunk.

Later I got a right bollocking from Mr McKeag, one of the Newcastle directors. I was told this would be my last warning.

Jimmy and I had so many laughs together, doing daft things, egging each other on. Jimmy's mates once got a crossbow from somewhere and Jimmy put an apple on his head while I tried to hit the apple. Then we got hold of an air gun. Jimmy stood twenty yards away with his pants down and I fired at his bare arse. For each of the pellets I managed to hit him with, I had to pay him £25. His arse ended up looking like the end of a watering can. We used to drive that old Mini right through hedges, just for a laugh, though we did take the precaution of wearing crash helmets in case we got injured. Eventually, the car fell to pieces.

I had failed my driving test several times, so I took my next one in another area, where I was told it was easier. Jimmy found out that the examiner might accept some money to pass me. I offered him £50 and he said, 'Make it £75.' The examiner kept the money but failed me. Bastard. I later sat it again elsewhere and passed.

I was still having trouble with Colin Suggett, the youth coach. I was doing well in the youth team, and we were winning things, but he was on my back all the time, going on about my weight, about getting into trouble off the pitch, getting injured, the usual stuff. I suppose that was hardly surprising, but it got me down, made me depressed, and then I'd feel guilty and ashamed at my own behaviour, about eating all this junk food, but because I was depressed, I'd just eat even more.

Colin was still making me do extra laps after everyone else had finished training, to get my weight down, which I hated, especially when the others hung around laughing at me. I remember Wes Saunders standing there having a milkshake while I was sweating like a pig. One day, after the coaches had gone, I was getting changed on my own when I felt so fed up I went out on the pitch again and got on to the groundsman's tractor. I didn't really know how to drive it, but I aimed it straight at the dressing rooms and jumped off just in time. It knocked about twenty-five bricks off the dressing-room wall. I was fined £75 for that.

I worried, all the time, that the club would get rid of me, not because of my football but because of my behaviour. At home I would moan constantly that I was being picked on, it wasn't fair, Colin Suggett was being a bastard to me. My dad said he'd go up to the club and thump any of the coaches who were picking on me, but I managed to stop him. What I didn't know was that my mam had written to the club saying everyone was being horrible to me, making my life a misery; that the club was making me depressed and unwell. I was called in and her letter was read out to me. That was really embarrassing.

I knew that only a small percentage of apprentices ever get through into the first team and make it as professionals. But I was confident enough of my football to think I would be the one to make it. I believed I was better than the rest. Well, most of the rest. I have to admit I was a bit jealous of Ian Bogie. He was a year younger than me and had played for England Schoolboys, which I never did. That was the real reason why I was jealous. Not that I told him that, or anyone else.

I realised that to be the best player among the youth players, which I was determined to be, I had to be stronger. So I did a lot of extra training with weights and things to build up my upper body. Jimmy used to borrow weights and medicine balls from the training ground and I'd go out in the evenings to Dunston Park and train there on my own. Then, late at night, Jimmy would return the equipment and sneak it back where it belonged.

Ian Bogie was probably the one that was better than me at the time, for his age, but there were other good talents as well – Joe Allon, who went on to play for Chelsea, and Tony Haytor, who was a brilliant tackler. Tony Nesbit was a right workhorse, but he got a nasty injury and the last I heard of him, he'd become a policeman. Jeff Wrightson was good, as was Paul Stephenson. Some made it, some didn't. Some showed early promise and then didn't develop. I always thought that, because he had played for England, the pressure of expectation hung over Ian Bogie. It worked against him, and then he got an injury, which didn't help.

You just can't tell who'll come through. It takes determination as well as talent, and I had plenty of that.

I had worked on my natural ability. When I was younger, I'd injured my right ankle once, so for weeks I did almost everything with my left. I ended up being able to kick with both feet. My dad had always been on at me to use my left foot more, and I built on that, practising tricks for hours. Now I was playing on through injuries, scared I'd miss a game. And there were people who encouraged me. My dad would shout at me to get me out of bed on the days I didn't fancy it, and players like Waddler and Beardsley were very good to me. Waddler may have called me a fat shit, but I knew he'd taken a liking to me.

Working on my upper body paid off. It helped me get physically mature more quickly. When I began to play with the senior pros, they couldn't knock me off the ball or intimidate me, which they can easily do with a young boy who's perhaps not very strong or confident. I was strong in my body and also in my head, always confident of my own ability.

But of course I might still not have come through, for the other non-football reasons. And if I hadn't become a professional footballer, if I hadn't had the talent and determination, God knows what I would have done. I'd probably have ended up as a carpenter – if I was lucky.

I had been quite good at woodwork at school. I

once made this very thin board which I stuck down my shirt. I told everyone I'd been exercising to control my weight and now had a rock-hard stomach. I asked this kid to punch me as hard as he could in my stomach, just to test it. He did – and broke his knuckles.

If I hadn't become a footballer, my life, obviously, would have been very different. And my problems would have been much worse, I'm sure of that. I believe football saved me from a far worse fate than I've experienced.

Paul came back one day after a meal at a Chinese restaurant to say he'd brought me some fried rice. I said, 'How lovely.' He gave me the packet and it was still hot, so I thought I'd eat it straight away. I opened it – and found it was a load of maggots, which he'd bought for fishing. I dropped it, screaming and shouting. They were crawling all over the place. I shouted at Paul to get rid of them – now! – and he was just lying on the floor, laughing and laughing. No, I wasn't really upset. Aye, it was funny. Typical Paul.

Carol Gascoigne

FIRST TEAM, FIRST SUCCESSES

As I approached my seventeenth birthday in 1984, I was starting to fantasise about being in the first team, even if no one else at the club was doing so. I was in the dressing room once, finishing off some jobs, when I noticed that Arthur Cox had pinned up the first-team selection for a game. He'd written out the list himself. I traced the names on the list with my fingers, still wet from washing the toilets, imagining mine was among them. I didn't know that Arthur was in the shower. When he came out he realised I was responsible for the grubby, wet fingerprints on his list. He told me never to touch it again.

In those days, the first team marked a win with a bottle of Harvey's Bristol Cream Sherry in the dressing room. Hard to believe now, when a side is more likely to celebrate with a bottle of vintage champagne. I'd nip into the dressing room after they'd gone, empty all the dregs into one glass and drink them. Arthur caught me at it one day. I said I was just clearing up the glasses, but he knew I was lying. He offered me a drink, as there was still some left in the bottle. I said no, I didn't drink. Which I didn't, really, then. I just liked the sweet taste of the sherry.

He poured me some out, in a plastic cup, not a glass. He said I would get a glass when I got into the first team. I think Arthur quite liked me deep down, and was hopeful I'd succeed – if I didn't mess it all up.

Arthur signed another very good pro to help us get promotion, and that was Glenn Roeder. He was a natural leader and very good to the young players, someone you could go to for advice. He was also a very snappy dresser. He'd come up from London with all the latest styles. He wore a sheepskin coat which reached right down to the ground. I offered to carry his stuff for him if he'd let me wear it, which would have looked pretty funny, as he was about six inches taller than me and as thin as a rake.

In the 1983–4 season, I did well in our youth team. We beat Hull, Leeds and Southampton in the Youth Cup and got into the fifth round, where we were unlucky to be beaten 2–1 by Everton. Then, at the end of the season, the first team were promoted to the First Division. Things were really going great, for the club and for me.

But then, out of the blue, Kevin Keegan announced his retirement. We were still reeling from that when a second blow came. Arthur Cox resigned. None of us could believe or understand that. I think it was something to do with the board not offering him a long-term contract, and that he resigned as a matter of pride.

In June 1984, just after I'd turned seventeen, we found we had a new manager – Jack Charlton. I liked the idea of having a Geordie in charge of the Toon. But he obviously didn't like the idea of me, from what he'd been told or from what he'd seen of me. He hadn't been there long when he called me into his office. He didn't ask me to sit down, so I just stood there, waiting to find out what he had to say. He reached out and patted my stomach, as if I were a woman expecting a bairn.

'I hear you're a cheeky chappie,' he said.

I just mumbled.

'And I also hear there's a bit of skill underneath all that fat. Well, you've got two weeks to get it all off. If you don't, you're out of the youth team and out of the club.'

I left the room in tears and ran home, feeling really

scared. To be fair to Jack, he did try to help me as well as frightening me. When I went to the Oven Door Tea Room near the training ground, where I used to go every day after training and stuff my face with cakes, I discovered they'd had orders not to serve me. I had to eat lots of salads, not hamburgers and chips. I managed to do it, though not without a struggle. I also did lots of running wearing a plastic bin-liner under my clothes, to get me sweating, and I got my weight down. Jackie Milburn, one of Newcastle's greatest-ever players and Jack Charlton's uncle, came to the ground to have a look at me, and he thought I was really good. That was nice. He even told Bobby Robson, the England manager, I was one to look out for.

The next season, 1984–5, Jack made me captain of the youth team and we set off on a really good run in the Youth Cup, doing even better than we had the previous season. We thumped Everton 6–0 and beat Leeds and Manchester City. What was especially great was that we were getting big crowds at home for all our youth matches. We hammered Coventry 3–0 in the fifth round and in the semi-final we trounced Birmingham City 7–2 on aggregate, earning a place in the final, where we were due to meet Watford, then managed by Graham Taylor.

I'd also been playing quite often in the reserves, which was tough, as they tend to be full of old pros on the way down who know all the tricks, including how to flatten any cheeky seventeen-year-olds who think they are smart. Towards the end of that season, in March 1985, I was given my first chance to travel with the first team – for their game at Ipswich – which I suspect I enjoyed more than they enjoyed having me with them.

Chris Waddle had been injured and was on the subs' bench, replaced by Neil McDonald. Jack Charlton, who was never very good with names, thought Neil's first name was Gary. In the dressing room before the match, Jack instructed that Gary was to play wide on the right. I thought he'd said Gazza, so I rushed off to get the number 7 shirt. The gaffer asked what the hell I was doing. 'Sit down,' he said. 'I was talking to Gary, not to you.'

So I sat on the bench that day, in my ordinary clothes, as I was just travelling with the team, next to Chris Waddle. I kept offering him emergency rations, such as Mars bars and Twixes, which I wasn't even supposed to be eating myself. I insisted that he waved back at the crowd when they shouted his name, which he didn't want to do as he was concentrating on the game, knowing he might have to go on. I always find it hard to sit still and watch a game when I'm not playing.

Then, a few weeks later, on 8 April, I was named as a substitute, number 12, for what was usually Newcastle's biggest game of the season: Sunderland. As a member of the first-team squad, I was expected to turn up in a suit. You didn't get it free, or provided by sponsors. It was meant to be your own best suit. I went out and bought one at Top Man. I think I made it last a year before I got another one.

I didn't come on that day, but I was again named as a sub for the visit of QPR to St James' on 13 April. I couldn't believe it when big George Reilly came off after scoring the only goal of the match and Jack told me to get stripped off. I was greeted with a huge cheer when I came on for my debut. Many of the 21,000 there that day had seen me playing for the youth team, and the local papers had been going on about the need to try out new young talent, such as me.

I do like to talk to people on the pitch, always have done, even to members of the opposition. I found myself standing beside Robbie James of QPR, a very experienced Welsh international. I had been saying something like, 'Isn't this great, man? The atmosphere is unbelievable!' Then I got the ball, and he immediately tackled me. His elbow hit me in my throat, sending me flying practically out of the ground.

I was so excited that I can't remember much else about the game, except that we won 1–0. It all seemed to be over far too quickly, almost as soon as I'd come on. But I was thrilled that I did manage to get the ball into the net, even if the goal was disallowed.

Almost straight afterwards came the Youth Cup final. We were expected to hammer Watford but they held us to a goalless draw at St James' Park. However, in the replay at Vicarage Road, we beat them 4–1 in front of a crowd of 8,500, many of whom had come down from Newcastle. I scored twice and so did Joe Allon, who went on to play well for Hartlepool among others before injury cut short his career. It just shows that you can't tell what will happen in football.

As captain, I received the trophy, holding it high in the air, imagining I was at Wembley, winning the World Cup. For many in the team that day, it was the only thing they ever won. For me, it's still one of the most satisfying-ever games – being captain, winning the match, earning the cup. I was full of such hope for the future.

On the coach back to Newcastle, we were allowed fish and chips, still wrapped in newspaper, as a special treat. And before we got off the bus, Jack Charlton told me he was going to offer me a two-year contract as a full professional. I was going to be eighteen in just a week or so, so I'd been on tenterhooks about whether or not I'd be signed. I never asked him about the details. I had no agent or adviser to discuss it with or negotiate the best terms. I just said yes. At once.

My wages went up from £25 as an apprentice to £120 a week as a pro. I was thrilled. I would also earn another £120 a game in appearance money, which seemed even better. In my contract, Newcastle insisted on a further two-year option on me. I should never have signed the contract with that clause in it. Needless to say, I didn't fully understand it. But having said that, if I were eighteen again now and being offered that contract, I would probably do exactly the same. I'd have signed anything they stuck in front of me.

Big Jack was brilliant to me. He took me fishing with him one day. I'd just bought some new gear which had cost me £120. I'd had to take out a loan to get it. But he took one look at it and threw it in the river, saying it was rubbish. He then told me what sort of gear I really should have for proper fishing.

I'd always enjoyed a spot of fishing, since I was about

seven, in ponds and that. I caught my first fish, a perch, when I was ten or so. Once I got to eighteen, and could afford it, I took up trout fishing. At the time I much preferred fishing to golf as a form of relaxation. I found it more lively. With golf, you take one shot and then spend the rest of your time walking to find your ball.

I got another run-out in the first team before the end of the season, coming on as a sub in our last home game, against Spurs. I thought I did quite well. I discovered later that a Spurs fan called Irving Scholar, who happened to be sitting in the stand that day, also thought I had done quite well.

I began the 1985–6 season with great hopes that I would get into the first team on a regular basis. I was so full of confidence that I got engaged to Gail. Then various developments suddenly changed things at the club. First Chris Waddle left for Spurs. It wasn't that he was a particular mate of mine at the time, as I was still hanging around with players I'd been in the youth team with, like Ian Bogie and Paul Stephenson, both of whom had been offered pro forms along with me. Chris, meanwhile, was an established star. But he had always been good for advice when I had problems or wanted help, and I did miss him. He was also a brilliant player, of course. I felt it was a bad sign that Newcastle had let him go.

Then Big Jack resigned. I'd been sitting beside him on the bench for one game, for which I was a sub, and had listened to the crowd starting to chant, 'Charlton out.' I could hear him saying, 'I don't need all this.' Not long afterwards, he jacked it in.

Big Jack was never one to take criticism or stay anywhere he wasn't wanted. If he wasn't wanted, that was fine by him, he would just be off. He wished me all the best when he left. I was sorry he never managed England rather than Ireland. I feel he would have done a good job, but I could see that the establishment would never take to him.

Willie McFaul took over as manager. I'd known him since I first joined the club as a schoolboy, and he'd served the club in almost every capacity, apart from tea lady. I always got the impression he liked me, so that was reassuring, at least.

I was picked for the first game of the season, away to Southampton. It felt a bit odd, pulling on Waddle's number 11 shirt. It seemed strange to me that I was preferred to David McCreery, who had been a good friend to me. When I came off, ten minutes before the end, David gave me a big hug as he replaced me.

Peter Shilton was in goal for Southampton. I tried to dribble through the whole of their defence a few times, on my own, thinking, this is the life, this is football. I'll just get through this lot and then I'll tap it past Shilts. I could hear Glenn Roeder behind me, shouting 'Fucking calm down, Gazza!' I was like that in all my early games, trying to do too much. I relied on people like David McCreery to do all the boring work of tracking back.

After we got a draw in that match, I played in the next four. We won three and drew one of those, moving into fourth place in the league. Then we went to Old Trafford to meet Manchester United, managed by Ron Atkinson. There were 51,000 in the crowd, the biggest I'd ever played in front of. I didn't quite freeze, but I have to admit I didn't play to the best of my ability. We were battered 3–0 and I fully expected Man United to win the title that season.

I was bitterly disappointed to find myself on the bench for the next match, with Spurs: I'd been looking forward to playing against Waddle. But I was young and still hadn't played many first-team games. Willie brought me on when we were 5–1 down. Our fans had been chanting for me. Because we were so far behind, I was able to play with no pressure and sprayed the ball around.

I got my first goal for Newcastle against Oxford, in our 3–0 victory over them at home. I stayed in the team for most of the season and was twice made North-Eastern Young Player of the Month. When I was injured against Man City and was out for three weeks, I was worried sick that someone would get my place and keep it.

I managed to get fit in time to play Liverpool at Anfield. I'd always admired them, especially Kenny Dalglish. As I ran out on to the pitch and saw the sign proclaiming 'This is Anfield', I thought I'd like to be part of them one day. They had an excellent team, much better than Newcastle's. And the club seemed to be forward-looking, unlike Newcastle in those days.

On the field, I said to Dalglish, 'Hiya, Kenny, all right?' – and of course he didn't know who the fuck I was. He was standing by a post at the time, waiting for a corner to come over, concentrating hard, so he wasn't too pleased with me rabbiting on. We got a draw that day, which was good, considering that Liverpool went on to win the league.

Although I was playing regularly, I was still struggling to keep my weight down. Perhaps I'd grown over-confident, having established myself in the first team, or so I thought. In any event, I'd lapsed into my old bad eating habits. The gaffer threatened to fine me for every pound I was overweight, so I went on the bin-liners again, trying to sweat it all off. I found not eating at all for a few days was the best way to lose it, and I managed to shed half a stone.

Against Man United at home, Remi Moses was marking me, following me everywhere. To annoy him, I said to him, 'Man U don't need you,' because that was all he was doing, nothing else useful. But not all my chat in that match was designed to needle the opposition. They got a penalty, which Bryan Robson took. I was so thrilled to be playing on the same pitch as a world-class player that after he scored from that penalty and was walking back, I said to him: 'Great penalty, Bryan.' If the Newcastle fans had heard that, they would have lynched me, particularly as we lost 4–2.

In a game against Everton, I took the ball into the corner flag and shielded it for about ten minutes while Peter Reid tried to kick me up in the air. He'll deny it was ten minutes, of course, but it was a very long time, and he was getting mad with me, a young kid doing this to him. Thanks to all the weight training, my upper body was strong enough to keep him off.

I had no fear of anyone, even people like Terry Fenwick, who could be pretty hard, and clever with it.

He marked me when we played Spurs, but I still scored. Of the hard men, Mick Harford was probably the toughest I ever played against. We had one very tough player of our own at Newcastle called Billy Whitehurst. He was a really physical tackler. In training one day I beat him by putting the ball through his legs and he grabbed me and said, 'Whoa, son – do that again and I'll break your fucking jaw.'

I didn't actually mean to do it again – I wasn't that stupid – but a ball came to me very quickly and bounced off me and through Billy's legs. Billy hit me which made John Bailey laugh and I said to him, 'You're a has-been, John.'

In the dressing room afterwards, when I was putting my clothes on, John came up and thumped me. I went home in tears and stayed there for the next three days.

It was all part of growing up, finding out how things worked, how to behave. Perhaps I had been a bit cocky, taking the piss out of senior players. I soon realised that was a bad thing to do and I came to respect them, as I have always done since. They have been there, done it and survived, so you have to respect them.

Between December and April I had a run of seventeen games in the starting line-up and my game improved a lot. I was much more consistent, and scored the odd goal. I was still trying too hard, of course, and attempting too many tricks. I once caught the ball on my shoulder, but the ref couldn't believe it and declared it a hand-ball, which it wasn't. The other side got a free kick out of it all the same. John Anderson, our full-back, gave me a right bollocking for that, telling me I had been stupid. I told him to fuck off.

But the team wasn't doing so well after its decent start, and we were sinking down to mid-table. We'd bought nobody, apart from our hard man Billy Whitehurst, from Hull, who wasn't exactly the best striker in the country.

In a game against Birmingham City, I seemed to be getting whacked all the time. I finally saw red and punched Robert Hopkins, right in front of the ref, and got myself sent off for the first time in my career. I ran off the pitch crying. I went straight past the bench and into the dressing room, where I kicked every bit of furniture. Stupid, I know. It's hard to describe what happens in those moments on the field. It's a cliché but a red mist really does seem to descend, clouding the big picture, making you unable to stand back and consider the likely consequences of your actions. All you see is what has upset you, and you lash out.

Because of suspension and injury, I missed quite a few matches at the end of that season. Unable to play, I grew depressed and started pigging out again. I had too much time on my hands. I went out with Jimmy a lot, or played snooker with all my old mates. We got ourselves involved in another motor accident when a bloke ran in front of my car. It was his fault, and I couldn't avoid him but, panicking again, we drove away at top speed. I hadn't realised that someone had taken a note of my registration number. I was tracked down and fined for failing to stop after an accident, failing to report an accident, and other stuff. The club was furious with me. They said I was tarnishing their good name.

Newcastle finished only eleventh in 1985–6, but it had been a great season for me personally. I had played thirty-one league games, even though it was only my second season in the first team, plus four Cup games. With nine goals, I was top scorer after Peter Beardsley. I'd also acquired an adviser, Alastair Garvie, who had been assistant secretary at Newcastle before setting himself up as an agent. He was also looking after Chris Waddle, among others.

In the first team, I was playing against many famous footballers, people I had only previously seen on television. I was also playing on famous pitches, hallowed turf where the greats of the past had performed. I remember, when I first played at Old Trafford, sitting on a toilet and wondering how many idols had sat there before me. Would George Best ever have sat on this very seat? It was all quite hard to believe.

The established lads had been so helpful, right from the beginning, when I was only on the fringes of the first team. John Bailey may have been a joker in the dressing room, but he was kind to me and gave me good advice. When Tony Cunningham arrived for training in his BMW, I would call out, 'Can I park your car?' and he often let me. Both on and off the pitch, Glenn Roeder was probably the greatest support to me. 'You're doing well, keep it up,' he'd say to me all the time during games. And when I was still quite young, he took me home with him, to where he lived in Essex, for a bit of a holiday. While I was there, he drove me past this big, posh house. 'Look at that,' he said, pointing it out to me. 'Trevor Brooking lives there. One of these days, if you work hard, keep at it, and don't get distracted, you could have a house like that.' I was dead impressed.

At the end of the close season, Willie McFaul called me into his office. I thought I was in for a bollocking for some crime I had forgotten, but instead he said: 'Here, I've got a present for you.' He'd got an advance copy of the 1986–87 *Rothmans Football Yearbook*. I didn't twig why he was giving it to me till I saw the cover. The photograph on it showed me beating Mark Lawrenson of Liverpool. I appear to be pushing him off, bashing him on the face with my left arm, but, of course, I'm not – it's just the camera angle. It was sheer skill and determination.

I look so young. Chubby cheeks, floppy hair. But then, I was young, I suppose. It had been a very good beginning.

He can be a loony with a fast mouth. He's either going to be one of the greats or finish up at forty, bitter about wasting such talent.
John Bailey, former Newcastle colleague, 1988

George Best without brains.
Stan Seymour, Newcastle chairman, 1988

He is accused of being arrogant, unable to cope with the press and a boozer. Sounds like he's got a chance to me.
George Best, 1988

6

GRABBED BY VINNIE, BUT NOT BY FERGIE

The 1986–7 season was a good one for me: I played twenty-four games and scored five goals, though I was out for a while with a groin strain. And at the end of that season, I was picked for the England Under-21 team. It was my first representative honour and it made up for the fact that I never played for England Schoolboys, which I won't mention ever again.

I was selected for an Under-21 tournament in Toulon. It was the first time I'd ever been abroad, and for many years afterwards I used to wind people up by claiming that Toulon was the capital of France, because that was the only place in France I'd ever been to.

It was also the first time I'd ever been in an

aeroplane. I was shit-scared, convinced that the thing would crash and I would die. I had a couple of brandies beforehand to give me Dutch courage, but I was still worried about getting on the plane. The England doctor had to take me by the hand and physically lead me on board – and even then I held his hand for most of the flight, like a little boy, as I was still shaking so much.

Our first game was against Morocco, and I scored with a free kick. It was not only our first goal but the first goal of the whole tournament. We beat Morocco 2–0, so it was a good start, but the biggest pleasure for me was having been able to pay for my dad and a couple of his mates to come out to Toulon to watch me play and then enjoy a fishing holiday. I felt happy that I could at last pay back my dad in some way for all his support.

I was so excited during the trip that I could hardly sleep. Instead I used to go to other players' bedrooms at night, to talk to them, see what they were doing. For some reason, it didn't seem to please them.

I played in the draw against Russia, but then I got 'flu and missed the game against France, who beat us 2–0. I was back for the match with Portugal, which finished in a goalless draw. We ended up fifth in the tournament, which was disappointing.

Back in Newcastle for the 1987–8 season, one of the big thrills was the arrival of Mirandinha, the first Brazilian to play in England. On his first day at training, we all stood in a line and shook hands with him, one by one. After I'd taken my turn to welcome him, I nipped along the back of the line and rejoined it at the end to shake his hand again. He must have thought there was a set of Gascoigne twins playing for his new club.

I took it upon myself to teach Mirandinha English, starting with the days of the week. The lads tested him afterwards every day to see if he'd got them right. When it came to Wednesday, and the players asked him what day it was, he said 'Wankday'. The lads were practically in tears.

He played his first game away against Norwich. Hundreds of Geordies made the long trek to Norfolk wearing sombrero-type straw hats. Our Brazilian took a free kick from about sixty yards out and tried to score and all the fans went wild. He always tried to score, wherever he was: the one word I never got him to understand was 'pass'. In his next away game, at Manchester United, he scored two goals.

Mirandinha was given a sponsored car when he

joined the club, a VW Golf GTi. One day I asked him if I could borrow it. As yet he didn't really know much about me, except that I was in the team, so he agreed and I went out for a spin in it with Jimmy. As we were driving along we happened to pass a lad from Dunston we both knew, in his car, someone who always thought he was right flash. So I decided to race him, overtaking him as fast as I could and speeding away from him. Unfortunately, moments later I braked too quickly at a corner and went straight through a fence into a field.

Next day at training, Mirandinha asked for his car back. I said, 'Car? Car? What car?' Eventually, I took him to it – still stuck in the fence, its back wheels almost touching the front wheels. Despite all that, I got my own sponsored club car not long afterwards.

I felt a bit guilty about what I'd done to Mirandinha's Golf. When I heard that his two little kids were desperate for a dog, I bought them one, a springer spaniel. He was so delighted he called the dog Gazza. I responded by telling him I would call my goldfish Mirandinha.

That season I was chosen again for the England Under-21s, and I was desperate to play, even though I'd picked up a knock. So I didn't report for treatment, as

FAMILY ALBUM

Above, left to right: earliest snap of me, aged about one; me with sister Anna in the middle and Carl right, three blond bombshells; the four Gascoignes, Carl, Lindsay, Anna and me at the back.

Below: me aged about 13, very sensitive . . . or I could have hurt me ankle.

Previous page: I've always tried to help. In 1988, while in the Newcastle first team, coaching some lads at Chester-le-Street.

Opposite, top: in the team for Redheugh Boys, aged 14; aged 15, now a Newcastle United schoolboy, receiving an award from all-time Newcastle superstar Chris Waddle – he looks big and old enough to be my dad. *Below*: with my real and only dad, John Gascoigne.

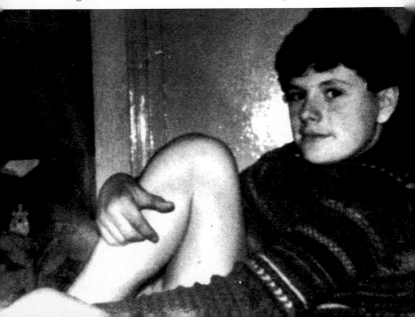

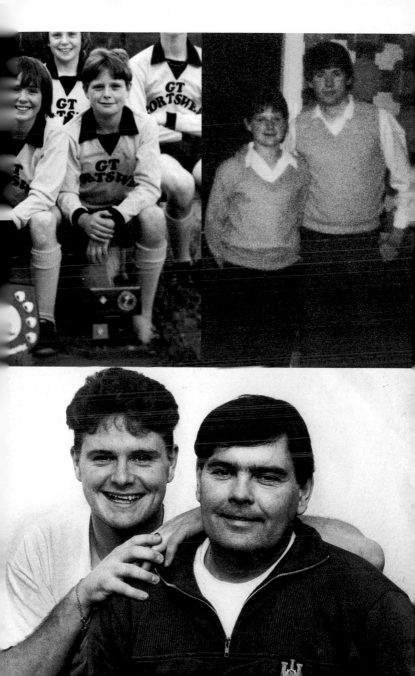

FAMILY AFFAIRS
Left: Lindsay's 21st birthday, 1994, with (left to right) Carl, Lindsay, me, Mam, Dad, Anna; *right*: Carl with wife Jane and children Lauren and Joe.

Me mam. I often go to bingo with her which leads to lots of autograph hunters, so she has her own handwritten sign.

With Anna, the famous actress, at the premiere of her film *Dream On* in Newcastle, 1990.

Sister Lindsay with her son
Cameron, already a brilliant player.

Anna's bairns, Harley and Jay.

While playing for Lazio in 1992, the Pope asked to see me. I didn't make
it but he presented Anna and Mam with rosary beads and my dad with a
gold cross.

Arriving back from yet another hol with Sheryl and her children Mason and Bianca, 1995.

My wedding to Sheryl, 1996; (*opposite*) with some of my England colleagues at the reception and with my mates Chris Evans and Danny Baker.

My son Regan, pride and joy: . . . and at his fourth birthday party.
as a baby in 1996 . . .

With Regan aged six and Mason, 12, on the pitch at Everton, 2002.

I should have done, or tell Willie McFaul or Dave Sexton, the Under-21s manager, and succeeded in hiding the problem in training. But by the time of the Under-21 match it was really hurting. I ran around the field like a nutter, and was taken off before I did something stupid. The gaffer was less than pleased when I returned home injured and missed two matches, including one with Man United.

I was dropped from the Under-21s, which woke me up. I got my head down, started working hard and regained my place in the team. At the end of October, I won the Barclays Young Eagle of the Month award and was back in favour with Dave Sexton. I worked my socks off in our 5–1 win against Yugoslavia, scoring twice. And then I went and got myself sent off playing for Newcastle against QPR in November. As always with me, things seem to be going well, moving forward, and then something happens to set me back and the depression sets in.

In a game against West Ham, I got a bit frustrated and lashed out at Billy Bonds, the Hammers defender. He was clutching his leg.

'All right, Billy?' I asked him.

'It's my ankle,' said Billy.

'That's all right, then,' I said. 'As long as it's not your arthritis.'

A bit cheeky, and also unwise, since Billy, despite being forty-one, was still one of England's toughest defenders. He proceeded to mark me out of the game and we lost 2–1. Mirandinha got our consolation goal. That'll larn me, I thought. But of course it didn't.

I was now in my third full season in the Newcastle first team and felt I was a fully-fledged regular. But I was beginning to suspect that the club itself wasn't moving forward, which was worrying. Liverpool had signed John Barnes from Watford and then taken Beardsley from us. That just seemed to sum up our lack of ambition. For a club as big as Newcastle to have won bugger-all in thirty years was a disgrace, really.

The game which was to change my life, though I didn't know it at the time, was on 23 January 1988 against Spurs at home. We beat them 2–0 and I got both goals. Terry Venables, the Tottenham manager, and Irving Scholar, who had by now become their chairman, told me later that it was one of the best performances they'd ever seen from a player of my age. I gathered from Mel Stein, my recently acquired lawyer, that Irving

Scholar had asked what it would take to bring me to London.

I wasn't bothered. I had never really fancied Spurs in particular or going south in general. There was also said to have been an approach from Manchester United, but I wasn't much interested in that, either. If I was going anywhere, I wanted it to be Liverpool. I'd spoken to Kenny Dalglish a few times and he seemed really keen on me, so I couldn't understand why nothing was happening there. I was told that Liverpool didn't have the money. Kenny, apparently, was hoping I would stay on at Newcastle for another year, during which time he would be able to get the transfer fee together.

Nothing continued to happen but I kept on playing well. I won the Barclays Eagle of the Month award again in January, and Newcastle crept into the top half of the table. Bobby Robson, the England manager, was quoted as saying that I was 'a little gem'. I've been called a few names in my life, not all of them complimentary, or repeatable, but at the age of twenty, for the England manager to say that gave me the biggest lift in my footballing life so far.

In February 1988 we were away to Wimbledon. They were known as a really tough team, because of

John Fashanu, Dennis Wise and Vinnie Jones. I'd been pleased with my performance when we'd met them at home, but Vinnie hadn't played that day. The press built up the return match into a personal duel between Jones, the hard man who took no prisoners, and me, the young kid full of fancy tricks.

I didn't really know much about Vinnie but he'd probably heard or read a bit about me being a new young player to watch, perhaps even a 'gem' in the making. During our warm-up, a lot of the photographers were taking pictures of me and I was generally getting quite a bit of attention. I could see Vinnie glaring at me. As I watched him in his warm-up, he looked huge. I'm always nervous and hyped-up before a game, but this time I was physically sick. As we walked out on to the pitch, and immediately after the kick-off, he made a point of talking to me. 'I'm Vinnie Jones. I'm a fucking gypsy. It's just you and me today, fat boy, just you and me . . .'

It's quite normal for more experienced players to try to intimidate you, sometimes by threatening to kill or maim you, especially if you're young and new or seen as a fancy-dan player. But one look at Vinnie and I believed his threat. I didn't think he was acting, though we know now what a good actor he has become. I was sure he meant it, and I was right.

The first time I touched the ball, he kicked me up in the air. He never left me alone all afternoon, except when he went off once to take a throw-in. 'I'm off to take a throw, but I'll be fucking back,' he snarled.

As a free kick was being taken, Vinnie was standing in front of me, waiting. I suddenly felt his hand come around and grab me by the balls. I screamed in agony. I thought at the time that nobody had seen what had happened, since we were not involved in the free kick, but a photograph was taken that appeared everywhere afterwards, becoming one of football's best-known images. Someone must have made a fortune out of that, and I must say it didn't in the end do Vinnie or me any harm, either.

The game finished 0–0 and after the final whistle a Newcastle fan presented me with a bunch of roses. I sent someone to the Wimbledon dressing room with a single red rose from the bunch for Vinnie. In reply, Vinnie sent me a toilet brush. It made me laugh, but I didn't quite get the joke. No one had yet called me daft as a brush, at least not in public. I now know, from Vinnie's own autobiography, that when my rose arrived he looked around the dressing room for something to send back to me, and the toilet brush happened to be the first thing he saw. Later on, Vinnie and I became good friends and I went fishing and shooting at his place.

Wimbledon had the last laugh on us that season. They beat us 3–1 in the fifth round of the Cup, having already knocked us out of the Littlewoods (League) Cup. They went on to beat Liverpool in the FA Cup final.

By this time I'd come to believe that the Newcastle board did not know as much about football as they did about the politics of being a director. We'd had no decent new signings and some of the board members didn't seem interested in putting much of their own money into the club. Stan Seymour, the chairman, liked to call himself Mr Newcastle – though I'm sure no one else would have called him that. Gordon McKeag, who took over as chairman from Stan, spoke as if he had a plum in his mouth and seemed to me stuck up. He rose to become League chairman, but I still didn't reckon he knew much about football, just the politics.

I was beginning to feel that I didn't want to stay at Newcastle any longer, though I didn't know where I would go. Perhaps I should have waited another year for

Kenny and Liverpool to make a bid. The uncertainty kept me awake at night, with everything going round and round my head, worrying about what was going to happen. I made endless lists. The frustration affected my game. When I played for the Under-21s against Scotland I got taken off because I was crap.

Towards the end of the season, Newcastle went to Derby, now managed by Arthur Cox, my old manager. I dreaded hearing his voice shouting at me, telling me exactly what he thought of my performance. He didn't need to tell me. I was awful and ended up getting sent off, for the second time that season.

As I stormed towards the dressing room, I kicked over the Derby physio's water bucket, soaking a woman from their staff. Then I trashed the dressing room, breaking the door. Arthur Cox was furious with me.

After a couple of days, when I'd cooled down, and before I got the bill for the breakages, I wrote a letter of apology to Arthur. I can't remember exactly what I wrote, but Arthur later told me that I'd gone on about wanting to win things, wanting to be the best player in the country, and my frustration when I played badly.

Eventually, Newcastle got the message that I wanted to leave and wouldn't be signing another two-year contract. They officially gave their permission for my advisers to speak to Tottenham. Some of the Newcastle fans weren't very pleased, naturally enough.

Alex Ferguson found out what Spurs were prepared to offer me. They couldn't match it, apparently, but said that I'd more than make up the shortfall in win bonuses if I came to Man United. Fergie saw me as the natural successor to Bryan Robson, or so I was told, though later on, when I told Robbo this, I learned that this wasn't the story he'd heard.

Fergie had discussions with my lawyer, Mel Stein, as if he was certain I would sign for them. The figures bandied around seemed enormous at the time, though they were nothing like those that change hands today. All I was really interested in was being able to buy a house for my mam and dad. In Fergie's autobiography, this somehow got turned into me saying that the club had to buy a house for them, but this wasn't so.

On 7 May I pulled on a Newcastle shirt at St James' Park for the last time. Nothing had been officially settled, but I knew, and most people assumed, that I wouldn't be playing for them the next season. The game was against West Ham and at the end of it, I ran to the Gallowgate End and applauded those fans who had been applauding me. I ran all round the ground and finally left the pitch in tears. In the dressing room, it was very quiet. A few of the lads wished me luck, but I could sense a distance between me and them.

There was, in fact, nearly a last-minute change of plan. John Hall, later Sir John, was mounting a bid to take over Newcastle FC, and he rang me up. He said that although he could make no promises about when and how he might gain control of the club, he wanted me to stay. But he understood that I couldn't wait much longer. As it turned out, he didn't take over till quite a bit later.

I was pleased to get away with the Under-21s in Toulon. We started with a 2–1 win over Mexico. In the squad we had Nigel Martyn, David Platt, Michael Thomas, David Rocastle, all of whom made the full national team. In the semi-final against Morocco I got our goal, which took us into the final against France. The French decided to man mark me. Once you've been marked by Vinnie Jones, there's not much that can frighten you. We tired in extra time and France beat us 4–2.

I got back to England to find that Newcastle had now decided that I was worth £2 million. It doesn't seem a lot now, but it seemed a fortune then, for someone who had just turned 21 and had yet to play for the national team, and also someone for whom they were only wanting to pay £250 a week. That was what Newcastle were offering, if I stayed and signed a new contract. Spurs, on the other hand, were prepared to pay about six times that and at Man United, so they said, I would get almost as much.

I hadn't actually met Terry Venables, the Spurs manager, yet. I agreed to go down to London to be introduced to him at Mel's office in Mayfair. I sat in a room with El Tel, cuddling a giant talking bear called Teddy Ruxpin, which Mel and Len Lazarus, my accountant, had given me for my twenty-first birthday. I let Teddy do most of the talking. I don't think Terry Venables could really believe it, but at least he could see what he might be getting for his money.

For my part, I was very impressed by what Venables had to say, especially when he told me that if I came to him, and was trained by him, I would be sure to get into the full England team. That mattered to me even more than the money being offered.

In the absence of any firm offer from Liverpool, just the request to wait a year, I didn't know what to do. I still hadn't decided against Manchester United. In fact, if anything I was veering towards them. I thought I'd feel more at home if I stayed in the north. Going south would be a big change. When I played for the Under-21s, a lot of the southern lads couldn't understand my accent, or so they claimed.

I was invited by Fergie to come and look round Old Trafford. I set out to drive myself to Manchester, but changed my mind and didn't go that day. I was in a very confused state.

Fergie phoned to say that he was about to go on holiday, but he really did want me to sign for him. I have to admit I did tell him on the phone, 'Don't worry, go on your holiday, and when you come back, I'll sign for you.' I know he was furious when I didn't, as he has since revealed. But while Liverpool remained my first choice, I just couldn't make up my mind. One day I would feel I should go to Old Trafford and the next I wasn't at all sure.

Irving Scholar of Spurs then made a smart move. He got Glenn Roeder to talk to me. We met in a pub in Newcastle and Glenn told me it would be good at Spurs. This only added to my confusion. I went down to London to talk to Irving Scholar and I was most impressed by his enthusiasm. He seemed to be a real football fan. Everyone at the club was friendly, and not at all stuck up, as I had thought they might be. There didn't seem to be a lot of difference between Geordies and Cockneys.

Mel tried to get hold of Fergie, by now away on holiday, to ask if Man United would match the terms Spurs were offering, but he couldn't get through. Mobile phones were not then as good as they are now, especially when it came to international calls.

Irving Scholar was offering me a very good deal, and lots of extras. Tottenham were then sponsored by Hummell, and I was wearing their boots at the time, so that was another factor. Chris Waddle had convinced me I'd like it at White Hart Lane. I liked the look of Venables and Scholar, and they had offered me the best terms. So, in the summer of 1988, I signed for Spurs.

I'm sure Fergie thought I'd behaved like a stupid little bastard, double-crossing him, and many people feel he's never forgiven me. He sent me a letter saying I'd been a silly boy, that he'd believed me when I'd promised I would join Man United. I don't know where that letter is now. There's no doubt he was upset at the time, but he later invited me to play in his testimonial, and I agreed. And he gave me a watch, which I still have somewhere. As for me, I never hold grudges against anyone or any club.

Now my immediate future had finally been resolved. I was sad to be leaving Newcastle, and in some ways I didn't want to go. They have the best fans in the world, but I could see that for the moment they were a selling not a buying club.

They [the schoolboys] asked me things like:
'How big are Gazza's balls?'
Vinnie Jones, after addressing the boys of Eton College, 1996

I had been determined to bring Paul to United ever since he had tortured us with a devastating performance for Newcastle at St James' Park. We sent out the powerful midfield of Moses, Robson and Whiteside that day but the twenty-year-old Gascoigne outplayed them, crowning his precocious display by patting Remi Moses on the top of the head like a headmaster mildly rebuking one of his pupils . . . What a performance, and what a player! 'I'm going to sign him,' I told my assistant, Archie Knox, on the way home . . .

The fact that he never wore the red shirt was his mistake, not ours. As far as I am concerned, I had a solid promise that he would sign for me and I think that his change of mind hurt both of us.
Sir Alex Ferguson, Managing My Life, 1999

7

FUN AT SPURS

I started at Spurs on £1,500 a week – compared with the £120 a week I'd been getting for the previous few years at Newcastle. I was also paid appearance money, which took my wages up to around £2,500 a week. There was another bonus if I played for England. And I got a good boot deal, too, worth £10,000. I didn't have anything in my contract about bonuses for scoring goals. A lot of players have those, but I've never asked for them. It puts too much pressure on you.

Spurs were known as big spenders at the time, and there was a lot of cash around at White Hart Lane. They were the top team for gate money. In 1985 they were taking £2.5 million a year, ahead of Manchester United who were on only £2.25 million, with Liverpool and Arsenal quite a way behind. Things have changed a bit since then.

When I was signing for the club, I asked about a car, and they agreed to give me one – a Merc, I think it was. 'What about me dad?' I said. 'I want to buy him one as well.' They said they'd see to that too.

'Anything else?' inquired Irving.

'Me sister,' I said. 'She wants a sunbed.'

'Is that it?' he said at last, throwing his chequebook and credit cards at me.

I thought for a moment. 'Fishing. I could do with some new fishing gear.'

There was a fishing shop not far away from White Hart Lane, so I went there with Irving's credit card and ordered all the best gear, plus new tracksuits for my mates.

The transfer fee was £2.2 million, which was the most any British club had ever paid for a player, plus I got £100,000 as a signing-on fee. I gave £70,000 of it to me mam and dad to buy a house. I just splashed out, threw it around, thinking I'd lots of years left to make more.

One of the things Irving Scholar promised me was that they would pay for me to stay in a hotel for as long as I liked. They booked me into a very nice hotel called West Lodge Park, near Hadley Wood. The England team used to stay there at one time, and traditionally it was a base for one of the FA Cup final teams before the big day at Wembley. Spurs used it all the time. Or at least they had done until I moved in.

I'd also been promised that some of my friends could stay with me at West Lodge Park, to stop me from feeling homesick, settle me in, so I invited my Uncle Ian, my friends Cyril and Kikki and, of course, Jimmy Gardner to come and join me. On the night they arrived, we decided to order champagne to celebrate me signing for Spurs. I'd never had champagne before. We chose Dom Perignon, which seemed to be about the best, or at any rate the most expensive. It didn't seem very strong – till I stood up to go to the toilet.

After every bottle, it seemed a good idea for Jimmy to have a swim in the fish pond. Naked, of course – he didn't want to get his clothes wet, did he? He wasn't a pretty sight, but he attracted a large audience, judging by the number of complaints that reached Reception.

The next night we thought we'd try the champagne again, as it seemed a very good vintage. In three days we got through thirty-eight bottles of Dom Perignon before the hotel threw us out. I was called to Irving Scholar's office in the West End and we all trooped down there, where we had to line up like schoolboys to be told off. Irving was certainly cross with us, but I didn't think he seemed too furious. And compared with his mood after we moved to the Hendon Hall Hotel, he wasn't.

I didn't realise their piano was so valuable, or that my trick with the lighted cigarette, the tablecloth and the food was going to go wrong . . .

We were then moved into the Swallow Hotel at Waltham Abbey, with some stern warnings about not mucking it up ringing in our ears. Many of Tottenham's staff and players used the health club there and they didn't want to be banned because of my behaviour. And I didn't mess it up this time. I got on brilliantly with all the hotel staff. Whenever I got into a spot of bother, with the press or girls or whatever, I always knew I could retreat there and they'd look after me. I stayed at the Swallow for about six months and became so much part of the furniture that I used to sit in on interviews for new staff.

There was just one bloke who wasn't so fond of me. He was going out with a girl and they used to meet at the back of the hotel, where they thought they couldn't be seen. We spotted him one day from my bedroom window, in a compromising position. His trousers round his ankles, basically. I couldn't resist taking a pot at his bare arse with an air gun. What a shock he got. He was screaming and shouting. We, on the other hand, were pissing ourselves.

The *Sun* somehow found out about this incident. I did a deal with Kelvin McKenzie, who was the editor at the time. I'd talk to him exclusively provided that he said that it was Jimmy who fired the shot and not me. I always liked Kelvin. He was a straight talker and you knew where you stood with him. I remember him once asking me if I'd had a fling with a girl. 'It's dead simple,' he said. 'All I want to know is whether or not you sank the sausage.'

Having Chris Waddle at Spurs was a great help. When my mates all went back to Newcastle, I'd often go and stay with him and his wife Laura if I got fed up on my own in the hotel. I was also very friendly with Paul Moran and Paul Stewart, who signed for Spurs at the same time as me. I did get a bit homesick and often returned to the north-east.

Jimmy drove me all over the place. He would come down to the training ground and wait for me to finish, or collect me after a match at White Hart Lane, then he'd drive me back up to Newcastle for the night, if we had the next day off, or for the weekend.

His car broke down once, about halfway home. We

decided to hitch-hike the rest of the way. A Mother's Pride bakery van stopped to pick us up but we had to sit in the back, because the driver had no room for us at the front. After about two hours, we began to get hungry, really starving. Then it dawned on us that of course we were surrounded by loaves of bread. So we tucked in, tearing open the packets.

When we got out, we paid the driver for the bread, making sure we took away the loaves we'd only half finished in case we got peckish again.

I eventually bought my own house, at Dobbs Weir in Hertfordshire, which cost me £220,000. Gail came down from Newcastle and joined me there for a while, but it didn't last. I got caught with another girl, and that was it. We split up and she went back to the north-east. My moving south and seeing the bright lights of London was what really brought it to an end. But I didn't actually go on to have another regular girlfriend. I was really more interested in going out with the lads, drinking, living it up, having a good time with my mates. Gail and I had been going out for about six years, so it was a shame, I suppose. I gather she's now happily married – and probably quite pleased she didn't end up with me.

I first turned out for Tottenham on their pre-season

friendly tour in Sweden. As we ran on to the pitch for a game at Trelleborg, I patted the head of one of the pretty Swedish girls lined up to greet us. I honestly didn't take in what she looked like, and could never have recognised her again, but she remembered me and when we got to the next stop on our tour there was a steaming love letter waiting for me, together with a very revealing photograph. We passed the photo round the bus and all had a good laugh. At our hotel, a bunch of red roses arrived for me, and then she started phoning and asking for me.

Then she rang me in my room, saying that she was in the hotel, had booked into a room and wanted me to join her there. I made Waddler take all my calls after that, reckoning that one Geordie voice would sound very much like another to her. But she wouldn't take no for an answer. I told Terry Venables what was happening: that I was being stalked. The hotel register was checked and there was no trace of this girl. The letters and phone calls suddenly stopped, so I decided it had all been a hoax and forgot all about it.

But a few weeks later, a Sunday paper ran a piece claiming that I'd had a night of passion with this girl. Her photograph was in the paper. I still didn't recognise her. I don't know to this day whether she set the whole thing up herself or whether a newspaper had put her up to it. Either way, when it hadn't worked, somebody – she or the paper – had decided to go ahead with it anyway.

It was the first time anything like that had ever happened to me, but it certainly wouldn't be the last. I realised that I would have to be very careful from then on, constantly aware that girls making eyes at you are not always what they seem. It was a depressing prospect. It's awful to feel you have to be suspicious of people until you know for sure that they are genuine.

My first proper match for Spurs was a pre-season game against Arsenal in the Makita tournament, held at Wembley. I got plenty of stick from the Gunners, but when we were beaten 4–0, the Spurs fans booed as well. I could hear them chanting: 'What a waste of money.' Chris Waddle told me not to take it to heart. He'd needed time to win the fans over, too.

I hadn't even got off on the right foot with all of my team-mates. In one training session, I went to the toilet and found myself standing beside Paul Moran. He later became a good mate but I didn't know him yet, and he seemed very young. 'Are you an apprentice?' I asked him.

'Are you fucking joking, mate?' he retorted, and stormed out. I also had a bit of a ruck with Vinny

Samways in training, when we grabbed each other, though it wasn't serious. It was nothing really, just over a daft tackle, either I had made or he had made, can't remember which of us now. It was in Norway, on our pre-season tour. You get these rucks in training. They flare up suddenly but don't mean much. It shows that you're taking the training seriously.

My first league game for Tottenham should have been at home against Coventry, but it was postponed as the new stand wasn't ready. So as it turned out, my debut in a competitive match was at St James' Park. It's the sort of coincidence that always seems to happen in football.

I hoped the Newcastle fans, particularly the Gallowgate End, would understand why I had left and go easy on me, but the best thing you could say about the reception I was given was that it was mixed. When I took a corner, someone threw a Mars bar at me. My usual response to this was to treat it as a joke, pick up the Mars bar and bite a chunk out of it. I did try, but on this occasion, whoever had thrown it must have had it in his freezer for months, because it was rock hard. I've spent enough money on my teeth over the years, so I was relieved not to break any of them on that frozen Mars bar.

After drawing that match 2–2, we faced Arsenal at

home. I lost a boot after a tackle from Paul Davis, when he accidentally stood on it. I still had one shoe on and one shoe off when Chris Waddle put the ball through to me, but I managed to steer the ball past John Lukic and into the net with my stockinged foot. That pleased the crowd. I think the Spurs fans took to me more after that.

One thing I'd noticed about the Tottenham crowd was that they only got behind you if you were doing well. When you were not doing so well, there could be silence – or worse. At Newcastle, we could have been 5–0 down but the crowd would still be singing 'We'll support you ever more'. I also noticed that a large number of season ticket-holders in the West Stand always left well before the end. You could see the large gaps where they'd been sitting. You'd never get that at Newcastle.

I was dead excited when I moved into my new house. It was great getting it all just as I wanted it. But as I was getting ready to leave for the game one Saturday morning, I found the bath taps weren't working properly.

The problem nagged at me all the way to the ground. In the dressing room I was very quiet, which is not like me. Usually I'm jumping around all over the place, playing tricks, doing stupid things.

Eventually Venners came over to me and asked what the matter was, what was I depressed about? I said it was nothing, really, but he could see I was low. I just couldn't get it out of my head. I like things neat and tidy. I tick off jobs when they're done, and when they're not done they hang over me and start to worry me.

I'm always anxious. Even when larking around, there's a bit of me still anxious. There's almost always something on my mind which is about to concern me and which I'm trying to forget. Then it gets me depressed that I should be so stupid.

I told Terry about the problem with the bath. I would have to sort it out when I got home, and it was bugging me. He said: 'We've got water here. Have as many baths as you like.' But I just grunted and held my head in my hands. When someone gets into that state, it's hard to talk them out of it. They know it's trivial, but that doesn't make it go away.

Terry knew that however ridiculous the cause of the worry, it was the effect that mattered, and he could see that my anxiety was genuine. So he got out his mobile phone and checked my address with me. Someone managed to track down an emergency plumber and Terry talked him into going to the house there and then. It was still about an hour before kick-off. Just before we went out on to the pitch, the plumber rang Venners. Terry passed the phone to me, so that I could talk to the plumber myself and would know that it really was him and my bath really was working. Then I ran out on to the field with my head clear – and played a blinder.

Fierce and comic, formidable and vulnerable, urchin-like and waif-like, a strong head and torso with comparatively frail-looking breakable legs, strange-eyed, pink-faced, fair-haired, tense and upright, a priapic monolith in the Mediterranean sun – a marvellous equivocal sight.
Karl Miller on Paul Gascoigne in the London Review of Books, *1990*

Tyneside's very own renaissance man. A man capable of breaking both leg and wind at the same time.
Jimmy Greaves, Tottenham and England predecessor, in his Sun *column, 1996*

He's still lovable, even when he does something diabolical.
Gary Lineker, Tottenham team-mate, 1991

8

ENGLAND CALLS

Terry Venables was right. I got my call-up for England not long after I joined Spurs. It was in September 1988, for the game against Denmark. Terry called me across in training to give me the news. At first I thought he meant the England Under-21s. When he made it clear he was talking about the full England squad, I couldn't take it in. Everyone was shaking my hand and congratulating me.

I checked into the England hotel at Burnham Beeches and manager Bobby Robson made a special announcement welcoming the new members, including me, David Rocastle and Des Walker, and the whole squad clapped.

It sounds a bit schoolboyish, and it is in a way. You go up through the ranks till you achieve your lifetime's ambition: to get into the top class, with the big lads.

Bobby asked me if I'd brought a white shirt and tie with me. I'd been notified about this in advance, as there was some dinner we had to go to. I said: 'Yes, I've brought one white shirt, but I leave the other white shirt to you.'

In training, I sprinted up and down like an idiot, trying so hard. I was in awe of the senior players, like Bryan Robson. Just being in the same room as him was a thrill. Peter Shilton was winning his 101st cap. I wondered if I could ever get as many as that. Perhaps I'd never get more than one. Or even one. I loved being with Peter Beardsley, because of course I had played with him at Newcastle, and at least he understood my accent.

I knew I wasn't going to make the starting line-up this time, but I was pleased just to be one of the four subs, though of course I was desperately hoping I'd get on to the pitch. Walking out on to the Wembley turf for the preliminaries was brilliant. It was what I'd dreamed about, ever since I'd become a professional and long before: wearing the England shirt, walking out at Wembley. Tan-tan-tarrah.

Every time someone went down after a tackle and looked as if they might have to come off, I got all nervous. I was concerned that one of our lads might be seriously hurt, but at the same time excited at the thought that I might be sent on and worrying about how I'd perform. But as the game went on, I realised that the chances of me getting on at all, let alone having any time to touch the ball, were fading.

Towards the end, Bobby sent me and Tony Cottee to warm up. I ran up and down the touchline with Tony. 'Are you excited?' I said to him. 'I know I am.' I don't think he was really listening.

I finally stepped on to the park about five minutes before the end, replacing Peter Beardsley. By this time we were 1–0 up. Neil Webb had scored. I told the ref not to blow his whistle. Give us a bloody chance, ref. I got only about two touches, but I still felt so happy. I'd done it: I had won an England cap at the age of twenty-one. The crowd had been fantastic. Such as it was. Only 26,000 had turned up, this being a friendly. To most spectators, it probably seemed pretty boring – but to me it was the most exciting game the world had ever seen.

As I came off, I grabbed a handful of the Wembley grass and took it back to the dressing room with me. I put it in my sponge bag and kept it there for about a week, till it rotted and started smelling and I had to chuck it away. Back at Spurs, when I arrived for training, they all shook my hand again.

I was on the bench for the next England game, against Sweden, and didn't make it on to the field. This was the match in which Terry Butcher got a bad head injury – there was blood everywhere – and famously played on wearing a massive bandage. When he was rushed off into the dressing room for stitches, Bobby Robson made me go with them. I was mystified as to what they wanted me there for. When Terry was eventually patched up, looking like a mummy with that bandage round his head, desperate to go on again, Bobby turned to me and said, 'Gazza, this is what it's all about, playing for England.'

I was in the squad again for the next game, against Saudi Arabia in Riyadh. Everyone who was in the starting line-up was promised a brand-new car from Ford, an XRi Cabriolet. But again I was just one of the subs. I was gutted, missing out on a free car, and really jealous of the players who'd been picked. The wealth in Saudi Arabia was amazing. I'd never seen houses like it before. Everyone seemed to live in a palace, whether they were royal or not. We were all warned about drinking. If we got caught with alcohol we would really be for it – and not just from Bobby, either.

On the sidelines, I did my warm-up routine for about twenty-five minutes, going through my stretching exercises right in front of Bobby, so that he could hardly see what was happening on the pitch. But still he didn't send me on. At last, about ten minutes before the end, I got the call to replace Chris Waddle. It was as if the manager had taken a vow that his Geordie sub could be used only in place of another Geordie.

'Gazza, go on and give us a goal,' he told me as he pushed me on.

'Fucking hell,' I said. 'You've only given us five minutes.'

We played poorly that day. Don't ask me why. Perhaps it was the heat. Or not being able to have a drink. We were lucky to manage a 1–1 draw, with Tony Adams saving our blushes. When we got back to England, we found that Bobby was being rubbished in the press: 'For the Love of Allah, Go Now.' Some of the papers were arguing that if we carried on like this, we wouldn't have a chance of qualifying for the World Cup, so we might as well have a new manager now. The football press, of course, are absolutely brilliant at predicting what will happen. They are always spot-on. Or not.

In the qualifying rounds for the 1990 World Cup, we had to play Sweden, Poland and Albania. Albania was awful, so backward and primitive. Our hotel was very basic and the phones were useless. We were allowed to make only one call home and we were all given a set time to do it. Mine was five o'clock in the morning. I was still with Gail at the time, so I rang her in England. Fuck knows what time it was there, but I woke her up. She shouted at me, 'Why the hell haven't you rung me before?' I explained that we were only allowed one phone call. 'You're a liar,' she said, and hung up on me.

Out in Albania, we were followed everywhere by kids begging. We had some little England badges and stuff to give away but the minute we showed them, we were surrounded and practically torn to pieces. There was nothing for it but to throw them all up in the air and run like hell back to the hotel. Looking over our shoulders, it was like a scene from Hitchcock's *The Birds* with all these kids swooping on the ground trying to grab those trinkets.

Stuck in the hotel, it was so boring. There was nothing to do, no facilities. From my bedroom window, in a sort of yard down below beside the hotel, I noticed some hens and chickens. While the rest of the lads were at a meeting, I went round their bedrooms and took all their little packets of soap, which was about the only luxury the hotel provided. Back in my bedroom, I amused myself by throwing the soap at the chickens to see how many I could hit. Chris Waddle joined me, and we laid bets on who would hit one. Soon John Barnes came in as well, to see what we were doing, what all the shouting was about, and then some of the others.

In all the commotion, I didn't see Bobby Robson walk in. Just when I'd scored a really good hit, practically killing a chicken. He stared at me in amazement, then asked what I was doing, which was pretty obvious, really. I said I was trying to hit the chickens with bars of soap.

I hurled a piece of soap out of the window, but missed this time. Bobby gave a funny smile. Then he walked out of the room, shaking his head.

I didn't get on the pitch in that game, except at half-time, when I took to the field to offer some of my goalkeeping impersonations, but we won 2–0 and I was beginning to feel a real part of the England squad.

In the return game against Albania, in April 1989,

I got to play for about twenty-five minutes. Bobby told me to keep to the right, as Waddle was doing a great job down the left, but in my excitement I immediately forgot his instructions and ran around like a kid in a playground, chasing every ball.

Fortunately, I didn't do myself any harm, setting up one goal for Waddler – and scoring one myself, with my left foot, after beating two men. It was my first goal for England and it felt fantastic. I ran across to acknowledge the cheers of the crowd. What I really wanted to do was hug me father, but he wasn't there: he was watching on telly at home. We won that match 5–0. As we came off the pitch, Chris Waddle said to me: 'That's it, you've cracked it now. Work hard and you'll be going to the World Cup.'

Bobby Robson didn't give me that impression, though. He gave me a bollocking afterwards for disobeying his instructions. I told him I thought he was playing me out of position by shoving me on the right. He told me, pretty firmly, in straightforward Geordie, that if and when I played for fucking England again, I'd play where he fucking well told me to play. But even if he didn't say so, I had a sneaking suspicion he had quite enjoyed my performance.

My debut in the England starting line came the following month, in a friendly in May against Chile at Wembley. When Neil Webb was injured, I got his place in midfield. It hadn't bothered me, being sub for all those games. I had been injured quite a bit myself, so I wasn't always available anyway, and I believed my turn would come. As qualification for the World Cup grew closer, I was enjoying an injury-free run and played in most of the games. I remember jumping for joy into the arms of David Seaman, against Poland I think it was. He was just beginning to step into Peter Shilton's boots, though he and I were both subs that day.

I wasn't in the starting line-up against Sweden in Stockholm, which depressed me. Bobby made it clear I had to grow up, or I wouldn't be chosen for the squad going to Italy, if we got there. He played Steve McMahon and Neil Webb in the middle instead. I didn't get on till twenty minutes or so before the end, but this time I did what I was told to do by Bobby, playing a holding role, doing nothing daft, and we secured a vital 0–0 draw. Bobby put his arm round me at the end and told me I'd done well. He's never been one to hold grudges.

All the same, I worried, as I always did, that some of my off-the-pitch adventures would bugger up my

England chances. Even some of my on-the-pitch antics, come to that. When Spurs were away to Crystal Palace in the 1989–90 season, before the kick-off, while we were warming up, there were these mascots mucking around, three blokes dressed up as cartoon characters: Postman Pat, Jess the Cat and Yogi Bear.

Jess the Cat came over and shook my hand, which I thought was funny. I decided to go one better and have a wrestle in the goalmouth with Yogi Bear. While I was cavorting about with the Bear, I kicked the Cat up the backside. It was only meant to be a friendly tap, but of course I was wearing football boots, so I struck her – it turned out to be a woman – a bit harder than I'd intended. All the same, I never thought she'd claim I had injured her, which she did afterwards, demanding an apology.

The match itself got into a bit of a punch-up when I lashed out wildly at Eddie McGoldrick. It was a bout of handbags that resulted in me getting booked. I was terrified I would be suspended and out of the England reckoning.

Around that same time, in a Cup game against Tranmere, I hit a ball which went straight at a cameramen and broke his glasses. The papers claimed I had done it deliberately. I'm not that skilful. It was an accident, but no one believed that. I apologised to the photographer and promised to buy him a drink, but that didn't stop some Tranmere fans writing to Spurs and the FA about my behaviour, saying I shouldn't be picked for Spurs or England.

On the World Cup trail, England ended up second in our group, one point behind Sweden. England were on their way to Italy, but was Paul Gascoigne going with them? I was starting to get worried.

Bobby came to see me a few times for Spurs, to check me out. I was picked for a B international against Yugoslavia when I thought I should have been in the first team, but I did what manager Dave Sexton wanted and afterwards Bobby said at a press conference that I had behaved myself. But then he was pushed into talking about who he would pick in the middle for England alongside Bryan Robson. 'The man who plays with Robson,' he was quoted as saying, 'has to have brains and discipline. He has to be able to work out when to go and when to stay, when to take chances. I'm not saying Gascoigne hasn't got a brain, but he still has to learn when to use it.'

Well, that was a bit of a sickener. The tabloids

naturally took this to mean that I didn't have a brain, and I began to fear that Bobby was going to prefer David Platt or Steve McMahon in midfield to me. Bobby, to be fair, did take me aside before the Czechoslovakia game in April 1990 to tell me that I would be playing from the start, which was good of him, and reassuring for me. But I got the distinct feeling this might be my last chance, which was less reassuring.

Tottenham played Man United at White Hart Lane before that England match, and not surprisingly, I was very hyped up, wanting to show not only Bobby but also Alex Ferguson how good I was. I played one of my best games for Spurs, especially in the first half. I got a good goal and made one for Gary Lineker. The look on Fergie's face at half-time was a reward in itself. We held on in the second half and won 2–1.

Bobby Robson had first described me as 'daft as a brush' when talking to Dave Sexton during the Albania match, but in the run-up to our clash with Czechoslovakia he repeated this pronouncement in public. I turned up for England training the next day with a brush stuck down my sock. He did laugh at that. Later he had a quiet word with me, and told me that this was my chance to prove myself, to let everyone see how good I was. As he had promised, I started against the Czechs.

For the first twenty minutes I ran around like a headless chicken and was lucky not to get booked, but then I settled down. I set up two for Steve Bull and took the corner from which Stuart Pearce scored. Then I did a one-two with Tony Dorigo, beat two and thrashed it into the net. We won 4–2, and some of the papers which had earlier called me a 'chaotic presence' were now saying I was an 'irresistible force'. It was no doubt that match that secured my place in Bobby's final World Cup twenty-two.

Before we left for Italy I went up to Newcastle to say cheerio to my family and friends. We had a farewell drink in a local bar. I was quite sober when this lad came up to me in the car park as I was leaving and said he was going to get me. I replied that I never hit a man with glasses, and he took off his specs and had a swing at me. I hit him once, on the nose, to stop him hitting me any more, and he ran off. The next day there were headlines about 'World Cup wallies' all over the place. Looking back, I think that incident might have been a set-up. But that didn't occur to me at the time. In spite of my brush with the Swedish stalker, I was not yet wise to the ways of the media world.

I discovered on the evening of 24 May, the night before the England squad was due to fly out to our World Cup camp in Sardinia, that I'd left my passport in Newcastle. We were leaving first thing in the morning. I rang Jimmy and he drove through the night to bring it to me, arriving just in time.

So my World Cup didn't get off to a brilliant start, but it wasn't as bad a start as Bobby Robson was having. Just as he was trying to get us all organised to go off for the finals, there had suddenly been lots of stories in the press about his personal life. Then I felt the FA handled his contract very badly, and there had been leaks to the press suggesting that they were already looking for a replacement for him.

The upshot was that before the World Cup finals had even begun, we knew that he was going; that he would no longer be the England manager after it was all over, whatever happened. Instead he would be going abroad, to manage PSV Eindhoven. It was not the ideal atmosphere in which to launch a World Cup campaign, and I felt very sorry for him.

Two days after we arrived, it was my twenty-third birthday. The lads presented me with a special choco- late birthday cake beside the pool at our hotel. Chris

Waddle did the handing-over honours – and smashed it right in my face. It's a good job I've always liked chocolate. In the evening, at the team dinner, I found that Bobby Robson had ordered a special birthday cake for me as well. This one had a brush on top.

On 2 June, we went off for a warm-up game in Tunisia. When I gave the ball away and they scored, I was convinced I'd blown it, that I wouldn't be in the starting team for the first game. But afterwards Bobby saw how depressed I was and put his arm round me. He was good at man-management. He knew when to be ready with a joke, and when to boost your confidence.

Our first game in the World Cup finals was to be in Cagliari in Sardinia, against the Republic of Ireland, managed by Jack Charlton, my old boss at Newcastle. After taking the job he'd asked me if I had an Irish wolfhound. I said no, I hadn't – but why was he interested? 'If you had an Irish wolfhound, you could qualify to play for Ireland.'

During the World Cup, I roomed with Chris Waddle, which was of course a big pleasure for him. At least he already knew what he was dealing with: that I could never sleep without the light and the TV on. He moaned, of course, but we were good mates, so he put up with me. He'd wait till I'd fallen asleep, then he'd get up and switch off the light and the television.

In the mornings, he'd get his own back. The moment he woke up, he'd put on his sound system really loud. You could hear people all down the corridor, Shilton and Butcher and all the others, telling him to turn the fucking thing down.

I was always up early, usually straight out of the patio door and into the pool. Then I'd be looking for someone to play a game with – table tennis, snooker, golf, whatever. I loved being at the World Cup. It was everything I ever wished for, how I wanted life to be. Not just the football, and being in the finals, but being with the lads twenty-four hours a day. I always had someone to play with, and there was always some sort of activity going on. I didn't have to worry about boring domestic things or me house or girlfriends. I could escape all that, leave my responsibilities behind.

At Spurs, when training was finished, I'd come home and have nothing to do. Feeling bored, I'd do daft things just to avoid sitting around, stuck on my own with my awful thoughts and worries and obsessions. Often I'd just have a drink to blot it all out for the rest of the day, till it was time for training again. So being away at the World Cup was brilliant for me.

One day, wandering round our hotel in Sardinia, Peter Beardsley happened to spot the secret place where Norman Medhurst and Fred Street, the physios, kept their bars of chocolate. They used to give us one each in the evenings, that was our allowance, for sugar and energy. They had also stashed away various World Cup goodies, wallets and things, to be given out to kids, visitors and VIPs.

When Peter told me he had discovered this secret cupboard, I begged him to show me where it was. I begged and begged, promising, of course, that I would tell no one. The minute he showed me, I went straight back to my room and told Chris. We both immediately went to the cupboard and helped ourselves to some of the stuff. Not too much – we didn't want them to notice. We kept on going back to what we called Gazza's Aladdin's Cave. We were pissing ourselves every time we came back with our treasure.

Beardsley came into our room one day, spotted some of the England stuff and realised instantly where we'd got it from. He was terrified he would get the blame. Norman and Fred did find out in the end. We were told off and they moved their stash to another hiding place.

Being at the World Cup, or at any big tournament, is like being on holiday. I loved everything about it, even all the training. I was first on the pitch and last off it every day. I'd get local kids to take shots at me in goal when everyone else had packed up. I wanted it to go on for ever, and then I'd never have to face real life. And it hadn't even properly begun yet.

> **If he were a Brazilian or an Argentinian,**
> **you would kiss his shoes.**
> **Arthur Cox, Derby manager, after Gascoigne had inspired**
> **Tottenham to victory over his team, 1990**

> **Paul Gascoigne has done more for Mars bars than**
> **anyone since Marianne Faithfull.**
> **Patrick Barclay, Independent, 1988**

> **Gazza is the hardest trainer I have ever seen. His**
> **problem is that he does not understand the**
> **concept of pacing himself, whether in training or**
> **in a match. Gazza gives everything from the start.**
> **John Barnes, The Autobiography, 1999**

9

WORLD CUP 90

We played Ireland in our first game of the 1990 World Cup finals on 11 June and drew 1–1. Gary Lineker scored our goal. It wasn't a brilliant game, but it was very tough. Then we got a 0–0 draw against Holland, who were viewed as the favourites as they had such wonderful players, people like Van Basten, Ruud Gullit, Ronald Koeman and Frank Rijkaard. During that match, I asked Van Basten how much he was earning. I also pulled Ruud Gullit's hair to see what it felt like. He had dreadlocks at the time. 'Is that nice?' he asked me. 'Lovely,' I replied. I did my Cruyff turn, which some of the papers thought was new. Others thought I was doing it as a wind-up. But I had performed it before – it was just

| 133

that it had never been commented on. The score, 0–0, makes it sound a dull game, but we played with poise and concentration and I felt at home on the world stage.

In the bath afterwards, we were all singing and shouting, having got through what we thought would be the toughest games. In the evening, some of us decided to go out and have a small drink as a modest celebration, which of course we weren't supposed to do. Waddler, Chris Woods, Steve Bull, John Barnes, Terry Butcher, Steve McMahon, Bryan Robson and I sneaked out and found this local pub full of local Italian fans, who challenged us to a few rounds of arm-wrestling. Chris Woods, who was massive, had trouble with an equally massive opponent. It took all his strength to beat this bloke, but he did it in the end. We all cheered and ordered more drinks. Suddenly, we heard the sound of police sirens. Bobby Robson had found out we'd gone missing and sent the police to look for us. We ran like hell to get back into the hotel before he caught us. Chris Waddle and I made it back to our room, where we were joined by Bryan Robson, the England captain, a fellow Tynesider. I threw myself down on the bed, still laughing and messing around. 'Come on, you Geordie bastard,' Bryan was shouting at me. 'You can't take your fucking drink.'

Bryan began to try to tip me off my bed by lifting it up and turning it over. In the process he slipped – and the bed fell on his toe. There was blood everywhere. 'Quick,' I said, 'wash it in the bidet.' We rushed to our bidet and as the water cleared the blood we could see it was a really serious gash. Immediately we all sobered up. We knew it was so bad we'd have to call one of the physios to treat it. He came, took one look at Bryan's toe and announced that he would have to call Bobby Robson. Oh God. Bobby was furious, of course. He was well aware we had all been drinking, and then mucking about, and that we must have done something really stupid. He demanded to know how it had happened.

I said that Bryan had been washing his feet in the bidet and had slipped. That was all it was, a pure accident. There'd been no larking around . . .

'I don't believe you,' said Bobby. 'I'll speak to you later.'

Then he went off with Bryan to find the doctor.

And that was it. Our captain and key player was out of the World Cup, injured in a stupid prank. We never told Bobby the whole truth, and it never emerged elsewhere. Bryan was reported as having Achilles' tendon trouble, which he suffered from anyway. He had to return to England, and David Platt flew out to take his place.

The very next day, I was running across the grass as fast as I could, preparing to do a running dive into the pool, competing against Waddler to see who could do the longest dive. I fell and stubbed my toe. Oh fuck, I thought, I've broken it. Bobby was livid with me. 'Now both my midfielders have buggered up their toes by being bloody stupid.' Luckily, there were no bones broken and mine was OK the following day.

We had to beat Egypt to progress to the next stage, which we did, 1–0. I set up our goal with a free kick for Mark Wright, who headed it in at the far post.

We then left Sardinia for Bologna, where we were to play Belgium in the next round. On the plane, for something to do, to take my mind off the flight, I went into the cockpit and persuaded the pilot to show me how to fly. He explained which switches you flicked to make the aircraft go up, down or sideways. I wasn't supposed to touch any of them myself, of course, but I grabbed one and pulled it, just to see how responsive it was, and the plane immediately went into a dive. Back in the cabin, Chris Woods had just started to stand up, and was thrown violently back into his seat. When he heard it was me who'd caused the plane to dive, he said that once we landed, he was going to really thump me.

The game against Belgium turned out to be very exciting, despite the fact that there were no goals after ninety minutes. In extra time, we managed to summon up more energy and more inspiration than the Belgians, though it was extremely difficult to unlock their defence. About two minutes before the end, I made a surge from midfield which caught them on the hop, and they had to foul me to bring me down. I took the free kick, chipping in to Platty, who had come on as a sub, and he lashed it into the net. So we won 1–0, and we were in the quarter-finals.

In the bath afterwards we were all in high spirits, me especially. Shilts told Steve McMahon and me to calm down. McMahon told him to fuck off. There was a slightly nasty atmosphere for a bit, but not for long. Soon we were all the best of friends again. Everyone in the squad got on well, and there were never any rows. I suppose Chris Waddle and I were the daftest two, and Terry Butcher and Chris Woods could sometimes be pretty wild. As you might imagine, Gary Lineker was the most sensible one.

As in any team, there was plenty of good-humoured

baiting. Steve McMahon and John Barnes used to try to wind up Waddler and me by saying, 'Show us your medals.' Playing for Liverpool, they had won shedloads of silver while Chris and me, with Newcastle and Spurs, had won fuck all. Paul Parker was picked on once, just for being little. Some lads put a cover over him and pretended to wrap him up. It was a silly joke, nothing serious. Everyone liked him. It was just the sort of horseplay you get in any dressing room.

One evening Terry Butcher and Chris Woods were sitting having their team meal wearing their clothes back to front. Jackets, shirts and baseball caps, they had all of them on back to front. They started their meal with coffee, followed by pudding and ice cream, a main course and finishing with soup. They also drank a huge amount from some wine bottles, which actually contained nothing stronger than water, just to wind up Bobby and the coaching staff. When they had finished, they stood up and we noticed for the first time that they had no trousers on, just jockstraps. They walked backwards out of the dining room. They had kept straight faces throughout. Everyone cheered and clapped.

I got a cheer myself one day for diving into the swimming pool totally naked except for some toilet paper.

I'd wrapped myself in it. I can't remember why now. I think I'd just been to the lav, noticed all these rolls of toilet paper and thought I'd make meself a cossie.

I know they sound stupid now, all those daft things, but they amused us then and helped to release the tension. You do have a lot of time on your hands between games, and people can get nervous or irritable or worried, so laughs and diversions that can break all that up are essential.

There was a lot of betting going on, too, with some of the lads running a book. People took punts on other games, not on ours. Right at the beginning I put some money on Cameroon to beat Argentina, just to be sociable, join in with the lads. No one expected it to happen and I won £800. We also used to gamble on horse races. We had videos of races sent out to us, and Shilts would tell us the names of the horses and the odds and we'd all put our bets on. I don't follow the horses, or know much about the sport, but those who did were on the phone home to their mates, finding out which horse had won what race.

We had a lot of trouble with the press. They were printing all sorts of rubbish about us, including some shite about an Italian hostess – she was actually a translator –

who was helping to look after us. It was claimed that some of the lads were sleeping with her. I remember poor old Steve McMahon being named. It was all bollocks. Nobody slept with her. To cheer everyone up I made up a song we used to sing on the team coach, 'Let's All Shag a Hostess'. I can't remember the rest of the words now, but I'm sure they must have been good.

The truth was there were no girls at all in our bedrooms during the whole of that World Cup. We might have had a few drinks when we were not supposed to, but there was no sex, please, even though we were British – not till the wives and girlfriends arrived. They were allowed to join us during a short break. Now that they couldn't accuse us of sleeping with other women, the press tried another tack, suggesting that Bobby Robson was eyeing up one of the players' wives, which was more bollocks. These attacks were pretty nasty, but in many ways enduring them together helped to unite us even more.

I had fallen out with Gail by this time, so I didn't have a girlfriend to visit me. I was a bit pissed off about being left on my own to amuse myself while my team-mates spent time with their partners. I suppose I was jealous of the wives, and felt that they were taking their husbands away from me. The couples started playing charades together. Eventually they asked me if I wanted to join in. I stood up and said, 'Two syllables.' After a pause I gave them the answer, 'Fuck Off,' and stormed out of the room. Yeah, it was childish. I was just fed up.

We were due to meet Cameroon in the quarter-finals. On the eve of the match, Bully, Chris Waddle, John Barnes and I decided to sneak into town. We couldn't order any drinks in our rooms, and our doors always had to be left unlocked, so that Bobby could just walk in at night and check we were there. We were not supposed to leave the hotel without permission, either, but we just fancied a little break and a soothing pint. That was all. By chance, we'd bumped into Mick Harford, who wasn't with the England camp, but had come out to watch the World Cup. He'd told us about a quiet place he knew, where, he assured us, we would not be spotted. And we weren't.

But when we got back to the hotel, we saw Bobby Robson at the front door, waiting for us. Chris Waddle and John Barnes took a run and a jump over a wall and just disappeared in the dark. I thought, fuck me, I'm not doing that. I managed to work my way round the hotel, found a side door and crept in – only to walk straight into Bobby Robson. 'Go to your room,' he said,

'I'll see you tomorrow.' On the way, I came across Chris Woods, just sitting on some steps with a bottle of wine. God knows how he'd got that.

It might sound as if some of us weren't serious about playing football, but we were, we all were. We were desperate to do well in the World Cup. Chris and I used to fantasise the whole time about getting to the final and winning the trophy. None of us were looking for a wild night out before a game. We just wanted to relax for an hour away from the rules and regulations and hothouse atmosphere of our hotel base.

In the team meeting before the Cameroon game, Bobby showed us a video of Cameroon beating Argentina which, of course, had been a sensation. I don't really enjoy team meetings – I find them pretty boring – so to pass the time, whenever Cameroon made a good pass, I went 'Mmmmmmm,' giving a sort of low hum of appreciation. When they gave the ball away, I groaned, 'Oohhhh' in disappointment. I was sat at the back, with Chris Waddle, who was soon joining in with my sympathetic noises. It wasn't long before others took up the chorus, and eventually almost the whole room was going 'Mmmmmmm' when Cameroon did well and 'Oohhhh' when they made a mistake.

It took Bobby a while to twig what was going on, and when he did, he was absolutely livid that we were messing around in his team talk. He soon worked out that it was me who had started it.

'Oh yes,' he raged at me, 'you can go fucking "Hmmmm, hmmmm" now, but you'll be the first to go "Oohhhh" if we get fucking beaten by Cameroon!'

It's not that I don't listen or pay attention. It's just that, as a player, I've never bothered much about opponents. I've always been more interested in my own game, and my team's game. I have total faith in myself, and in the England team. So I have to admit that, when I was younger, I did often muck about a bit in team meetings.

In Italy, I also used to get bored when John Barnes came to our room and he and Chris Waddle started going on and on about formations and tactics, recapping team talks, and generally talking football non-stop. They would ask my opinion, partly to wind me up, because they knew I hadn't been listening and didn't really care. I'd put my fingers over my ears, say 'I'm not listening, I'm not listening,' and leave the room.

Well, in the Cameroon match, you can guess what happened. After disrupting the team meeting and being told off by Bobby for not paying attention, I gave away a penalty. I fouled Roger Milla. I felt terrible about that. But on the plus side, I did help Gary Lineker to win his two penalties, and I could have scored myself. We eventually beat them 3–2. It was a good team performance and, my responsibility for that penalty apart, I enjoyed it. Most important of all, we were in the semifinals.

We all wanted to celebrate afterwards, but Bobby wouldn't let us. He said the tabloids would hammer us if any whisper of us drinking was heard. I had an idea. They served good milkshakes in the hotel bar, and I'd noticed that one variety looked very like a Baileys. So I asked the barman to give us Baileys in milkshake glasses, and to make them look like milkshakes by putting in umbrellas and all the other bits and pieces. I'd had about five of these when Bobby walked in.

He asked what I was drinking. I said a milkshake. He remarked that it looked good, and he would have one as well. I had to pull faces at the barman to make sure he made Bobby a real one, not the Baileys version.

One of the running jokes of the 1990 World Cup centred on David Platt, who'd flown out to replace Bryan Robson. He was for ever going on about Doug

Ellis, the chairman of Villa, who had this brilliant boat, or so Platty was always telling us, boasting about how he'd been on it. So whenever we saw some scruffy old boat, we'd all shout to Platty, 'Hey, Platty! That must be Doug Ellis's!'

We went to the seaside on one day off in Sardinia, and Chris Waddle, John Barnes and I went for a swim. About 300 yards out we came upon this big yacht. I said, 'I bet that's Doug Ellis's.' And fuck me, it was. We were invited on board and, with the help of other guests, got through about twenty bottles of his champagne.

Several visitors arrived that afternoon, including Nigel Kennedy, who played his violin. There was a pop star as well, who played the piano, but I can't remember his name. Gary Lineker and his wife, Michelle, were there. She was standing sipping her champagne in the sun when I decided to leap on her as a friendly gesture. I landed on her back and we both went overboard. Gary was in a state of shock, seeing his wife disappear over the side of the yacht. But we were fine, though I admit we had a bit of a struggle getting back on board.

One of the jokes at Bobby's expense was his fondness for military references. He always seemed to drag the war into his team talk. 'Get stuck in, it's a war, you know,' he'd say, or, 'You have to fight as if it were a war-time battle.' Gary Lineker opened a book and we all took bets on how many minutes it would be before Bobby used the word 'war' in his next team talk. Gary wrote 'The War' on a sheet of paper and pinned it to the wall, with the writing facing inwards so it couldn't be seen. We all waited expectantly. Even I was listening intently for once to all Bobby's tactics and stuff. The moment Bobby mentioned the war, as we all knew he would eventually, Gary jumped up and turned over the paper. Everyone cheered. Bobby took it all in good humour.

Before the semi-final against West Germany, Bobby told me privately, 'You do realise you'll be playing against the best midfielder in the world.' By which he meant Lothar Matthäus. I said, 'No, Bobby, you've got it wrong. He is.' Then I walked off. I think it took him a few minutes to work out what I'd just said. I might have been nervous and hyped up before a game, but I was always confident of my own ability.

The semi-final was to take place on 4 July in Turin. The night before, I just couldn't relax. I knew I would never get to sleep, so at about ten o'clock I sneaked out of my bedroom and went to the hotel's tennis courts. I found two Americans and persuaded one of them to have a game with me. We'd been playing for about twenty minutes when I heard this Geordie voice shouting, 'Gazza, where the fuck are you?' It was Bobby Robson looking for me, having discovered I wasn't in my bedroom. I dropped my racket and ran like hell. We were supposed to be in our beds, if not sleeping, then at least resting. I could see Bobby questioning the two Americans, but it was obvious they didn't know who I was. The name Gazza meant nothing to them. They were not football fans, they just happened to be staying at the same hotel as us. Before Bobby returned, I managed to reach my bedroom, get into bed, and pretend to be asleep.

The game against West Germany went well for me. I felt I got the better of Matthäus, and I had one of my most disciplined games. After ninety minutes the score was 1–1. The Germans had gone ahead with a lucky deflection but Lineker pulled us level with about ten minutes to go. Then we were into extra time. All I wanted to do was win for England, for me, to keep it all going. It was in the first half of extra time I think, and I got the ball near the halfway line. I beat off two German players and was going really strong, heading towards their goal, when I overhit the ball a bit, which gave Thomas Berthold the chance to nick it off me. I lunged towards him, to get the ball back, no intention of trying to get him as he wasn't a threat in that area of the field. I just wanted my ball back. As I stretched to get the ball with my left foot, my right foot must just have caught him. But it was nothing more than that. I hardly touched him.

But he went down in a heap. Like I'd hit him with a sledgehammer or something. Rolling over and over. The moment he went down like that I knew I might be in trouble, even though we'd barely made contact. So I wanted the ref to know straight away there was nothing nasty. A foul maybe, but nothing more. So I put my hands right up and headed over to Berthold. Just to show there was nothing in it. He was probably still rolling. I can't quite remember. And then I saw the ref holding the card up. I couldn't believe it. I was devastated. I realised what it meant the minute it happened and the tears just came. I'd already picked up a yellow card so that was me out of the next game. I wouldn't be playing in the World Cup final, if we got there. And I was sure we would, we were doing so brilliantly. At that moment, when I looked down at the German still on the ground play-acting, I could have slapped him.

I've since seen the television pictures relayed to the viewers at home. In one shot, Gary Lineker signals to the bench, a gesture taken by most of the TV audience to mean that he thought I should be pulled off in case I did anything else daft. But in fact this wasn't what he was communicating at all. He was just alerting them to the state I was in, and suggesting that someone on the bench would have to calm me down. Chris Waddle told me settle down and get on with it.

I didn't need telling twice. I resolved to give my all for England in whatever time there was left; to do my utmost to get them to the final regardless of the cruel fact that I wouldn't be there myself. So I played my heart out. We came so close – Chris Waddle hit the post – but at the end of extra time there had been no further score. Now it was all going to come down to penalties.

I was supposed to take one of the kicks: that had been the arrangement. But I was still so worked up that I decided it wouldn't be wise. Platty took the one that would have been mine. At least he scored with it. Poor Chris Waddle and Stuart Pearce missed. I was heartbroken for both of them. In a way, I suppose it was better that two of them missed rather than just one of them, otherwise he would have felt he had to shoulder all the blame. Either way, that was it. The Germans had won. By the time the final whistle blew, I was in floods of tears.

I felt even sorrier for Stuart afterwards when he was called for a random drugs test and had to go and give his sample straight after the game, leaving the rest of us in the dressing room, either crying or trying to comfort each other. At least we had each other; Stuart, poor sod, had to suffer on his own.

I was so disappointed that England hadn't made it to the final. Had we got there, I was sure we would have won it, whether or not I had played. But losing the semi was not the only reason for my tears. I was also crying because it was the end of the tournament for us; the end of those terrific six weeks or so in our World Cup camp. I didn't want to go home. I wanted to stay in Italy playing in the World Cup finals for ever. That would have suited me champion. So the realisation that all this was over was deeply depressing. I was wondering whether I would ever have this sort of fun again in my whole life. The suspicion that I wouldn't made me cry even more.

That evening, we all had a drink, of course, to drown our sorrows. Now that it was all over, we had Bobby's permission. In fact, there was quite a party, with Nigel Kennedy playing his violin. We chucked Bobby into the hotel pool, with all his clothes on. We threw him so hard he nearly split his head open. I think most of the players got pretty drunk. If the press had seen us, they would probably have said it was disgusting, how could we have a big party when we'd just lost our chance to win the World Cup? Of course we were gutted to be missing out on what we'd worked for for months, all our lives, really. But at the same time, we genuinely felt we hadn't let the country down. We'd done our best. We'd all played well. So why not let our hair down?

Before we could go home, there was the anticlimax of the third-place play-off to be faced. Our opponents were the other losing semi-finalists, Italy. Because of my yellow card, I could only watch as they beat us 2–1.

On the plane back to England, I remember Gary Lineker warning me that life would change from now on. I didn't really know what he meant, whether he was referring to me or to all of us. He'd been a hero of the 1986 World Cup in Mexico, scoring six goals and winning the Golden Boot, and when he came home he was staggered by all the attention. But I didn't expect much excitement on our account. I thought there might be a few hundred people waiting to welcome us at Luton when we landed, and that would be all.

I couldn't believe the sight that greeted us. It was bedlam. There must have been about 100,000 fans at the airport, and the noise was incredible. And people were singing and shouting my name. I hadn't, of course, seen myself on telly, so I didn't know about all the close-ups of me crying. I soon discovered that over 30 million viewers had been riveted by my tears. I suppose they identified with me, understood what I was going through and felt sympathy for me, though at the time I'd been completely unaware of that.

As we shoved our way through the airport, someone gave me a set of joke plastic breasts which, of course, I immediately put on. It was said later that it was some pressman or photographer trying to set up a stunt picture that he had planned in advance, but I don't think it was. The lad who gave it to me looked like an ordinary punter, an England supporter who had brought it along for a laugh and just handed it over. Apart from big, bulging plastic breasts, it had a huge stomach, though you couldn't see that as clearly in most of the photographs that appeared in the papers. The joke was that I was overweight, a fat bastard, a jibe which, of course, I'd had to put up with in England from rival fans for some while. At the time, it was what I was best known for, being fat – that and for Vinnie Jones grabbing my balls. But after the World Cup I was known by everyone, inside and outside football, for my tears.

From the airport we went on an open-topped bus for a little parade around Luton. As I was leaning out of the bus, shaking someone's hand, my medal was pulled off my neck. We had all come home with a World Cup medal – for coming fourth – including me, even though I wasn't able to take part in the third place play-off. I don't think this bloke was trying to steal it. He was just trying to kiss and hug me, and accidentally dragged it off. I screamed at him to give me back my fucking medal, but the bus was moving on. Luckily, someone else picked it up and handed it back to me.

Back at the airport, my father was waiting for me. I'd just bought him one of those motor home things. I got in along with Chris Waddle, who we were taking up to Newcastle, and we drew all the curtains and got out of the car park without being mobbed. I don't suppose anyone was expecting to see two England foot-ballers in a camper van.

Halfway up the motorway, I suddenly felt starving. I was dying for a burger or chips or something. Me father pulled up at a McDonald's and I opened the door to get out and fetch myself a burger. The minute I was on the pavement, I was surrounded – yet no one could possibly have known I was going to stop there, or could have recognised the motor home. In seconds, I was mobbed by people shaking my hand, wanting autographs, grabbing me. There was no way I could get my burger, so I had nothing at all to eat till we got to Newcastle.

That little incident was the first sign I had of what life was going to be like from then on. It was my first experience of what was to become known as Gazzamania.

Before Paul Gascoigne, did anyone ever become a national hero and a dead-cert millionaire by crying? Fabulous. Weep and the world weeps with you.
Salman Rushdie, Independent on Sunday, *1990*

A dog of war with the face of a child.
Gianni Agnelli, Juventus president,
admiring Gascoigne during England's World Cup run, 1990

I was amazed by our reception on our return to Luton Airport. There were tens of thousands of people there to greet us as if we had won the World Cup. All of the squad were greeted almost as conquering heroes, particularly Gazza.
John Barnes, The Autobiography, *1999*

10

GAZZAMANIA

In the north-east, I was offered free champagne in all the best hotels. I discovered that no one wanted to take money from me for anything, which was also nice. But what happened nationally became a sort of madness. Offers came flooding in from every conceivable company and business and media outfit, all competing for a bit of me, wanting my presence at events, my endorsement of things, or just my name on any old tat. It was overwhelming. Mel Stein and Len Lazarus, my advisers, could hardly cope with all the requests and turned down far more than they accepted.

I hadn't really much of a clue about what was going

on, and what all these deals meant, but I was endorsing all sorts of things, from lunchboxes, calendars, bedroom rugs, T-shirts, keyrings and shell suits to stuff which I was told could bring in hundreds of thousands of pounds, such as videos, TV series, records, books, newspaper columns and boots. I can't even remember half the products now. Over the next few months, I was invited everywhere, from 10 Downing Street to Buckingham Palace. Madame Tussaud's made a waxwork of me and *Spitting Image* had a Gazza puppet. Although it was all a bit of a whirlwind, I enjoyed being in the limelight. It was certainly very exciting.

We had to take on more staff to cope. We'd set up a company called Paul Gascoigne Promotions and a fan club. I tried to get my family involved as much as possible in working for these companies, as I knew I could trust them. We also took on another lawyer. But, of course, Mel and Len supervised everything. The name Gazza had been registered so that people couldn't instantly rip us all off. On my return from Italy, the *Mail on Sunday* was desperate for an exclusive interview, so we demanded a fortune, and we got it. I can't remember how much money it was now, but I know it seemed a colossal amount for doing very little.

Later on, we made what I thought was a big mistake by signing up to the *Sun* for a huge sum. It meant their rivals did everything they could to rubbish me by digging out or whipping up scandals – and although I was working for them, even the *Sun* weren't always nice to me, either.

The money and the offers just kept on rolling in. I've no idea how much I made during the year after the World Cup, but it must have run to several million. Mel and Len have since been accused by the press of taking advantage of a young lad from Gateshead who didn't know what was going on, but I tried to keep an eye on things, to have the final say. Mel made it clear that he and Len didn't take any commission from any of the commercial deals. Mostly it was a question of them charging me for their services by the hour, at a rate I think was usually about £200, plus, of course, expenses, and what it cost to hire or pay other people to handle various matters. It's all my own fault that I didn't keep as tight control as I should have done, or didn't read all the small print or check all the bills and statements. I am in fact quite good at sums and can add up quickly, but I couldn't be arsed. I would rather give people the money, or whatever else they want, than argue the toss.

I mucked up a lot of deals myself, by being daft, or

just not bothering. One endorsement my advisers lined up for me was with Brut, the aftershave firm, who previously used Henry Cooper to advertise their toiletries. They now wanted a younger sporting hero to be the figurehead for all their promotions. The deal had been worked out and agreed, and I went along to a press launch to announce to an astounded world that I was the new face of Brut.

'How long have you been using Brut?' someone asked me at the press conference.

'I don't,' I said.

'What aftershave do you use then, Paul?'

'None. They bring me out in a rash.'

It was true. So I couldn't lie, could I? I've also never worn underpants in my life for the same reason. They bring me out in a rash as well.

Anyway, the damage was done, and we lost the contract, which I think could have been worth around £500,000. But I merely shrugged it off. It didn't mean that much to me at a time when I was getting something like £1,200,000 from just one boot deal.

I did a skills video, which I enjoyed, and another video with a commentary by Danny Baker. That's how I met Danny, and after that we became good friends. Then there was a TV series for Channel 4, which was

OK. I also went on the *Wogan* TV chat show. I remember having a few brandies to steady my nerves before that. The crowds outside the studio had gone wild when I arrived, screaming and shouting as if I were a pop star. A doorman told me it was the worst racket he'd heard since they'd had David Cassidy on. I turned on the Regent Street lights that Christmas and the hordes of people there were hysterical as well. I'd never seen so many young girls screaming. Some of them were yelling: 'Gazza, Gazza, show us your chest.' Obviously I obliged.

I had always taken the piss out of Chris Waddle about that single he'd made with Glenn Hoddle, 'Diamond Lights', so I was a bit worried I'd get a taste of my own medicine when I agreed to record 'Fog on the Tyne (Revisited)' with the Tyneside group Lindisfarne. It got into the Top Ten and earned me a gold disc, selling over 100,000 copies, but as I had feared, I had to take a lot of flak in the Spurs dressing room.

Although I enjoyed being so popular, a lot of the stuff I had to do annoyed me. I get nervous in public, and hate being bound by arrangements, having my life all tied up and having to be at a certain place at a certain time. It was exciting, yes, but all I really wanted to do – all I'd ever wanted to do – was play football. And some of the attention was just plain daft. Naming me Best Dressed Man of the Year for 1990, for example, seemed mad even then.

However, I was well chuffed when, at the end of that year, I was voted BBC Sports Personality of the Year, particularly as it was an award decided by the viewing public. I was presented with my trophy by another Geordie footballer, Bobby Charlton, who spoke about the pride the country had taken in their team out in Italy.

I managed not to have any brandies before this television appearance, but I had a hard job keeping back the tears. I said I was so honoured to be given the award by such a great man as, er . . . I had nearly said Jackie, for some reason. Then I just grinned and said to Bobby: 'I haven't won anything in the game as yet. But the World Cup did help to put England on the world map again.'

After the World Cup, the whole squad had been invited to Downing Street. It had always been one of my ambitions to get into Number 10. When we were introduced to the prime minister, Mrs Thatcher, I said, 'Is it OK, pet, if I put my arm round you?' She just smiled; she didn't seem to object at all, though I could see that her husband, Denis, was a bit alarmed. I pretended I didn't know who he was and remarked to

Mrs Thatcher: 'Your security bloke doesn't look too happy.' She took it all in good humour.

I also met Princess Diana, before the Cup final at Wembley in 1991. The Tottenham team were all presented to her by Gary Mabbutt, who was the captain that day.

'This is Paul Gascoigne,' says Gary.

'Hello,' she says.

'Can I kiss you?' I asked.

She smiled, but she looked a bit embarrassed, not to say taken aback. But she hadn't said no, so I leaned forward – and kissed her hand. The incident was common knowledge because it was covered in all the papers, so when I was due to meet Princess Diana again some time later, at a charity do at the Dorchester Hotel, word came from Buckingham Palace that I was not to be presented to her after all. Instead I was kept waiting in another room. I was well pissed off by that. I blamed the Queen, or one of her courtiers at the Palace.

Before another England match I was, however, introduced to the Duchess of Kent. She was well clued up. I was standing beside Ian Wright, and she said to him: 'I hope you score a goal for England today.' When she reached me, I said, 'Hi, I'm Gazza.' She replied: 'Yes, I know who you are, Paul. I do hope you have a good game.'

And I met the King . . . no hold on, Prince Philip, that's it, at Buckingham Palace. I was presented to him at another charity function. He was doing the queue, walking along it, saying hello to each person. When he got to me, he asked: 'What's your name?' I was gutted by that. At the time, the papers were saying that I was the most famous person in the country after Princess Diana. A High Court judge had recently inquired during a hearing, 'Who is Gazza?' and everyone had taken the piss out of him for being so out of touch.

Prince Philip then asked me: 'And what do you do for a living?'

That was me well and truly in my place. I don't think he was being funny. I think he genuinely didn't know who I was. I did meet him again, a few months later, at another event, something to do with the Duke of Edinburgh's award, and he did know me this time. We had a good chat about fishing. He seemed a very relaxed bloke.

Besides royalty, I met a lot of showbusiness people, of course, as so many of them love football. Rod Stewart is a huge football fan. He wanted me to come on stage at one of his shows and help him kick footballs into the audience. I was at the concert with the Spurs lads. We all had seats, but I was the only one to get this invitation to go on stage and then meet Rod in his dressing room afterwards, and I wanted it to be all of us, not just me. So I declined.

I did meet Rod later at the Pharmacy restaurant, when I was with my mate Chris Evans, the television presenter and producer. I rang me dad and asked Rod to talk to him, and he sang a few songs to me dad over my mobile. He asked me if I had ever had a Kamikaze. I said I was game for any drink. Famous last words. I don't know what was in it, but I practically collapsed in Rod's arms. He arranged for me to be taken back to Chris Evans' house and made sure I was safe.

And Phil Collins I would consider a friend. He once offered to sing and play at a birthday party I was having, without me asking. In the end, the date clashed with another engagement he had, but the thought was there.

After I played in Paul Walsh's testimonial at Portsmouth, I got talking to Robbie Williams. I said to him, 'Come on, let's go and have a few drinks,' but he said, 'No, I'm on the wagon, I haven't had a drink for six weeks.' All the same, I persuaded him and we went out in this big limo. On the radio, we could hear one of his records playing. He shouted: 'Turn that off, it's shite. I'll sing it to you better.' And he sang us the song, in the back of the car, as we drove off to find a pub.

Having a few bob gives you the means to go and do daft things, which otherwise I suppose might not occur to you. Although I don't know. Having no money had never stopped me.

> He wears a number 10 jersey. I thought it was his position, but it turns out to be his IQ.
> *George Best, 1993*

> If he farts in front of the Queen, we get blemished.
> *Paul McGaughey, adidas spokesman,*
> *on the risks of a sponsorship deal with Gazza, 1996*

> I'm extremely grateful to Gazza because at least now people are going to spell my name properly.
> *Bamber Gascoigne, former*
> *University Challenge presenter, 1990*

> Literally the most famous and probably the most popular person in Britain today.
> *Terry Wogan, introducing Gascoigne on his*
> *TV chat show, 1990*

11

CUP FEVER

Whatever my commitments with England or the distractions of my new-found fame, my first loyalty at that time was always to Spurs. In my first season with them, 1988–9, we had finished sixth in the old First Division. In all competitions, I made thirty-seven appearances and scored seven goals. I like to think that the Spurs fans had taken to me, perhaps even seeing me as a replacement for their hero Glenn Hoddle, who had left the season before I arrived. In my second season, 1989–90, we shot up to third, which was even better.

The 1990 season, after my return from the World Cup, did not begin so well as far as the league was concerned, and the club had a lot of problems. However, we did set off on a good run in the Cup.

There was a lot of criticism of all the commercial work I was doing and a story went round that Terry Venables was going to stop me from taking on any more. That wasn't true, but what was agreed was that I would not involve myself in any commercial or non-club-related activities seventy-two hours before a game. I did nothing in the way of business on Sundays anyway, as that was my day off, the day I liked to go out with my mates, but the seventy-two-hour rule did help me to get a grip on some of the outside stuff and concentrate on my football.

I always got on well with Terry Venables at White Hart Lane. He knew everything that was going on behind the scenes and could handle players without getting nasty and, unusually, without swearing. In fact, I think he's the only manager I've ever known who didn't swear.

I swore at him once, though, after one game. It pissed down the whole time and we were well beaten. Afterwards, in the dressing room, I was going around moaning at the lads. 'Too fucking cold for you, was it? Couldn't stand the rain? Fucking soft southerners . . .'

I was in a right foul mood, and when Terry told

me off for my behaviour, I retorted: 'And you can fuck off as well.' Very quietly, he instructed me to come to his office when I'd got dressed.

I was shitting myself, wondering what he was going to do, so on my way I went to the players' lounge, collected two pints of lager and took them into Terry's office, handing him one as a peace offering. I told him I was very sorry. I shouldn't have spoken to him like that, and I wouldn't do it again.

'I could fine you,' says Venners. 'And by rights I should fine you, for bringing me beer and not wine. But I'll let you off this time. Now, get out.'

Gary Lineker, who joined Spurs in 1989, the year after me, was the total professional, and so was Gary Mabbutt. You couldn't find better players, on or off the pitch. You might think, judging by Lineker's squeaky-clean image, that he never let his hair down. Now and again he did relax and enjoy himself, and have the odd drink, but even so, he was always the proper professional.

When he first arrived, he wasn't scoring. I said to Venners, 'I thought you said he was a goal machine?'

'Just wait, you'll see,' Terry replied. 'When he starts scoring, he won't stop.'

And he didn't. He got his first goal against Norwich in his sixth match – and then three in the next game with Queens Park Rangers. Terry was right: he was a phenomenal scorer. He notched up a total of twenty-six goals in his first season (compared with my seven) and nineteen the next, 1990–1. I matched his tally that year, but most of mine came in Cup games.

I loved playing with Lineker. We worked out a series of signals. When I had the ball, he would nod his head towards our opponents' goal, as if he were going to run forward for me to lob the ball over to him. He actually meant the opposite. He would appear to start a run, but then stop and come back and I'd play the ball short to him. When he made a spinning gesture with his finger, he was telling me to put it over the top, and he would then spin round and run forward.

Lineker made the mistake of inviting me to his house once, in a very posh Georgian terrace in St John's Wood. His mistake was letting me know where he lived. When I came up to London for the day from Hertfordshire, I'd leave my car in his front drive and go off into town. Gary would come out to find I'd blocked his car in, sometimes for the whole day, and he'd be really furious when he saw me the next day.

Paul Walsh was another great player, even though he was a short-arse. All the girls loved him, and he loved himself. That's what we used to say to him in the dressing room when he was combing his long hair, putting all the gel on. He became a good friend of mine and I later played at his testimonial.

Chris Waddle left White Hart Lane for Marseille in 1989, but while he was still at Spurs, he and I were the naughty ones. The hard bastards were Terry Fenwick and Paul Stewart. I mean on the pitch. They knew how to get stuck in. Then there were what I call the daft lads, like Steve Sedgley. Along with me, of course. It was a strange dressing room, throwing together this whole range of personalities, from the very serious and solid and sensible Garys Lineker and Mabbutt to the crazies, like me.

John Moncur came into the daft category, too, which used to worry his dad – especially when Moncur Senior found out that John was going out somewhere with me. I'd often ring his dad and say, 'Hi, I'm just with John. We're going off to the City Limits in Loughton for a few rounds of the chicken game.' He would go mad, and demand to speak to John, so that he could warn him on no account to go out drinking with me.

But John wouldn't even be with me – I was making it all up. His dad would eventually track John down and then he'd get a telling-off about going out drinking with Gazza.

We did used to go to the City Limits a lot, though. The chicken game was this machine it had which you put money into and tried to catch chicken eggs. According to our rules, whoever lost the game had to make as loud a chicken noise as possible and buy the winner a B52. This was a mixture of Baileys and Grand Marnier. After three hours of playing the chicken game, we'd more often than not be stotting.

Next door to the pub was a playground, right on the road, with lots of traffic flying by. 'Now let's go to the arena!' was the usual rallying cry after we'd been drinking for a while. We'd leave the City Limits and stage our own version of the Olympics in this playground. You had to slide down a slide, or swing on a swing, jump over some bars, then land on your feet in the 'arena' and give a big smile to the crowd, while the others gave you marks out of ten.

For some reason, it always ended up with one or other of us taking our clothes off. I suppose footballers do spend a lot of time naked, getting in and out of their kit, having showers, and so we're used to seeing each other in the buff. But I never went in for mooning or any of that kind of thing. I don't like being seen with my clothes off in public. People like John and Steve Sedgley, on the other hand, didn't seem to think anything of it. Steve once stood on the roundabout near the arena, bollock-naked, pretending to be a traffic policeman and directing the traffic.

John Moncur put up with a lot from me. We went to Portsmouth for an important fifth-round FA Cup tie in February 1991. The night before, I couldn't sleep, as usual, so I got John up and out of his bed. I'd discovered that the hotel had a squash court, so I begged him: 'Just play one game with me. Come on John, please. Then I'll be tired out and I can get back to sleep.'

One game led to another and we played about eleven in two hours. We were both knackered at the end, and aching all over. We shouldn't have been playing squash at all, of course. The night before a football match you're supposed to take it easy and rest.

On the coach to Fratton Park I could hardly move, my legs were so sore. I tried to do some press-ups when no one was watching to get them going. John wasn't actually due to play, but Terry Fenwick broke his leg in a freak accident, and he was called on to the subs' bench but didn't play.

In the first half, I felt terrible, really stiff and sore, and at half-time we were 1–0 down. In the second half, I felt and played better. I got two goals and we eventually won 2–1.

Afterwards, Venners somehow found out that two players had been playing late-night squash on the eve of the game and launched an investigation to find out who they were. It didn't take him long to come up with my name. I got a telling-off, but I don't think he was too bothered. He said I was hyperactive and that work-out probably helped me. But he was worried about who the other person was. I don't think he ever found out.

When Nayim first joined Spurs, in 1989, he didn't drink at all. When he arrived, he was put up at the Swallow Hotel, just as I had been. I told him I'd look after him. 'Don't worry, you'll be safe with me.' I took him out and ordered Long Island iced tea for him, explaining that, as its name suggested, it was a type of tea. He had no idea it was a cocktail, containing about five different white spirits, plus a Coke. I got the barman to put an extra Coke in it to disguise the taste of the alcohol. After five of these, Nayim was staggering, so I took him out and bought him a kebab.

At the players' Christmas party, at a place in the West End, I managed to spike his drink with spirits, and he was well away. Everyone was worried about him, so I got him into a taxi, promising to take him home. Instead I took him to Gary Lineker's house and dumped him there, without telling Gary. He had to spend the night there. He was still sleeping it off when Gary got home.

Another Christmas Phil Gray and I had a drinking competition with a young player. Not surprisingly, we won easily and he was soon totally pissed. We put him in a taxi, took him to King's Cross and made for the first train we saw. We put him in a carriage and took all his clothes off. He woke up, naked, in Cambridge. There was then a call to the Christmas party hotel saying that a lad claiming to be a Spurs player had been found naked in a railway station. Gary Mabbutt had to get some clothes and go and collect him. Venners wasn't pleased by that incident.

The other players weren't my only victims. There was a Spurs fan who became a friend and used to come and watch me train all the time and generally follow me around.

He was at training one day when my dad happened to be there. He'd left his motor home in the car park, and someone had put one of those traffic comes we used in training on the roof. I asked my friend if he'd climb up on to the roof and get it down. As soon as he was up there, I got in the motor home and started driving it along the A1, going faster and faster. He was screaming and shouting, 'Please, please, Gazza, stop! I'm a married man, I've got a family! You're going to kill me!' He was clearly terrified, so I stopped. I'd only been having a laugh.

That motor home didn't last as long as I'd thought it would. I later drove it under a gate, misjudging the height, and took the roof off, so I had to buy my dad another one.

After we beat Portsmouth in the fifth round of the FA Cup, we met Notts County. We won that game 2–1, and I scored the winner. And guess who we found ourselves facing in the semi-final? Arsenal. They were top of the league and clear favourites to win everything, possibly the first Double twice.

I'd had hernia trouble for some time but I kept pushing myself on, even though I was often in agony. The club would give me injections before a game, and sometimes even at half-time as well.

I suppose some might say it's bad that clubs do such things, and that it's building up worse trouble for you in the future. I don't know about that. But when it happened to me, I never blamed the club. I wanted them to give me a painkiller or whatever. I was desperate to get back on, to get over injuries. I never objected – because I knew it worked. I did feel better afterwards – and usually played better.

Before we played Norwich, I think it was, I felt hellish in the warm-up, but Venners said, 'You've been picked to play, Paul – get on there, we need you.' In spite of the injections, I still felt terrible, and I gave away the first goal. The coaching staff realised I was in a bad way so they had an ambulance waiting for me after the game. At the hospital, I was told I had to have an operation for a double hernia, which would keep me out for six weeks.

While I was in hospital with my double hernia, my balls began to grow to twice their normal size. I was astonished. I shouted for the nurse one day. 'Nurse, nurse, come quick.' She came running, thinking there was something wrong. 'Look at these,' I said.

She held my balls in her hand and said, 'Yes, they are big, but what's the matter?'

'Nothing's the matter, pet. But don't you think they're massive?'

She went off, shaking her head. 'Ee, Gazza, what are you like?'

I think she might have been a Geordie.

I managed to recover from the operation in four weeks, and was rushed to full fitness in time for the FA Cup semi-final against Arsenal at Wembley. After just five minutes of the match, we were awarded a free kick about thirty yards from their goal. I took the kick. I hit the ball as hard as I could, managed to make it swerve and poor old Dave Seaman got beaten all ends up. I don't think he saw it till he picked it out of the net.

I then linked with Paul Allen to provide an opening for Lineker, which he didn't miss. Arsenal pulled a goal back before the interval. Our defence held well in the second half, despite intense Arsenal pressure, and then Lineker grabbed his second. We had done what most people thought was unlikely, if not impossible: we had thumped Arsenal 3–1.

Better still, we were in the FA Cup final; *I* was in the FA Cup final, for the first time in my life. The previous season had finished with the thrill of a World Cup semi-final, and this one was going to end on a high with a Wembley Cup final. Life couldn't have been much more exciting.

> I wonder if his advisers ever consider what a boob
> they made, taking a lad of Paul's background and
> temperament to London. Maybe his self-destructive
> nature would have brought him trouble anywhere,
> but it is my belief that if he had signed for United
> he would not have had nearly as many problems
> as he had in London. I know managing him would
> have been no joyride but the hazards that went
> with the talent would never have put me off. I still
> don't know Paul well but at our meetings I
> warmed to him. There is something strangely
> appealing about him. Perhaps it is his
> vulnerability. You feel you want to be like an older
> brother or a father to him. You might want to
> shake him, or give him a cuddle, but there is
> certainly something infectious that gets you
> involved with him. To this day I regret being
> denied the chance to help him to make better use
> than he did of his prodigious abilities.
> *Sir Alex Ferguson*, Managing My Life, 1999

12

ENTER SHERYL

Before the FA Cup final of 1991, two things had happened, or were happening, in fact – they kept on happening for quite some time after the Cup final. Each had quite an important effect on my life.

First, there was Sheryl Failes, who came into my life early in 1991. By that time I had long since finished my relationship with Gail, and she had gone home to the north-east. So as far as girlfriends were concerned I was fancy-free. But I wasn't really looking for anyone. Mainly I was just enjoying myself going out with the lads, having a few drinks, and a few more drinks, and only then, if I had the energy left – if I could walk straight, or see straight – might I take an interest in the opposite sex.

I met Sheryl in a wine bar in Hoddesdon, not far from my home in Dobbs Weir. I'd gone there with Mitchell Thomas and Paul Stewart. There was a live band on and I had quite a bit to drink, but the moment I saw Sheryl, I fell for her. She was stunning-looking. I asked her for her phone number, but she wouldn't give it to me.

I think at the time I might have been dancing on a table. That's what Sheryl said later, anyway, but I'm not sure. Whatever I was doing, I was no doubt messing around, and probably drunk. She says she didn't know who I was, but she wasn't very impressed by how I was behaving. She was with a friend, Wendy. Wendy knew straight away who I was, because she had three football-mad little boys. I gave her some autographs for her lads, and offered some to Sheryl as well, which was how, as I remember it, we finally came to exchange phone numbers.

Sheryl maintains she never gave me her number. She says it was Wendy who rang me and gave it to me. Wendy told Sheryl that she might as well have a bit of fun, but Sheryl was furious, so she says. Anyway, one way or another I got her number, and eventually I rang her.

We met up a few times, but it was on and off for a while, and I had other girlfriends. I wasn't put off when I discovered Sheryl was married, because I was told the marriage was over. The fact that she had two bairns didn't bother me, either.

Before long, it started to get more serious. One night I went round to her place, it got late, and Sheryl said I could stay the night, so I did. I was worried in the morning, when I came down to breakfast, that her kids would recognise me. She was, after all, still married to this other bloke, and I was concerned that if the kids started talking about me it might complicate her divorce.

Her son, Mason, was only about two years old at the time, so he was no problem. But her daughter Bianca was about five. When I appeared at the breakfast table, she just stared at me, stared and stared. Eventually she said, 'Mum, what's Gazza doing in our house?'

I knew she would be bound to tell her father – you couldn't expect a five-year-old not to talk about having breakfast with a footballer – and I did for a time get dragged into the divorce proceedings, even though the break up had occurred long before Sheryl ever met me.

Shel had grown up locally in Hertfordshire, in a council house, just like me. Her dad worked as a welder. Unlike me, she had had a decent education. She went for a while to a ballet boarding school in Sussex. She was awarded some sort of grant, but her dad had to pay fees as well. She hadn't really liked it, and had run away once. Her dad had offered to move house, to be near her, if that would help. Whenever she came home, she felt she had grown apart from her old friends. They thought she had a plum in her mouth, as she spoke with a posher accent than they had, and that she believed she was better than them, which she didn't.

She wasn't really the right height to be a ballet dancer or a catwalk model, but she did become a fashion model, doing demonstrations in department stores. She also worked part-time in a hotel till she got married. When her marriage, to an estate agent, ended, she worked hard to support herself and her kids.

We argued a lot. We fell out and separated, and I would go my own way for a few weeks. It was usually when I got depressed, when I was injured and fed up with hanging around all day, eating too much and getting drunk just to cheer myself up, to forget things. Obviously, putting up with that kind of behaviour wasn't much fun for Shel. But in the end she would take me back, when I apologised and pleaded with her. Women do. I suppose she thought she could help me and believed all my promises that I'd improve. And I meant them when I made them. I meant to be good to her, because I really loved her. I grew to love the kids as well, and looked upon them as my own.

The second drama in my life in 1991 unfolded even more slowly. In fact, I wasn't really aware of what was going on for some time, and even now I don't know all the details. Spurs had somehow got themselves into a financial mess, and they were running out of cash and building up debts. In 1983, they had floated the club on the Stock Exchange, which seemed to have solved their problems for a while. But then they had diversified, going into other businesses, such as clothing, which had done badly. The sale of Chris Waddle to Marseille for £4.25 million in 1989 had helped, but now they were desperate for money once again.

It looked at one stage as if Robert Maxwell might buy the club, which would have been terrible, so everyone said. As manager, Terry Venables was obviously caught up in all this, because it meant he had no funds to spend and instead had to look around for ways of bringing in more money. He tried to set up a deal to buy the club himself. It was that deal which, in the end, brought in Alan Sugar as chairman on what the press called a dream ticket: the brilliant football brain allied with the brilliant business brain. What could go wrong?

It was around February 1991 that I first heard that an Italian club called Lazio was interested in me. I didn't know what or where Lazio was at the time, but I remember being pissed off that discussions had been going on between Spurs officials and Lazio people, plus a lot of intermediaries and so-called experts who were sticking their oars in, looking for a piece of any action there might be, without my knowledge. I was upset that Tottenham had even contemplated selling me behind my back without talking to me first about any of it. I began to feel like a piece of baggage, just another load of goods for sale.

I imagine the interest from Lazio had probably been stimulated by my World Cup exploits in Italy. Various top Italians, like Gianni Agnelli, the famous industrialist and president of Juventus, had said nice things about me. Gian Marco Callieri, the owner of Lazio, had apparently fallen in love with me during the finals. He loved my image, that's what I was told.

GEORDIE BOYS
Left: with Glenn Roeder, 1986, Newcastle's captain, always there to give advice; right: helping Mirandinha to speak fluent Geordie, 1987.
Previous page: February 1988 against Wimbledon. Vinnie Jones grabs the attention of the football world – and me.

As captain of the 1985 Youth Cup-winning team, front row, fourth from right. Colin Suggett is in the back row, far left, with Joe Allon fifth from left. Next to me, third from right in the front, is Ian Bogie, with Paul Stephenson far left.

Left: my first appearance in the starting line-up for the first team, away to Southampton in August 1985.

Below: Newcastle's first-team squad, 1985–86, with me as the new boy, back row, third from right.

BIG DAYS AND BAD DAYS AT SPURS, 1988–92

Left: scoring the vital free kick against Arsenal in the FA Cup semi-final, 1991. Seaman never saw it. Then celebrating our 3–1 win with Gary Lineker.

Below: the Cup final, 1991. I made a mad lunge at Nottingham Forest's Gary Charles, which resulted in me knackering my cruciate ligament, having to come off and missing the rest of the game. My whole career now appeared to be shattered.

Left: before the Cup final I kissed the hand of Diana, Princess of Wales. Afterwards, in the Princess Grace hospital, I kissed the FA Cup, which I'd helped to win but I felt I had let everyone down, myself most of all.

LIFE AT LAZIO, 1992–95

Left, top to bottom: arriving at Lazio, already looking the part, and a welcome message from the fans – I felt quite at home; the dramatic derby against Roma in 1992 ended with me scoring the vital goal that got us a draw – and feeling very emotional.

UP THE 'GERS, 1995–98

Opposite, top: waltzing through the Celtic defence, 1995. *Below*: a hat-trick to be proud of against Aberdeen, 1996, but nothing to be proud of playing the flute, which led to death threats from the IRA.

GAZZA'S BOYS...are here...
...SHAG Women...DRINK beer!

Signing for Middlesbrough and Bryan Robson, March 1998.

Playing for Everton
against Newcastle,
October 2000.

Spurs said they wanted £10 million for me, which was of course ridiculous – five times what they had paid for me – but obviously it would have solved their financial problems. Lazio had offered £5 million, and so the negotiations started. Mel and Len went out to Rome to check it all out. Maurizio Manzini, Lazio's general manager, was on the blower all the time. They eventually seemed to reach agreement on a price of £8.5 million, by which time news of the negotiations had leaked to the press.

A lot of Spurs fans were very upset. They thought I was being disloyal and was just trying to make a lot of money, but none of these talks had been my doing. Spurs and Lazio had begun it all without reference to me. Spurs desperately needed money, while Lazio had new owners with a lot of cash to spend and were desperate for a big signing. The Lazio people had been going round in public saying they were going to buy a new star. When the story hit the press in Italy, they were even more determined to keep their promise. When I was asked what little extras it would take to attract me to Lazio, apart from the money, I said, half-jokingly, that a trout farm would be nice, and they instantly said fine, no problem.

Discussions and arguments and secret meetings, in London and in Rome and elsewhere, went on for months, against the backdrop of the struggle between Irving Scholar and Terry Venables for control of Tottenham Hotspur. Venables was now saying that if his bid was successful he would like to keep me, but of course by this stage he couldn't afford the kind of personal deal which was on offer from Lazio. I had enough to worry about with my hernia, and then trying to get fit for the Cup final, in which we were due to meet Nottingham Forest. I knew it was going to be my last game for Spurs, but I hadn't actually signed the forms. They were all there, ready and waiting, with all the details agreed, but I wanted to go into the final feeling that I was still a genuine Tottenham player.

I was determined to go out on a high, to show the world how good I was, to please the Tottenham fans and my own family, too. I bought about seventy extra tickets for practically all the people in Dunston I had ever known in my life. So not surprisingly, I was a bit revved up, even before I got on the pitch.

People said later that Terry Venables should have calmed me down, not let me run out to play a Cup final in such a state, but that hyped-up condition was normal for me. It was how I usually went on to the field: desperate to do well, all wound up. Terry knew that, and he knew how to handle me.

Within minutes of the start, I charged into Garry Parker. It wasn't a nasty or vicious challenge. I got the ball, but my leg carried through and banged into his chest. The referee told me off. Perhaps it might have been better if he'd given me a yellow card there and then.

Ten minutes later, Gary Charles, Forest's young full-back, powered through and cut across the edge of the penalty area. It looked to me as if he would have a clear run on goal, with no one else to stop him, so I lunged in. I thought I had got the ball, but he was too quick for me and I just scythed him down. At first I worried that I had hurt him, a young player just beginning his career, but he got up and seemed OK. Our trainer, Dave Butler, came on to check my leg and I told him I was OK, I'd manage. Somehow, I struggled to my feet, assuring him I'd run it off.

The ref had given a free kick so I lumbered towards our wall and joined in, though I was feeling groggy and didn't quite know what I was doing. Stuart Pearce, my World Cup team-mate, was taking the kick. The ball flew past our goalie, Erik Thorstvedt, and into the net. I toppled over, unable to stay upright. I just sort of collapsed in a heap, like a rag doll. We were 1–0 down and I was out of it – out of the game and also out of my head. I couldn't quite concentrate on what was happening around me. I just felt numb. As they put me on a stretcher silly things came into my head. Where had I parked my car? Who would collect my loser's or winner's medal?

The doc had a look at my knee. He was obviously very worried. As I lay there, waiting for an ambulance, I could hear the roars of the crowd. In the ambulance there was a radio on, so I listened to the commentary as the lads fought back. Nayim had come on for me and he helped set up Paul Stewart's equalising goal. The massive cheer from the fans was ringing in my ears as the ambulance made its way to the Princess Grace Hospital.

I even managed to catch the last bit of the game on TV from my hospital bed, as it had gone to extra time. I saw poor old Des Walker head the ball into his own net from a corner. We had won the Cup, the biggest achievement in my football life so far, in that I'd ended up with a winner's medal. But I felt I didn't deserve it. I'd acted like a mad bastard.

All the players came to visit me in hospital straight after the game, bringing me the Cup and my medal, but I could hardly look at them. It's true I'd probably done more than anyone to get them to the final, with all those Cup goals, but I felt I'd let them down when it mattered most.

It turned out I'd shattered the cruciate ligament in my right knee. It would have to be operated on and I was told I could be out for months, if not for ever. Officials from Lazio had been in the crowd to watch their new star. Would they now want me? Would Spurs want me? Would anyone? I spent my twenty-fourth birthday in my hospital room, feeling pretty sorry for myself, terrified that I had finally buggered everything up for good, all through my own stupidity.

A lot of people at the time said that was it, my career was finished, but I honestly never thought that for one moment. Once I knew it was my cruciate ligament I was concerned, but not too much because I knew other players who had recovered from it. As for those people in the press who still say that I never properly recovered from that injury, that it was downhill from then on, that's total bollocks. My career got better and better after that, and so did I as a player. No question.

But at that time, I was shitting myself. I was in a right state – but mainly because I thought I'd mucked up the Lazio deal, that it would now never happen.

I went with him to Wembley for the Cup final. We were in this limousine and every time we passed some Spurs supporters, with their scarves hanging out of the window, Paul would draw abreast and hand them sandwiches through the window. It was so funny, seeing their faces, when they suddenly realised who it was.

Carol Gascoigne

He took them to the final almost singlehandedly. He was the player we were most worried about because we knew he could turn a game on its head . . . That wild tackle had a massive effect on his career. He was never quite the same player afterwards.

Stuart Pearce, Psycho, *2000*

13

LEAVING FOR LAZIO

Maurizio Manzini, Lazio's general manager, and Carlo Regalia, another member of the management staff, came to visit me in hospital. They brought me a birthday present: a Lazio shirt and a gold watch engraved with a special message from their president. Apparently, it was worth £7,000. I was about to go down for an operation and had just had the pre med. When I woke up, the watch had gone. I thought at first someone from the hospital had pinched it, but it was me father who had taken it. Until then, he had never asked me for anything in my life, apart from a house, a car, a holiday, a wage. So taking a watch was nothing very much, really. I'm only joking. I probably told him to take it. I was so woozy I could have said anything. My mother took my medal.

Jimmy Gardner came to see me as well, bringing me a pellet gun, which came in handy for pointing out of the window at the photographers waiting down below in the street. But mostly we just dropped water bombs on them. At least they stayed outside. Some reporters tried to sneak into my room, pretending to be old friends from Newcastle.

My surgeon, John Browett, did a brilliant job in reconstructing my shattered knee, but it was clear it could be up to a year before I could do much with it. After a couple of months, I went out to Portugal to convalesce with John Sheridan, the Spurs physio, who put me through some intensive exercises and lots of swimming. But when I wasn't exercising, I was still hobbling around on crutches. Jimmy came out as well, along with John-Paul, my sister Anna's husband. Jimmy and I woke him up one night by pouring a fire bucket full of water over his head. You should have seen the look on his face. I nearly fell off me crutches laughing.

Terry Venables used to say, after I first came to Spurs, that I wouldn't be affected much by the culture shock of moving from the north-east to London because I had brought my own culture with me. Many young players get homesick, and feel lost and out of place. Some are so unhappy they decide to go back home, as George Best did when he first went to Manchester United from Belfast, or Graeme Souness when he moved to Spurs from Edinburgh.

It was true. I never felt lost. From the beginning, I had friends like Jimmy staying with me in the hotels I was living in, or my dad, plus other family who came to visit me. I planned to do the same thing when I went to Italy, if it ever happened. If I ever made it.

At that point Sheryl and I had split up, so the plan was for Anna and John-Paul to come out and live with me in my villa in Rome, to keep me company. That all fell through, obviously, when I got injured and it became clear that I would need several months to recover. But Anna had already given up her house in Dunston. So instead of going to Italy, she and John-Paul moved into my house in Hertfordshire.

As it turned out, this suited Anna, because she was keen to audition for a part in *The Phantom of the Opera*, which was then on stage in the West End of London. So while she was living in my house, she was singing all the time, practising her material. John-Paul also played the guitar a lot. I was supposed to be resting and recuperating, trying not to do my head in with all my usual worries. In the end, I moved out of my own house and left them to it. I went to live in a hotel for a while. Actually, I'd always enjoyed hotel life, so it was no hardship for me.

After weeks and weeks of physio and special rehab training, working my bollocks off, riding millions of miles on a training bike, I went up to Gateshead for a break. I was walking back from the pub one night with Lindsay, my little sister – we'd had quite a few drinks, but we weren't drunk – when some kids started hassling us, shouting at me and calling me names. Then a workman on his way home got involved – and I think he *had* had a few drinks – and there was a bit of pushing and shoving. In the midst of this fracas, one of these people punched Lindsay in the stomach. I wrongly thought it was the workman, so I lashed out at him and he fell to the ground. I had to do something: to have failed to protect my little sister would have been cowardly. It led to the police being called and me being taken off to the police station and kept in a cell for a few hours. I rang Mel Stein, and he arranged for a local lawyer to come and help me, and eventually I was allowed home. The incident was, of course, splashed all over the papers, and some of them made me out to be a right yob, describing events as if I'd been in a drunken brawl. In the Italian press, on the other hand, I was presented as some sort of hero going to the rescue of my endangered sister.

In August I went out to Rome to meet the Lazio management and be officially introduced to the club. My dad and some of the family came, along with Glenn Roeder, my old team-mate from Newcastle. He was planning his retirement from football and was looking to get into coaching. Although he's ten years older than me, I'd always got on well with him and he had been great to me since I'd come south to Spurs, sheltering me when I was in trouble, giving me helpful advice and showing me real kindness. It had been decided that he and his wife Faith and his family would come and live in Rome while I was there, to keep an eye on me. Glenn would be my football friend and companion and stop me from doing anything too daft. It was also an opportunity for him to have a close look at Italian coaching methods, to see how they did things, which he thought would be useful to him in his future career. So there were advantages all round.

We arrived in Rome to be greeted by amazing

scenes. We were mobbed at the airport, and there were screaming fans everywhere. I did a press conference, and some interviews, and was taken round the sights of Rome. There were Gazza posters and photos everywhere, even though I still hadn't signed for Lazio, the negotiations having been put on hold while they waited for me to get properly fit again. At the club, I met Dino Zoff, the Lazio manager – or coach, as they call them over there – for the first time. He, of course, had been one of Italy's most famous players and one of the world's best goalies. I was told they still wanted me, and were willing to wait till I was back in peak condition, whenever that might be – but not at the original price of £8 million-odd that had been agreed before my injury. They were still arguing the toss about what the new fee should be and who would get what share of what.

Glenn and his family made inquiries about schools in Rome for their kids and started looking for a villa. They liked the city and were impressed by the whole set-up at Lazio. I went to watch a Lazio game, where I was introduced to the crowd. They went wild. I gave them a little thank you, in Italian. All round the stadium there were banners, in English, welcoming me with messages such as:

Gazza's Boys are here
Shag women and drink beer.

It made me dad and me feel quite at home.

Before I left, it was agreed that I should make the move to Rome very soon, now that my knee was on the mend and I was getting really fit again. So finally, at the end of September, with all the arrangements in place, I went up to Newcastle to say goodbye to some of my old Dunston friends. As far as I remember it, after a few drinks at various watering-holes, we went to a club where a lad I had never seen before in my life comes up to me and says, 'Are you Paul Gascoigne?' I say yes – and he just whams me. As I crumpled to the floor I could feel my kneecap giving way. I put my hand down to feel my leg, to see what had happened, and my thumb practically sank into my knee. The hole was huge. The results of my operation had just been ripped apart. After all that work. I thought, fuck it. All the weeks and months of agony I had been through to recover, all the help I'd had from doctors and nurses and coaches and physios, and now this had happened. There seemed no way my career would recover this time.

When Glenn Roeder heard what had happened, he said, 'That's it.' He didn't even want to hear my explanation. It had not been my fault: a stranger had lashed out at me for no apparent reason. But Glenn said I'd promised never again to get in scrapes like that, and not to put myself in any situation where it could happen. So I shouldn't have been going to the sorts of pubs and clubs where there was a danger it might. I argued that this wasn't fair. It could have happened anywhere, and to anyone. But he wouldn't listen. He said this was the end, that I'd had me last chance. And he cancelled all his arrangements for Rome.

I know it was stupid not to have seen this daft kid coming after me, but the point was, I didn't want to stay away from the people or places I'd come from. I've never wanted to grow away from my roots. I want to live as I always have, not dropping old friends and old haunts, not moving away, not pretending I'm any different from them, that I'm something I'm not. And I like to think that, despite everything, I haven't changed. I'm still the same Geordie lad.

It was, though, a high price to pay. I had to have my third major operation in five months. Afterwards I returned to my house in Dobbs Weir, where Anna helped to look after me. Trying to recover all over again seemed to take for ever, but once more I worked like hell. In the meantime, a new president took over at Lazio, Sergio Cragnotti, who seemed tougher than the last one, but they still appeared to want me. Of course, it meant all the financial negotiations started again, with yet another series of deadlines and endless visits from doctors and specialists, both English and Italian. Lazio sent their experts over several times to check how I was doing, and I went over to Rome as well, to another triumphal welcome, so that they could all see me, and to show the fans they could expect me soon.

The deadline for the transfer was set for May 1992, a full year after my Cup final disaster – depending, of course, on me being passed fit. I was by now training again, and having treatment at Spurs, as I was still a Tottenham player.

At training one day, Steve Sedgley was showing off his new car, and being really flash. I happened to have a 2.2 air gun in my car, so I got it from the boot and shot out the back window of his car. I had to pay the bill for the damage, but it was worth it just to see the expression on his face.

When the Italians were over to check up on my

progress, Maurizio Manzini came to watch me training. One of the youth players was sent off to bring him a pot of tea. This lad was heading towards us, carefully carrying the teapot, cup and saucer and all the other bits and pieces on a tray, and for a laugh I got out my rifle and shot the teapot right off the tray. I think by that stage Lazio were beginning to wonder what they were signing.

When it was time for my new club's final check, I was so worried that I wouldn't be fit that I arranged an extra practice session for myself after normal training was over. I paid all the Spurs youths and young reserves £50 each to stay on and play a game with me, just so the Italians could see for themselves that I was OK.

I was finally transferred to Lazio at the end of May 1992 – the end of the football season in England and in Italy. I thought I deserved a break, after all the agonies and exertions, so I took the whole family off to Disneyland in Florida. There was my mam and dad, Anna and John-Paul, Lindsay and her boyfriend, my brother Carl, Jimmy, of course, and a couple of other friends as well as Sheryl.

Before my transfer, Sheryl and I had parted once again, but I soon realised how much I was going to miss her, on my own in Italy, with no Glenn and his family to give me company and support. I drove round to Shel's house. I pleaded with her to come with me, bursting into tears, telling her how much I loved her, missed her and needed her.

I had never lived with Shel when I was at Spurs, but she lived near me so I was often at her house. I had my own place at Dobbs Weir. Anna continued to live there for some time, while I was away, then I eventually sold it. I decided I didn't need it any more.

It took a while, but she agreed to come in the end. It was decided that Bianca, who was then aged about six and was at school, should stay in England and live with her father. Shel and Mason would come with me, and Bianca would come out during her school holidays.

With a party of that size, the Disneyland holiday wasn't cheap – and that was before anyone went shopping. Shel managed to buy herself some nice bits of jewellery. It wasn't a total success, though. I have to admit that my family didn't exactly hit it off with Shel.

My transfer fee from Spurs to Lazio was finally settled at £5.5 million – quite a lot less than the sums being bandied around when negotiations had first started, but of course I'd had all those injuries and lost over a year of football. The club offered me a signing-on fee of £800,000. I didn't care much about money – coming from a poor background, you know what it's like to have nothing – but you have to get as much as you can while you have the wherewithal to earn it. Around that time, there were approaches from Japan, offering me something like £2 million over two years, so I thought I'd try it on with Lazio. I spoke to them on the phone and said I wanted a £2 million signing-on fee, clear of tax, and I wanted a yes or no in five minutes, or the deal was off. Before the five minutes were up, they came back – accepting it. I was totally amazed.

My wages started at £22,000 a week, and were due to go up by about 10 per cent every year. So I was well and truly in the money and I was determined to spend it, mainly on my family. I bought them all houses and cars and holidays. It seemed the least I could do, after all the support they had given me.

When I had first watched Lazio training, on that visit with Glenn Roeder and my dad before I signed, I was a bit nervous. Their technique and fitness did seem better than ours in England, and I wondered whether I would be able to keep up.

When I eventually arrived, I was also, of course, worried about the language. I had had a couple of Italian lessons in England before I left, but I didn't bother with anything after that. The club did offer me more lessons, but there didn't seem much point when I had a translator available when I needed her, to help me get settled in, an Englishwoman whose name I'm not going to mention as she later wrote a book about me. In the end, I just picked up a bit of Italian as I went along, enough to get me by on the pitch or in shops and restaurants. The first words I learned were swearwords. I reckoned I'd be needing them.

Lazio employed about sixteen bodyguards, just to look after the players. I was told I would be guarded night and day. I thought it was a joke till I learned how intense and passionate Italian fans are. In Italy, footballers can't go anywhere without being pestered. And if your team is doing badly, they'll wreck your car, attack your house, throw things at you in the street, beat you up.

When I first moved into my villa in Rome, I was amazed to see two blokes hanging from the trees at the front, beside the gateway. I didn't dawn on me at first that they were my own personal security guards. When I realised who they were, I invited them in and got them pissed.

One of them nearly shot me one night. I'd got up to go to the toilet and, as always, I had to shut each door five times after me. He heard the doors being banged about and thought there must be a burglar in the house. Suddenly I found a gun being held to my head and this thug saying to me, '*Non ti muovere!*' – don't move – before he noticed it was me.

Before long, though, they got to know me better, and the same two guys were usually assigned to me, Gianni, who I called Johnny, and Augusto, who spoke good English. We all became good pals.

On the first day of proper training, when I was going to meet the whole squad, I went into town and bought twenty copies of a Teach Yourself English book. I got into the dressing room early and put one each on their benches. They thought that was hysterical.

> I'm very pleased for Paul but it's like watching your mother-in-law drive off a cliff in your new car.
> *Terry Venables, Tottenham manager,*
> *after Gazza finally joined Lazio, 1992*

> When he was at Spurs, and had bought his house in Hertfordshire, he was driving past this garden and noticed a man with a baldy heed who was bending over digging his garden. Paul went off and bought some eggs from a shop. Then he drove back to the man's house and threw eggs at the baldy heed.
> *Carol Gascoigne*

14

ROMAN DAYS

My debut in Serie A eventually came on 27 September 1992 at home to Genoa, sixteen long months after I had last played a competitive game. It was shown live on TV, in Britain as well as in Italy. Just before half-time, Mario Bortolazzi whacked me in the knee and I went down like a sack of spuds. The crowd fell silent, thinking I'd been badly injured, but I got up and shook the guy's hand, 'Thanks, mate,' I said. In Italian, of course. The game ended in a draw. I didn't actually manage the second half as I'd got a dead leg after another knock, which hit a nerve, but I was OK for training on the Tuesday.

I was in the starting line-up for the next game, against Parma, who were the Italian Cup-holders, and we thumped them 5–2. My new team-mate Giuseppe Signori recorded his first hat-trick in Serie A and I like to think I helped him get it. I came off about twenty minutes before the end, as I was getting tired, but I got a standing ovation. I felt great, played great and, most important of all, my knee felt great.

In the dressing room, Valerio Fiori, our goalie, spoke good English, as did Claudio Sclosa, who was my room-mate when we played away. Maurizio Manzini, the general manager, was very fluent and he was always helpful. Dino Zoff, however, didn't speak any English at all, so my conversations with him had to be translated. One of the first questions I asked him was if it was OK to have a pint of lager now and again. He said it was OK by him, as long as I did the business on the field. He gave me the number 10 shirt, which is considered a big honour in Italy. Many of the best players in Italy have worn number 10, including Platini, Maradona and Roberto Baggio.

Next we played away to AC Milan at the San Siro. They were the league champions and had an unbeaten run of forty games behind them and stars like Van Basten,

Gullit, Rijkaard, Maldini and Baresi in their ranks. That game was live on TV everywhere. We scored in the first five minutes, but after that we never touched the ball. We were stuffed 5–1 and Van Basten got a hat-trick. It was probably a great one to watch on TV, and a good advertisement for Italian football, but I certainly didn't think it was that terrific.

In the dressing room, I went mad. Our team was a fucking joke, I said. They were all useless. What were they thinking of? In England, we would always fight, fight, fight to the end, even when we were being outclassed. Dino Zoff told me off. '*Stai zitto*,' he said, which means shut up. '*Tu non capisci uncazzo del calcio Italiano*.' You know fuck all about Italian football. Which, of course, was true.

I think the other players probably realised I was over-excited, and deep down, they knew as well as I did that we'd let ourselves down. None of them held it against me. In fact, I never had any trouble with any of my Lazio team-mates, no rows or fights or anything. They were all very good, and we got on well.

The more games I played, the more I became aware that the players were not as technically brilliant as I'd first thought. They just did some things differently.

They'd keep the ball at the back for hours, so you thought, fucking hell, get a move on; then, suddenly, they'd come to life once they reached the last third. That's when you saw their speed and skill and cleverness. That's when they did the business.

Johnny and Augusto, my security guards, remained great friends of mine. All Lazio's bodyguards worked for Italy's leading security firm, Mondiapol, who also looked after the country's money. When I found out that one of their jobs was guarding some huge bank vault, I got them to sneak me in with Jimmy. I sat on this huge mountain of money, about £50 million. I started chucking wads of it in the air, which wasn't part of the deal – Johnny and Augusto had made me promise not to touch it. Jimmy has a photo of me throwing that money about, unless he's lost it, the dozy sod.

The club paid for my accommodation. I hadn't long moved into my first villa when I found a nine-foot snake by the pool. I immediately insisted on moving. In my next villa, getting up one morning to get ready for training, I found a two-foot snake in the bedroom. I wasn't as scared this time, because it wasn't so long, so I just whacked it with a broom.

I took the dead snake with me to training, and

when everyone else had got stripped off and gone out, I put it in Di Matteo's jacket pocket. Yeah, Roberto Di Matteo, the one who later went to Chelsea. He comes in after training, has a shower, gets dressed and puts his hand into his pocket. He went apeshit. It was hilarious. But no, he didn't get too mad with me. He was just relieved it wasn't alive.

I went to training one day on a motorbike, a sort of mountain bike scrambler thing, which the owner of my villa had left behind. I hadn't intended to use it, but my Mercedes had a flat tyre and I'd had a row with Shel, who'd gone off in her car, so in desperation I just jumped on this bike and rode off in a temper. I had no insurance, no helmet and I didn't really know how to ride it. The club had hysterics. All that money they'd paid for me, and I could have killed myself.

I did have one nasty driving incident, towards the end of that first season. The fans, as usual, were all over my car, hanging on, and in trying to get clear of them I ran one of them over. There were tyre marks on his leg and he was badly bruised. I gave him my number 10 shirt, by way of an apology, to keep him quiet, but he told the press anyway and everyone had a go at me, including the president.

I later met, on a plane, a reporter who had written some of the worst things about me. I smiled at him – and then punched him in the bollocks. I told him that was for writing lies about me when he didn't know anything about me. He said he would tell the police. Nothing happened, but it didn't help my relationship with the press.

Another time I was out shopping with Shel and we were being followed everywhere by this photographer. He'd already got loads of pictures, so I told him enough was enough. 'When I come out of this shop,' I said to him, 'if you are still here, I'm going to thump you.' I came out and he was still there, smiling a silly smile, so I hit him. He called the police and Shel and I had to give a statement. I apologised, and forgot about it, but of course the press didn't. Overall, you'd have to say I didn't handle the press very well in Italy.

During that first season I got the 'flu at one stage and had to miss a few days' training, so I wasn't surprised I wasn't picked for the upcoming league game. I was, however, surprised to find I was in the line-up two days later for some sort of benefit match with Seville, in which Maradona was due to play. I couldn't understand why I was thought fit for one and not the other. I came to the conclusion they didn't want me to play in the league game in case I got injured, but needed me for the Maradona extravaganza as they were making a lot of money from it. So I thought, fuck it, and went off to EuroDisney in Paris for a couple of days, taking Shel and the kids as a treat.

Manzini rang me at my hotel and said I'd got to come back for the Seville game. I said I wanted £120,000 extra to play in it, otherwise I was staying, to recover from the 'flu. He agreed, so I flew off to Spain. I had quite a bit of champagne on the plane, being afraid of flying, and arrived half-cut. All the lads cheered when I appeared in the dressing room. We were a goal down when I beat five players to score, even though I was still half-drunk, and the game ended 1–1. I didn't shake hands with Maradona afterwards. I was still furious with him for his hand-of-God goal against England in the 1986 World Cup.

I didn't get my £120,000. Instead the club said they were going to fine me £20,000 for going off to Paris without permission. I said to Dino Zoff, 'Fuck off, that's it. I'm leaving, then.' He was, I hardly need to say, disgusted by my behaviour. He had been one of Italy's all time greats: he was a World Cup star, he had a record number of caps, and yet he had to put up with all this. Mostly, I did get on with him well, though, and I think he liked me. He told me his plan was to make me captain of the team. He would buy me a racehorse, and I could always have the odd day off. But that was in my early days at Lazio, the honeymoon period.

I wasn't match fit, again, when we met Juventus, but I was there, in my Lazio blazer, in the VIP seats. And so was David Platt, in his Juventus blazer – he wasn't playing that day, either. As we were walking to our seats, there was this bloke pestering us, sticking a microphone in our mouths, up our arses. We were not supposed to talk to the media at all at that time – there had been some row or something. Platty, of course, being smooth and polite and well brought up, said nothing, and just smiled. I decided to give him a big belch. Jimmy would have been proud of me. It was simply a joke, the sort of thing I could have done in England and no one would have been bothered. What I hadn't realised was that my belch was going out live on prime-time TV, just as the whole nation was sitting down to dinner and waiting for the big match. The reaction was incredible, unbelievable. There were front-page headlines everywhere and it made all the TV news broadcasts. It was even raised in the Italian Parliament, where it was condemned as an insult to the Italian nation. Lazio were furious with me. My main crime was that I had belched while officially representing the club, wearing their blazer. I had therefore disgraced the club, let down its good name.

Signore Cragnotti, the club owner, was livid. He'd spent a great deal of money on the club and saw me as the vital element in bringing them success in Italy and in Europe. I'd already upset him once, at the training ground, when he'd made one of his grand entrances along with other officials. I'd gone up to him and said: '*Tua figlia, grande tette.*' Your daughter, big tits. At least, I think that's what I said. There were some embarrassed giggles from some of the bigwigs, but Signore Cragnotti wasn't amused. I only discovered later that I'd mixed up the daughters. I'd been thinking of his brother's daughter, not his. I'd never even met her. Luckily, that incident didn't make the papers, but the Belchgate scandal went on for weeks. The Italian press hammered me, and used it to criticise me, as proof that I was a yob, as well as overweight, never properly fit, a waste of money and a disgrace to Lazio and Italy, and all that shit. The Lazio fans, though, were brilliant. I never fell out with them. At the next game, against Torino, I could hear them singing, in English, 'Gazza, Gazza, give us a belch.'

The big event every season for all Lazio supporters, officials and players is the local derby with Roma. I was very nervous about playing in my first one because I'd already picked up on how much it mattered. All week the fans had been going on about it. On the day there was a crowd of about 75,000, all going mad.

We were 1–0 down when we got a free kick near the penalty area, towards the end of the game. I told Signori to get in the box, and I'd put it on his head. He said he was not much good with his head, so he'd take it and put it on my head. I replied that I wasn't much good with mine, either. Anyway, he took it, and somehow I managed to get my head to it, by leaning back, and it went in. I fell in a heap, just collapsed. It was about the biggest emotional high of my whole career up to that time. There was such a massive feeling of relief in the entire club that we had drawn this derby game. Afterwards, the president sent me about £10,000 in cash and a crate of Newcastle Brown. God knows where he got that from.

Comparing Gascoigne with Pele is like comparing
Rolf Harris to Rembrandt.
Rodney Marsh, former England striker, 1990

He is a very remarkable footballer. He may be the
greatest player Britain has so far produced, a Best and
Charlton rolled into one, a player with breathtaking
dribbling skills and a ferocious curving shot. His football vision is quite phenomenal.
Peter Barnard, The Times, *27 August 1994*

Gazza reminds me of Marilyn Monroe. She wasn't the
greatest actress in the world, but she was a star and
you didn't mind if she was late.
Michael Caine, 1998

15

SOME WEIGHTY PROBLEMS

Living with Shel in Italy didn't really work out. For two months, all we did was argue. Bianca came out for the holidays, but I didn't really know how to be a father and I was really ratty, shouting at the kids to keep quiet. I was under pressure, but all the same, I was being a horrible dad. One night I put them in the garage because they were keeping me awake and I just couldn't get a wink of sleep.

I didn't like Shel going out anywhere, even just out with other mums. She was once late back from seeing some of Mason's friends' mothers and I drove off to meet her, in a real temper, hurtling down the autostrada the wrong way on the wrong side of the road so that I would come upon her heading towards me. It gave her a terrible fright, and it was very stupid and dangerous.

Something was eating me away inside. There were all the problems of settling in, and trying to communicate in a new language, and if I was injured it made me ten times worse. It was, of course, tough for her, as it is for all wives and girlfriends of footballers abroad, cooped up all day, cut off from their own families, not knowing people. But it was mainly my fault. I didn't allow her enough space.

After about six months, she went home with Mason. I'd got £80,000 for some story about me in Italy from the *News of the World*, so we used that to buy a house back in Hertfordshire for Shel to live in with her kids. She came out to Italy often, and we spent all our holidays together, but without her there full-time I got bored and lonely. So my mates came out: Jimmy and Cyril came from Newcastle, and my mum and dad made regular trips to Rome.

On the field, meanwhile, that first season for Lazio went pretty well. I slowly got my strength back after the long lay-off and picked up only a few minor injuries. The worst was in April 1993, when I was playing for England against Holland at Wembley. I went for a challenge against Jan Wouters. We collided heavily and I felt my jaw lock. I lay there on the ground, unable to open my mouth. Ian Wright and Paul Ince were laughing, thinking I was putting it on. I didn't think it was all that serious myself. At half-time, I was asked if I was OK to carry on, and I said yes. The England doc thought it was just bruising.

Lazio were watching the game live on TV, keeping an eye on me. They were never very thrilled when I played for England, especially when I ended up with a bash like this. Lazio were due to fly out to Japan – or it might have been China, I forget – and I wasn't keen to go on the trip, so I thought I'd stay in London and get a doctor to look at me bruised jaw and sign me off as unfit to fly.

I didn't actually feel too bad, although it was a bit of a struggle to eat, and I'd been out to the pictures with Shel and had some popcorn which had made my jaw lock again. When I got to the doctor's for the appointment, fucking hell, there were two people from Lazio, sent over to check that I was telling the truth – and to take me straight back to Italy afterwards.

But the doctor discovered I had a broken cheekbone. I'd been walking around with it for two days, with no idea it was that bad. So that meant another operation.

When I came round from the op, someone was holding my hand. My eyes were still closed and I thought it was Shel, but when I looked up I saw that it was Gianni Zeqireya, my monster bodyguard, the one I called Johnny. He'd come to take me to China. I said, 'I've got a broken cheekbone. I'm not going nowhere now, Johnny lad.'

The next day, I felt a bit better, so I took Johnny out for a drink. I gave him some very strong beer, pretending it was gnat's piss, then took him for a Chinese and got him to drink two cans of lager, which I told him was a Chinese soft drink. So I didn't make it to China with Lazio, but we did have a nice Chinese in Newcastle instead.

When I eventually got back to Lazio, I played in a mask for a few games, like something out of *The Phantom of the Opera*. It was a bit awkward and sweaty, but it made a good photo. You could use those shots for frightening the bairns.

Despite that injury, and missing a few matches, I made twenty-six appearances for Lazio that first season, and scored four goals. Lazio ended up fifth and got into the UEFA Cup, their first appearance in Europe for sixteen years. So the club and the supporters were well pleased with what they'd achieved – and with me, as their big investment. All the time they had had to wait seemed to have paid off.

In the summer, I went on holiday with Shel, first in Italy and then to Florida. In the USA, I was eating rubbish, like ice creams and hot dogs, and my weight soared up to fourteen stone, the heaviest I've ever been. I had been warned by Dino to stay fit. Five days before I was due to return to Italy, he rang me up and reminded me about it, telling me it was time to start doing an hour's run every day. I said I was fit, I was fine, though by that time I was rolling out of bed with as many bellies as Jimmy had. But I put my kit on and went for a run. On the way, I saw a cocktail bar. It was very hot, so I thought, bollocks, I'll start getting fit tomorrow, and went into the bar and had a piña colada. It was still only nine in the morning. The thing is I like sweet things – piña coladas, for example – and once I have one, I can't stop.

When I got back to Italy and started pre-season training, I got a right bollocking from Zoff. He said he wanted two stones off me in the next month, and if I didn't manage it, I wouldn't be in the team.

Most managers have given me a weight to aim for. I've been down to 11st 8lbs, but personally I like to be about twelve stone. Having a decent upper-body weight has always helped me to ride tackles, shrug people off. It mattered a lot when I was young, being strong enough to keep my place in the side when other young players, often just as good, couldn't yet match me in that department. Terry Venables liked me to be 12st 3lbs. With Graham Taylor and England, I was over 12st 7lbs, which he did not like.

When I'm given an ultimatum, I like to go on a water diet, and that usually gets half a stone off. It's just water and lemon, plus a bit of maple syrup for energy. I throw a bit of cayenne pepper into the water to give it some sort of taste. I drink four litre bottles a day, all day long, for four days. On the fourth day, I'll have a chicken sandwich. Yeah, I know it's a mad diet, but that's what I do. I've always gone from one extreme to the other in everything.

During those weeks of trying to get fit and meet Dino Zoff's target, I also did a lot of running – wearing my trusty black plastic bin-liners, to sweat off the flab, just as I had as a lad.

When the month was up, I went for the weigh-in.

I knew I'd done it, but when they checked the scales, I was one fraction of an ounce still over. I was told I'd failed. I wasn't in the team for the next match. I went ballistic. But in the end they did play me.

When my dad came out to see me in Italy for the first time, with Jimmy and Cyril, I asked him to bring some English food with him. He brought some tins of beans, some mince pies and guess what? A load of packets of spaghetti. I couldn't stop laughing when I saw the spaghetti. 'Dad,' I said, 'they have spaghetti here. It's where it comes from.' But he said: 'Son, they won't make spaghetti Bolognese the way I do.'

We all scoffed the tins of beans and most of the mince pies in the first evening. About three mince pies were left over and I put them in the fridge. A bit later I decided I'd improve their flavour by adding a little bit of shit. I opened the pies, put some in each, then put the tops on again and put them back in the fridge. No one could tell they'd been touched.

The next night, after we've all been out drinking late, we come home and they say they're starving, what is there to eat? I mention that there might be some of those mince pies left. They go to the fridge and get them out, and put them in the microwave to heat up. It did create a bit of a smell, but they were too drunk to notice. I winked at me dad, warning him not to have any, but Jimmy and Cyril tucked in, scoffing one each, and then started fighting over the last one. When I told them what I'd done, Jimmy rushed to the toilet and was sick. But Cyril said he doesn't care – it was one of the best mince pies he'd ever had.

I did some awful things to Jimmy when he came to stay. He was lying on his bed once in my villa, bollock-naked, after a night on the tiles. There was a wild cat that used to hang around my garden, and I went out to look for it, tempting it with a burger. When I caught it, I threw it through the open window of Jimmy's bedroom, just for a laugh, to watch his reaction. It fell on his face, he screamed like buggery, and naturally the cat scratched him. Yeah, it was a bad thing to do, but I was bored. That was the reason.

Another time I drove my car at Jimmy, going about thirty miles an hour, just to scare him. Which it did, especially when I hit him. I thought I'd killed him, but he recovered. He did have a huge lump on his head, but I put a packet of frozen peas on it and it eventually went down – about a year later.

One of the nice things that happened when I played for Lazio was that I met Johan Cruyff, my boyhood idol.

We had a game against Barcelona, where he was manager. I told him afterwards that he'd been my hero, but I can't remember what he said to me. I suppose people tell him that all the time, so it probably wasn't anything out of the ordinary for him.

I also – though I wouldn't put the two encounters in the same category – met Colonel Gaddafi's son Saadi. He trained with us for a while and I was on his side, luckily. I didn't want to fall out with him, did I? He was a pretty good bloke – and not a bad player, either. He invited me out after training one day for a drink, but I didn't turn up. I was scared to, having heard stories about his dad and what happened if you got on the bad side of father or son, or played tricks on them – the sort I played on Jimmy, which they might not have appreciated in the same way. I later wished I had done. He went on to do a bit of training at Roma and one of their first-team players gave him his team shirt. In return, Gaddafi gave him a new car.

One day, as we were about to start training, Dino Zoff called me aside and said someone very, very important had been on the phone, wanting to meet me. He was so important, Dino had never heard of such a thing happening before.

'Oh, aye. Who is it, then?'

'The Pope,' he said.

'The *Pope*?'

I thought it was a wind-up, but it was true. Pope John Paul II actually wanted to meet me.

The Pope used to be a goalie, when he was young, and he was a football fan, so I suppose, with me playing for one of the Rome teams, it wasn't totally far-fetched that he'd been following my progress. After all, I had seen a photograph of him wearing a Lazio scarf.

Dino said that of course I should go and meet him – but not until after I'd finished training. I just had time to ring me mam and dad, who were staying with me at the time, along with Anna. I said: 'Get your arses into gear and get round to the Vatican as soon as you can.'

Training went on a bit longer than usual, and by the time I arrived at the Vatican the Pope had left for another appointment. I'd missed him by five minutes. But me mam and dad and sister had met him and been blessed. They'd been at the front of the handful of people who had been individually given a little present from him. My dad got a gold cross and me mam and Anna got special rosary beads.

At the Vatican, they told me that the Pope's right-

hand man wanted to see me, as the Pope had left something for me. This cardinal took me into a big study
with special phones all over the desk. One went direct
to the Queen, and another to the President of the USA,
so I was told. There was a photograph of the Pope on
the desk, and in the corner of the frame was a little
picture of me, in my Lazio strip. I don't know if the
Pope put it there, or maybe the cardinal had. Anyway,
he told me the Pope wanted me to have a special medal,
the sort he gives to the Queen, the US President,
Gorbachev, those sort of people. It's a big medal, in gold,
with the Pope on one side and the Vatican coat of arms
on the other. It looked really important and very precious.
I didn't know what to do with it. I was scared I'd lose
it, or it would get pinched.

So I rang Jimmy in Newcastle and told him to fly
out at once: I wanted him to come and pick up my
medal from the Pope, take it back and put it safely in
the bank. Of course, he didn't believe me. He thought
it was one of my stunts. 'It's true,' I insisted. 'Come
quick. I'll get someone to arrange everything for you,
the flights and that. All you have to do is get down to
Newcastle Airport and pick up the tickets.'

I sorted it all, just as I'd promised – although when

he got to the airport, he discovered he had to fly first to Heathrow, and then on to Copenhagen, Lisbon, Paris, all sorts, all over. He didn't know where he was ending up next till he picked up each ticket. It took him about two days. All first-class tickets, mind. But he did have to spend one night sleeping in an airport lounge because he'd run out of money, having left thinking he would be with me in a couple of hours. That was to teach him not to disbelieve me.

He did arrive in the end, and took the medal back to the bank, where it still is today, along with a few other bits of jewellery and medals and things I've picked up over the years.

I enjoyed that trick with the flights so much that I pulled it again later, with my brother. This time I was a bit more ambitious: when he got to the airport he found out that his first flight took him to Cambodia . . .

The referees were good to me in Italy. I talked to them all the time, and they didn't really mind that – except once, when I'd been giving him a lot of chat, a ref said, 'Here, take this.' It was a piece of chewing gum. 'Eat that,' he said, 'and shut up.'

I remember saying to another ref, when I was feeling

knackered, 'I'm done for, ref. You take over, you'll do better than me.'

'Will you referee?' he asked me.

'No chance. I haven't got the energy to blow the whistle . . .'

I was substituted not long afterwards.

The Italian football paper, *Gazetta dello Sport*, did a survey of the players by polling the referees. They all said I was no problem: always gentlemanly, never underhand or nasty. So that was nice. In one game, when I was performing very well, the ref said I was playing like a champion. I told him he was the best referee in the world.

I was sent off once, against Genoa, the team we had played on my league debut in Italy when that bloke Bortolazzi had nearly taken my leg off. In the same fixture the following season, I reacted badly in a clash with the same player, and I got a red card.

Before leaving the field, I smiled and shook hands with the ref and some of the players on each side, and went off to an ovation. I think it was behaving so well that kept my punishment to a one-match suspension. Sometimes it pays to make people smile.

He's a fat, ill-mannered Geordie who has urinated a glorious Godgiven talent against numerous walls. He bites every hand that seeks to restrain him and abuses those who would save him from himself. Not since the death of Princess Diana has a tragic figure so dominated the airwaves.
Ian Wooldridge, Daily Mail, 3 June 1998

He is under more media pressure than anyone in England except Princess Di. It can be argued that both of them have suffered from bad advice.
Peter Barnard, The Times, 27 August 1994

You have taken a place in our hearts, and we will always love you. Nobody is as great as you. Always by your side.
Amarando Sestili, Lazio fan club secretary, in a letter to Paul, 3 March 1992

16

ARRIVEDERCI ROMA

After the 1990 World Cup, when Bobby Robson left for PSV Eindhoven, Graham Taylor had taken over the England management. I played for him against Hungary that September and in the European Championship qualifier against Poland. We won both matches and I thought I did well, but then, although I was fit and available and not injured, he dropped me for the Ireland match in November, picking Gordon Cowans instead. It was the first time I'd been left out since I'd made the England squad, and I was devastated. Graham never really explained to me why. He told the press it was for 'tactical reasons'. All he said to me was that I wasn't in the right state to play, which really pissed me off. Obviously the public didn't agree with him, because it was the following month that I was voted the BBC Sports Personality of the Year.

The Ireland match ended in a 1–1 draw, and I was picked for the next fixture, with Cameroon at Wembley, in February 1991. We won that game 2–0, and I earned my twentieth cap, but after that came my hernia operation and my FA Cup final injury, and I was out of football altogether for about eighteen months. As well as delaying my move to Italy, all that meant I missed twenty-one possible England games, including the 1992 European Championship finals in Sweden. England crashed out of that tournament, finishing bottom of their group. They didn't win a single game. I'm not saying there was any connection between my absence and their poor performance. Me mam said so, of course, and me father. And Jimmy, and all the Gascoigne clan . . .

When I eventually recovered and joined Lazio, Graham Taylor came out to Italy to see me, to check I was fit again, and I was selected for the World Cup qualifier against Norway at Wembley in October 1992.

Two nights before the game, in the England hotel, I had a few drinks with Paul Merson. I wasn't drunk – I only had four bottles of Budweiser – but Paul was on the brandy, put away loads of it. I hadn't realised it all went on my bill. Of course, when Graham Taylor found out, he thought all the drinks had been for me.

Without telling me what he was going to say, he revealed at a press conference that I had problems because of my 'refuelling' habits. If he was going to say such a thing, he should have taken me aside first and warned me, not just come out with it like that in public.

Even so, I can't say I would have explained what really happened. I never told him the truth, so he probably won't know it until he reads it here. As everyone is now aware, Paul had serious problems, and at the time he was in a very bad state. The press were hounding him, and I was just trying to protect him from even worse publicity. But I lost respect for Graham Taylor after that.

At Wembley before the match, I was grabbed by a Norwegian TV crew and asked if I'd say a few words to Norway. So I did, I said, 'Fuck off, Norway.' It was quite obviously a joke. I was grinning like mad as I said it, and I immediately added that I was just being funny and asked them what else they would like me to say, but I could see they had taken the 'fuck off, Norway' seriously. Lawrie McMenemy, the England assistant manager, tried to laugh it off as well, and to persuade the TV people not to use that bit of footage, but they did. And after that I got hate mail from Norway for months.

The game ended in a 1–1 draw. The next month we had another World Cup qualifier, against Turkey. We beat them 4–0 and I scored twice.

Graham Taylor did usually pick me, but I never agreed with his tactics. He was a devotee of the long ball, the big whack up from defence to the forwards, whereas I believe in passing the ball. That's how football should be played. I think most of the players agreed with me, but Graham was the manager so we had to try and do what he wanted, which made for some dull games and some bad performances, such as the vital World Cup qualifier, against Norway again, in June 1993.

At half-time, I was going mad, screaming and shouting in the dressing room, raving that this was not the way to play football. I was having a go at everyone, even telling David Platt to pull his finger out. I didn't have a go at Graham Taylor directly, but he was in no doubt who it was I was unhappy with. Instead I lashed out at Lawrie McMenemy, his right-hand man. We ended up getting beaten 2–0.

About the only bright spot in Graham Taylor's

reign was having Steve Harrison as coach. I didn't really know much about him when he first came – like Graham, he had been at Watford. He was a great prankster. In the run-up to one England game, the whole squad went into the West End for a night out. We did some go-karting, and then we went to the theatre and saw the Buddy Holly musical, which was brilliant. Afterwards, we had dinner in a hotel. During the meal, this scruffy tramp came up to me, begging for money, his teeth all black, really stinking. I was a bit taken aback, wondering how the hell he'd got in. It turned out to be Steve Harrison, winding me up. He really got me there.

We had a karaoke competition after dinner. While Des Walker was giving us his version of 'Singing in the Rain' I poured a pint of lager over his head. That was pretty normal behaviour for me; Steve's tricks were often much better. One evening, at a team dinner, he burst into the room wearing a dirty mac. When he opened it, he was naked, except for a rubber chicken tied round his waist. Nobody could work out what the point was, but I got the joke: there *was* no point. I liked that kind of joke. He also played similar tricks to mine. He'd lead us on training runs round a circuit, then suddenly carry straight on, right into some bushes. He was a canny lad.

One thing that could be said for Graham Taylor was that he was good on team togetherness. He organised lots of outings and events, which I always think really helps to boost morale and team spirit.

In 1994, I got another really bad injury, a broken leg, and once again I was out for about a year. I missed fifteen months of England games. The only small consolation was that I didn't miss out going to the 1994 World Cup, because, of course, England didn't get there. And by that time, Graham Taylor had got the push.

This disaster struck at the end of my second season in Italy, 1993–4. Things had been going well, too. I got the Man of the Match award in January 1994 against Sampdoria, even though we were beaten and I had had to come off with a rib injury. They gave me a huge injection to keep me going for the next game, and I had a run of six consecutive matches, the longest I'd managed since I was at Tottenham, where in 1990 I played nineteen on the trot.

Against Cremonese, whom we beat 4–2, our captain in that match, Roberto Cravero, had to go off and I was given the captain's arm band for the first time in my professional career. I hadn't captained a team since I'd led Newcastle Youth to their Cup final victory.

Although the Italian press still didn't like me, it seemed the public still did. The Panini stickers people, who produce those little photos of footballers for people to collect, issued a voting slip with each packet sold in Italy, and I came out as their top player, beating Roberto Baggio and Franco Baresi.

So this new injury came at a really unfortunate time, when I was riding high. It happened in April 1994, on a day we were expecting to be a day off. Instead we were all told we had to come in and train, so I was pissed off. We were having an indoor game, which I was treating as just a bit of a kick-about, but when I made a mistake which gave away a goal, my side screamed at me. I hadn't realised they were taking it so seriously. Right, I thought, if they want a proper game, I'll give them one, and I went to tackle Alessandro Nesta, very, very hard. He was OK, but I went down in a heap. I just lay there, numb. I knew straight away that something was seriously wrong. The doc rushed over but I said, 'Leave it, leave it,' and began to feel my knee. There was a hole there about five inches in diameter.

I'd broken my leg. When they picked me up and carried me out, I was screaming in agony. I was taken to a hospital in Rome, but I persuaded them to let me have the op I needed in London, so that Mr Browett could do it, as he'd fixed my leg before. This time I had a double fracture of the tibia and fibula. I was put on a plane, all plastered and bandaged up, surrounded by photographers trying to take pictures of me. I went to the Princess Grace Hospital, which had become my second home. My first home was of course the Queen Elizabeth in Gateshead, but I'd got a season ticket at a new place now.

The Lazio fans gave Nesta dog's abuse for what had happened. They were convinced he must have been to blame, as he was known as a hard tackler. They loved me so much that one or two of them even sent him death threats. But it had all been my own fault.

I worked my bollocks off after the op to get back to fitness, doing exercises three times a day when I was only supposed to do them once. I think that made it my fifteenth operation. Feel free to check my chart.

I hated being injured, as all players do. I threw myself into getting fit again, doing everything I was told and more, but I got very low, and then I'd start taking pep pills or drinking or stuffing my face to try to comfort myself. I was out for practically a whole season. So, of my three seasons at Lazio, 1992–5, I only really played for two. In that time, I made forty-seven appearances and scored six goals. Not a lot, really. It was all a crying shame.

Things got even harder when Dino Zoff left Lazio and Zdenek Zeman took over as manager. He was a very tough Czech. Tough on all the players, not just me. He was a right bastard in training, making us work like dogs. Signori, our regular captain, complained to him that he was knackering us all, and it was too much. Zeman said, 'I'm not packing my bags and going, I'm staying, so you'll have to put up with it.'

Zeman informed me I was two stone overweight and he got me exercising on these bikes. When I'd done what he'd told me to do on the bikes, I was supposed to do a two-mile run, but once I did the equivalent on one of the bikes instead. He said: 'Get off the bike and do the run on your feet.' I was so angry I picked up five bikes and threw them down the stairs at the training ground. They didn't hit anyone, but they were ruined. The bikes cost about £300 each, and I had to pay for them.

The club doctor moaned on about my weight, saying I was only 50 per cent fit and couldn't manage two consecutive games because I hadn't got the strength. It was one thing to be told this in private, but the club let it out in the press, the bastards.

When I was fit, I wanted to play every game, but Lazio insisted on resting me for some of them, even though I was fine, in case I was injured again. They wanted to keep me safe, I understood that. But I always wanted to play.

But I have to say that I enjoyed Italy. I loved the football and never felt out of my depth. In fact, I felt I was a better player than most of them. I loved Lazio – the players, the club, Rome, the fans, the Italian way of life, everything. In the end I picked up quite a bit of Italian, enough for me to talk to Italian waiters whenever I meet them now. Or swear at them. And the lobsters were great.

The first New Year's Eve I was in Rome I went to this posh restaurant with Shel and ordered lobster because I'd seen they had a huge lobster tank. I pointed to the one I wanted and they went off to get it. They were taking so long I thought, what are they doing messing about? I'll get it myself. So I dived into the tank. I had on my best suit. The water was freezing cold and very salty. It took me a while, diving and swimming around, to catch the one I fancied. When I did, I hooked it out and said, 'There's the fucker I want.' Then I ate it sitting in me dripping suit.

I managed to see quite a bit of Rome without getting wet. I went to the Colosseum and did the historic sites. People think footballers have no idea where they are in the world, and care less. But because of Johnny and Augusto, I learned something about the country I was living in. They took me around and showed me places and told me about Italian history. It was quite interesting, actually.

I planted a tree while I was there, for the unification of Europe. Don't ask me what all that was about. I got this invitation from the British government, asking me to take part in a tree-planting ceremony, and I sent my reply to the prime minister, John Major. 'Dear John,' I wrote, which people thought was a bit cheeky of me, as I'd never met him, and he was, after all, the prime minister of my country. I said I would be delighted to help with the tree-planting, and invited him to come and watch me play for Lazio in a forthcoming friendly against Spurs at White Hart Lane. 'It will be a change from watching Mellor perform in a Chelsea strip,' I added.

I got a letter back about three weeks later. He called me 'Dear Paul' but said he was sorry, he had another engagement and couldn't make the match. In his own handwriting at the end, he added, 'Welcome back to the England team.' I was very pleased with that.

One of the things I enjoyed in Italy was the training. We did about twice as much as at Newcastle or Spurs, with an afternoon session as well as a morning one. But that didn't bother me. I liked it. Preferred it. I've always loved training.

With Zoff, the training was always fun, and we played a lot of football or worked on skills. It wasn't quite so much fun with Zeman. He put fitness before football, so I wasn't as keen on that. The hardest time I ever had was when they were getting me to lose the two stones. For 75 days, I did 35 miles a day on a bike and 8 miles a day running. That was truly knackering. But it worked. I got my weight down.

Italians are more dedicated and professional than we are, especially on things like diet. Players would worry if they had a Coca-Cola, in case it had a bad effect on them. And none of them drank, not like I call drinking, or British players call drinking. They'd have one glass of wine with their pre-match meal, and that was it. No drinking at all after a game. No going out getting pissed.

I didn't go out a lot with the players anyway, not socially. I got on with them all, liked them all, and I like to think they liked me, but I didn't socialise with them. I usually had Jimmy and Cyril or my dad staying with me. I preferred to be with them in the evening.

I didn't actually do a lot of drinking in Italy, not really, not compared with later. I suppose I picked up a bit of their healthy lifestyle. Italy did do me good – made me a better player and a better person. Made me determined to be the best player in the world.

I never made friends with the Italian press after that belching incident, and all my injuries buggered up a lot of my time at Lazio, but the Lazio fans never turned against me. So all in all, I have very fond memories of Italy and no regrets about moving to Lazio.

You'll have to excuse Gazza.
He's got a very small vocabulary.
*Lawrie McMenemy, England assistant manager,
after the player said, 'Fuck off, Norway,' on television, 1992*

Il suo amico Jimmy Cinquepance è convinto che alla fine Gascoigne si sistemerà a Glasgow. [His friend Jimmy Five Bellies is convinced that in the end Gascoigne will settle in Glasgow.]
Corriere dello Sport, 17 Maggio 1995

17

ARRIVAL AT RANGERS

Much as I loved Italy and Lazio, I had had enough of Zdenek Zeman, and he had probably had enough of me. When I did eventually manage to get back to full fitness, it became clear that I was no longer going to be an automatic choice for my place. There was a limit on how many foreigners a club could play, and Lazio had signed yet another one, Alen Boksic from Marseille.

The Italian press were declaring that I was finished, that my best years were behind me, and some of the British papers were saying much the same; worse, in fact: that I'd never been the same since my 1991 Cup final injury. I knew that was bollocks and I was determined to prove them all wrong. I was only twenty-seven, after all.

I'd heard rumours that Chelsea, Rangers and Aston Villa were all making inquiries about me. I didn't want to go back to London, so I didn't fancy either Chelsea or Rangers. Yes, I know Rangers are a Scottish club. But when I first heard the talk I thought it was referring to Queens Park Rangers. When I realised it was Glasgow Rangers, I was much more interested.

Glenn Hoddle came over from Chelsea to talk to me. I had a loose tooth the day we met and I was more concerned about that than about anything he had to say. Doug Ellis from Villa came too – without his boat, obviously. It was Glasgow Rangers that appealed to me, right from the beginning. I remember, as a schoolboy with Newcastle, a taxi driver telling me that there was nothing bigger and more exciting in the whole of football than a Rangers–Celtic derby. He said if I ever got a chance to play with either of them, I should.

I spoke to the Rangers manager Walter Smith on the phone, and then I met him. 'Drink that beer,' he said to me. 'Don't talk.' I thought, this is all right, so I agreed to join them. There was, of course, more to it than that, and negotiations went on for some time between Rangers and Lazio.

Around this time, my lawyer Mel Stein was charged in relation to some alleged financial scandal in the USA and Len asked me to help out with his bail security (which I did) – about £30,000. Mel was cleared of all charges in the end, but unsurprisingly the strain of the case had a terrible effect on him. He looked on the point of collapse.

In my last week at Lazio, I drove to training on my Harley-Davidson (I had nine Harley-Davidson bikes at one time – I'd learned to ride motorbikes by now) wearing shorts and flip-flops and smoking a big cigar. All the lads burst out laughing. As I knew I was leaving there seemed little point in making an effort, so I just mucked around all week.

On the last day, I arrived half-drunk. I crouched down at the side of the pitch, where Zeman was supervising training. I went down on one knee and asked him, 'O great coach, have you any tips, please, as I want to be a great coach like you one day.' I was clutching a Lucozade bottle full of wine. I was killing myself laughing, and fell over. I stayed on the ground, pretending to be asleep. In the end, Boksic had to carry me to my car.

I had several cars, as well as my bikes, in Italy. I pranged one of the cars once, and when the Lazio fans heard it was mine, it was taken apart where I had left it, in the middle of the road, by supporters pinching bits as souvenirs. Roma fans were, of course, not quite as adoring. Some of them spiked my drink once. I don't know what they put in it, but I began to see polar bears instead of trees. I had to tell the Lazio club doctor about it, in case I was called for a random drugs test.

When I finally left, I gave Johnny and Augusto a Subaru each as a farewell present. They'd been good pals to me all the time I'd been at Lazio. And then it was Arrivederci Roma from me, and from my 'amico Jimmy Cinquepance', as he was called in the Italian papers. Jimmy had become well known in Italy, for his gentlemanly, quiet behaviour, of course, and his slim figure.

When I'd first got together with Shel, back in 1991, I'd wanted us to have a baby. I looked upon Bianca and Mason as my children, and I was financially responsible for them, but I wanted my own child, too. But we had so many arguments while we were in Italy – we were always splitting up and getting back together. For about two years, I never mentioned it.

Shel came out at the end of the season for our holiday. We were driving in the car one day before setting off from Rome when she turned to me and said, 'I'm pregnant.'

My first thought was, oh shit. That's the last fucking thing I need. Yeah, I know it was horrible. It's not the way to behave when your girlfriend says she's pregnant. I know that, don't tell me. I should have given her a hug.

We went on holiday as planned, first of all in Italy, then to Las Vegas. I was hardly speaking to her. I was just stuffing my face all the time with ice cream and burgers and rubbish. I even suggested an abortion, but she refused to consider it. I was a total bastard, really.

Although I'd once wanted her to have our baby, over the years things had changed. I couldn't see us stopping the arguments and the continual break-ups, and it didn't seem right to bring a baby into that situation.

After our holiday, I went up to Scotland and Shel returned to Hertfordshire.

I arrived at Rangers in July 1995. The transfer fee was £4.3 million – almost the same as Lazio had paid for me, so they could hardly complain that I lost them any money. It was the most Rangers had ever paid for a player. It had been the same when I went to Spurs and to Lazio – they had each broken their transfer records to sign me. I was to receive £15,000 a week, with an increase every season, plus a signing-on fee.

I fell in love with Rangers right from the beginning. Thousands of fans turned up to greet me and watch me in training. I met Sean Connery, who happened to be at the club one day. I shook his hand and thought, I wonder how many boobs his hands have touched?

Rangers had a great team, with sixteen internationals from various countries: Brian Laudrup, Gordan Petric, Mikhailichenko, Mark Hateley. Ally McCoist was great – he took the piss out of me from the word go. Mark Hateley seemed a bit flash, with his big hair and his big Rolex.

I was told when I arrived that the tradition at Rangers was that you had to turn up for training in a suit and tie. You always had to look smart whenever you were on the premises, to maintain the good name of the club. So I went out and bought ten Versace suits – but in all the brightest colours: yellow and red and white. I was following the club rules, but not quite in the way intended. And I got my hair bleached. I can't remember why. It must have seemed like a good idea at the time. I suppose I thought I'd have a new image for my new club. Out of my signing-on fee, I bought myself a special BMW for £87,000, and a new Jaguar for my dad.

I also got my teeth done. My top teeth had always been at an angle, sort of slanty, and of course, with all the sweets I've eaten in my life, they weren't in perfect condition, either. I got the whole top row, sixteen of them I think, capped. It went on for weeks, getting them prepared and fitted, and cost me £12,000. At one stage, I had to wear some temporary caps, which were too big and stuck out. When I arrived in the dressing room, all the lads had a good laugh. Ally McCoist said I could now eat an apple through a letterbox. Very quick, was Ally.

Before the season proper began, I scored in a pre-season game against Galatasaray, and then in two other warm-up games. Three goals in four outings wasn't a bad start. One of these was a friendly at home against Steaua Bucharest. Celebrating my goal, I turned to the fans and pretended to play the flute. The lads had told me that this was what I should do to make myself popular with the Rangers fans. I didn't know at the time what it meant, and what they didn't tell me was the kind of reaction it would spark in Celtic supporters. But there wasn't too much of a fuss, not that time, since we were at home against a foreign team and the crowd were all Rangers fans. It was later explained to me that this imitation of flute players marching in the Orange parades mocked the Catholic Celtic supporters and was extremely provocative.

I made my competitive debut in the European Cup preliminary round against Anorthosis of Cyprus, a match which we won 1–0. And I got my first competitive goal for Rangers against Morton in the Coca-Cola (League) Cup. In the Scottish Premier Division, we won three of our first four games before we met Celtic away. We beat them 2–0 and I produced my first league goal. I ran about eighty yards from our penalty area to theirs and stroked home a through ball from Ally McCoist. That was what really endeared me to Rangers fans most of all, scoring against Celtic. Suddenly, Rangers kids all over Glasgow were having their hair bleached.

We won ten of our first twelve league matches, but we didn't do so well in the European Cup. We were up against some tough teams, such as Borussia Dortmund and Juventus. I wanted to do especially well against Juventus. I wasn't fit for the away leg, which we lost

1–4, but I played in the home game. In that one we were stuffed 4–0.

I got into the habit of having a brandy before I went on the pitch, just to relax me. There was a hip flask with my name on it, and fifteen minutes before kick-off, I took a swig. The club knew about this, but obviously they thought that if I was doing the business it couldn't be doing me much harm.

We continued to do well in the league. The vital match that would clinch it for us came towards the end of the season, on 28 April, when we met Aberdeen at Ibrox. We were 1–0 down early on, but I beat two men and hammered the ball into the roof of the net to equalise.

At half-time, I felt knackered, and in the second half I was running on pure adrenaline, not energy, but I managed another goal. I could hear Alan McLaren behind me yelling: 'Come on, Gazza, you can do it, keep going!' Somehow I found the resources to make it a hat-trick. That was probably my best feeling ever, perhaps an even bigger high than that derby goal for Lazio gave me.

So we won the title, finishing four points ahead of Celtic, and in the Scottish Cup final, we beat Hearts to do the Double. I had scored nineteen goals in my first

season, from a total forty-two appearances in all competitions, which was only five fewer than I had made in
three seasons at Lazio.

It was a great beginning to my Rangers career, and
I loved every minute of it. I was also voted Player of the
Year in Scotland and chosen for the same honour by the
press.

I was pissed before the award ceremony was even
underway, and I could see Walter Smith shaking his head,
knowing what would happen when it was time for me
to stand up and receive my trophy. He made the organisers present it to me early, and then sent it on home in
a taxi, just in case I lost it.

In my first season at Rangers, when Shel was about five
months pregnant, she answered the door at her home
in Hertfordshire to a woman who announced that I had
raped her. I was up in Scotland at the time and knew
nothing about this.

The next day at training, Walter Smith called me
over and said two people wanted to see me. The two
people were cops, a man and a woman. They told me
I had been accused of rape. I was put on a plane, escorted
to London and taken to a police station, where I was

informed that I was going to be charged with raping some woman. I was shaking the whole time. I didn't understand what all this was about, but it slowly began to dawn on me that the police were saying I might very well end up in jail.

The allegation was published in a newspaper and Shel called me all the names under the sun, and rightly so. But when I told her the full story of what had happened, she believed me and stood by me, which was brilliant of her. But would it be believed in a court of law? It could easily just come down to my word against this girl's.

I honestly couldn't remember the girl's name, or what she looked like, but I remembered the night she was talking about. I'd been drinking in Hertfordshire with two of my mates. It was during one of my splits from Shel, and she told me she didn't want to see me any more. We went to an Indian restaurant, where we met a couple of girls. One of them invited me back to her place. Her friend came too. At her house, the first girl asked me into her bedroom and suggested that I had sex with her. I was a bit scared, mainly about her getting pregnant, but she said, 'Don't worry, I've got a condom.' She fitted it on me herself, and then we had sex. And that was it. I never saw her again. I didn't call her and she didn't call me. I knew nothing about her and heard nothing at all of her till she knocked on Shel's door.

It was terrible waiting for the case to come to court. I became very depressed and started drinking even more than usual, trying to cope with the depression. Then I began to get awful pains in my head. I thought I was going to explode or go mad. I even had a brain scan, as I'd become convinced I was going over the edge, but it didn't show up anything untoward. I asked the doctor what it would take, how long it would be, before I flipped. What would make me decide to top myself? I could feel it coming on.

We had a barrister all lined up, and I kept on having to give my statement over and over again. I must say that the police were very friendly. I've no complaints there. And most of the papers were giving the girl a hammering, discrediting her story. My mam was, of course, constantly in tears and my whole family were extremely worried. It was terrible for them, when they went out and about, having to put up with all the looks and the gossip. It was bad for everyone at Rangers as well, being asked about me all the time. And of course it was horrible for Shel. For her most of all.

Just as I was beginning to think that the worst would happen, that the judge would believe this girl and I would be sent down, her friend, who had been there that night, decided to give evidence on my behalf. She confirmed that we had both been asked back to this house, and that I had been invited into the girl's bedroom.

So that was that. The case never got to court. I'd told the whole truth, 100 per cent, and thankfully Shel had stood by me, but it was very draining and tiring and worrying. This kind of thing has happened to me about nine times in total. Only one accusation ever went as far as resulting in a police investigation, but nine girls have come forward and said that I slept with them. It's what happens. You get offered all sorts, and if people are not married, and sometimes even when they are, they take what's on offer. Footballers are young, and they are human, and many girls will throw themselves at anyone who is famous. I'm sure it's always happened, but you have probably read more about it in the last ten years because of the huge sums of money girls can make from kiss-and-tell stories – up to £100,000 I've been told, if it's three in a bed, or if you can say you slept with two or more star players. Girls deliberately seek out footballers, no question. But at one time they would have been content just to boast about their conquests to their mates. Now it's practically an industry.

So you have to be very, very careful. When you meet a girl you have to do your best to make sure she's not the sort who is interested in you purely for her own financial gain. If she is, she'll sell you down the river, squeezing the maximum out of very little, twisting things round, making things up or making things worse. The clubs, of course, hate all this. It tarnishes their good names. And so they don't like the bad publicity they get if you are seen or reported to have been out on the town living it up when you should have been at home, resting.

I remember that after I'd split up with Gail, my first proper girlfriend, not long after I first came to London with Spurs, I met a girl in the West End one night and arranged to see her again. I said I'd meet her the following Friday at the main door of Harrods. It was the only place I could think of that I knew how to find.

She turned up on time and we went for a drink. Over the drink, I decided I didn't fancy her after all. She was really boring and irritating, in fact. So, after an hour, I said, 'Cheerio, pet, I've got to go. I've got a match tomorrow.' And I went straight home and went to bed.

The next day, before our game, Terry Venables calls me aside and says, 'Where did you go last night, Gazza?'

'Nowhere, boss,' I says. 'I was just relaxing. I went nowhere, honestly.'

'Then how come you were spotted with a girl in the doorway of Harrods?'

I couldn't believe it. I was gearing myself up to lie my way out of it, because of course nothing had actually happened in the doorway, when he explained how he knew.

I hadn't realised there was a security camera over the front door of Harrods. Somewhere, sitting in a little cubby hole, there's this security guard, probably dozing off. Suddenly, he happens to glance at one of his monitors and sees me with a girl. He recognises me at once because, as luck would have it, he's a Spurs fan. So he also knows we've got a game the next day. So what does he do, the bastard? He rings the club. Fortunately, Terry did believe me when I told him what happened.

Our baby was due in February 1996. Three days before the birth, Shel was at home in Hertfordshire and I was up in Scotland with Rangers. As we didn't have a game, Walter decided to take us down to London for the weekend, for rest and relaxation, which meant we had a very good night out on the Friday.

Over the years, I've actually not been a great womaniser, unlike some players I could name. I didn't really have a regular girlfriend after Gail, until Shel came along. I suppose I wasn't much bothered. So all those lurid tabloid stories about me give totally the wrong impression. I've always been more interested in being out for the night with Jimmy and the lads, with friends, or just staying at home on my own. I still am, really. Anyway, on this Saturday evening I went to Shel's house. I'd been on the piss and was still a bit drunk and argumentative. Even at this late stage, I was still going on about why we shouldn't be having a baby at all, and blaming her. We had a big row and she was soon in tears, and then I was in tears. I'd managed to upset us both. I thought, fuck it, I'm getting out of here.

I got in my car and started driving north, deciding I'd go home to Newcastle. Mel Stein rang me on my car phone. He said I should turn round and go back to be with Shel when she had the baby. I just told him to fuck off.

I drove to me dad's and went out on the piss all night. Next day, I went out to the pub in the morning to get drunk again, and it was there that I read in the paper I'd had a baby. That was how I learned about it, and found out the baby's name and weight. Shel had tried to discuss names with me, but I'd refused to talk about it. I was blanking it out. I didn't want to know or hear about a baby.

I didn't do anything for about two weeks, made no contact, sent nothing. By this time, I felt very embarrassed and guilty about what I'd done, or not done, knowing I really should have been there. Finally, I went down south and I saw my son for the first time. Shel was brilliant. She let me have him on my own, so I could cuddle and kiss him.

I quite like the name Regan now. I think Shel got it from a waiter in some hotel or restaurant. He had served her, and his name was on the bill, and she liked it. She looked it up and discovered it meant 'little king'. She thought that was a good omen.

Regan's arrival brought us together again and Shel took the plunge and moved up, with all three children, to join me north of the border. I bought a large house in Renfrewshire, near Ally McCoist's, which cost £510,000, a lot of money then in Scotland, or anywhere in Britain, come to that. It had six bedrooms, a swimming pool and a tennis court. I loved it. Lovely house. And to start with, we were happy there.

I was playing well for Rangers, and for England, loving life in Glasgow and Scotland, winning trophies – and I was injury-free. That was about the most important thing of all in my life at the time. Any time, really. It's when I get injuries that things become horrible. That I become horrible. But I had no twitches, I was sleeping OK, I had hardly any worries, hardly thought about death and other awful things.

He's a fantastic player when he isn't drunk.
Brian Laudrup, Rangers team-mate, 1997

He's an intelligent boy who likes people to think he's stupid. He doesn't have a bad bone in his body but he does some stupid, ridiculous things. That's what makes him so interesting.
Ally McCoist, Rangers colleague, 1996

18

EURO 96 AND
A DENTIST'S CHAIR

My England career had been massively interrupted by all those injuries. Remember, I lost over a year waiting to move from Spurs to Lazio, and then another one at the end of my time in Italy. But England hadn't done much to speak of during that time anyway, under Graham Taylor, notably missing out on the 1994 World Cup finals. And I hadn't done much when I did appear.

So I'd been well pleased when Terry Venables took over the England job in 1994. I had loved him at Spurs. The minute we all heard the news, people like Paul Ince and Ian Wright, who hadn't played for him before, were asking me, 'What's he like? What's he like?' I told them he was fucking marvellous.

I wasn't fit for his early games, but he picked me for the Japan match at Wembley in June 1995, just before I signed for Rangers. It was the first time I'd pulled on an England shirt for fifteen months. I came on as a sub and we won 2–1.

After that I became a vital part of Terry's Euro 96 preparation games. As the tournament was being held in England, we didn't have to qualify. I was on great form at Rangers, and playing well for England, so much so that Terry took me aside one day and said he was thinking he might make me the England captain.

I didn't think it was such a good idea. The press would be bound to dig out all the old cuttings about me drinking, the kiss-and-tell stories, the bust-ups with Shel, and would just hound me, looking for more dirt. Basically, they'd have a field day, which would be bad for me and my game and bad for England and for Terry. So I was quite pleased it didn't happen. I would, of course, have been dead proud. But I was proud enough to be going into the Euro 96 finals to be held in our own country confident enough that I would be in the team.

As part of our final warm-up for Euro 96, we went to play a couple of matches in Hong Kong and China. On the plane out, I tried to attract the attention of a

Previous page: I was well chuffed to score at home for Burnley against Bradford in March 2002.

Left: in China with Gansu Tianma, 2003.

Opposite: Jimmy Gardner, aka Five Bellies, with a helpful tattoo – in case he forgets his name; at the Legends versus Celebrities game at St James'. I didn't play in that outfit, I promise.

Lincoln versus Boston – the big derby. But have I spent too much time watching Jonny Wilkinson?

Below: Between 1991 and 2005 I've spent so much time coming and going from the Princess Grace I should have got a season ticket.

This last time, all the press said I looked terrible – but what did they expect . . . I'd just come out of hospital!

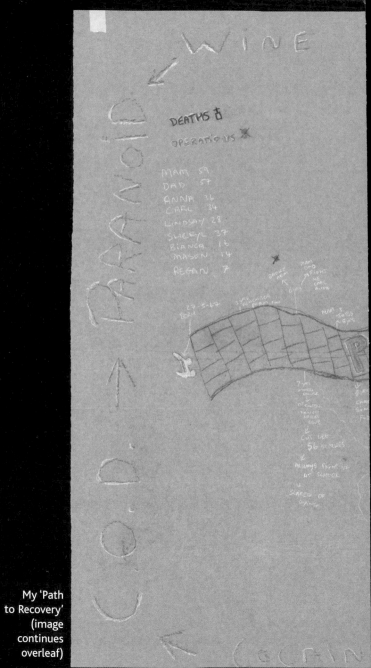

WINE

C.O.D. → PARANOID ←

DEATHS ☐
OPERATIONS ✻

MAM 59
DAD 57
ANNA 36
CARL 34
LINDSAY 28
SHERYL 37
BIANCA 16
MASON 14
REGAN 7

27-5-67
BORN

My 'Path
to Recovery'
(image
continues
overleaf)

COCAINE

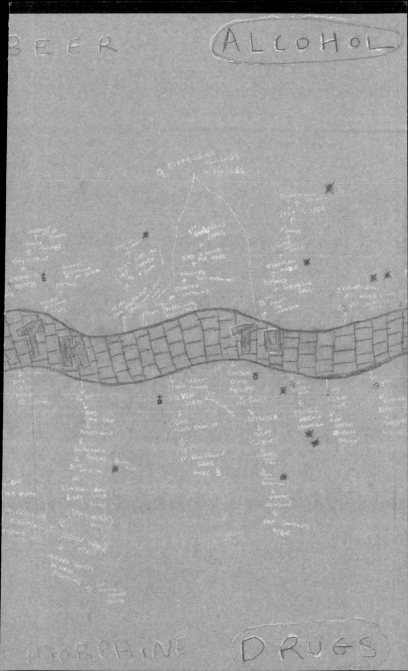

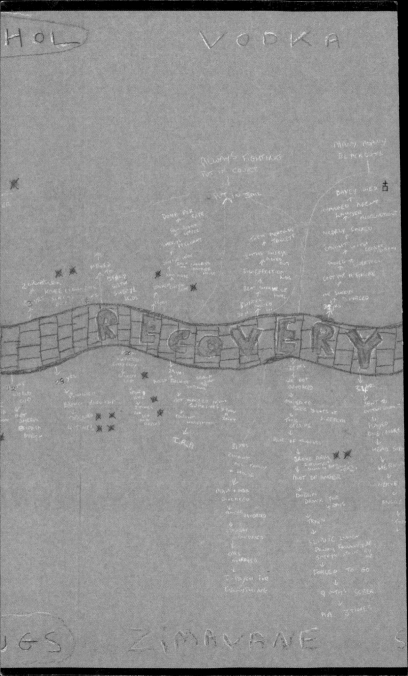

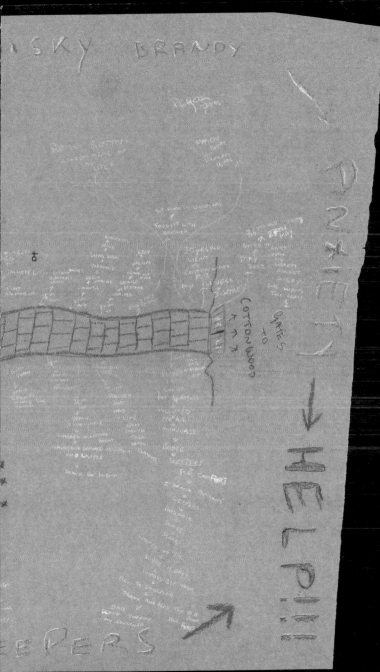

Me and Dave Seaman praying for an England victory in Euro 2004. I reckon Dave's also putting in a request to take my place on *Strictly Ice Dancing*.

'Wazza' fever took hold during Euro 2004. I hope young Wayne's paying close attention to that book . . . It's a cracking read.

Don't worry, Sven, if you're short in midfield I'm ready for a call-up.

steward standing in the aisle, just after we had taken off, to ask him to get me a drink. All I did was poke him gently in the back. But then things got out of hand and there was a bit of a scuffle. The pilot intervened, giving out a message that if there was any more trouble, he would stop the plane in Russia, drop me off and leave me there. An official complaint was later made to the FA about my behaviour. Luckily, none of that ever made the papers.

In Hong Kong, after we'd played both our matches, Terry said we could have a night out, so we all went to this club. I got drinking with Robbie Fowler at the bar and he saw this girl and said to her, 'Hi, what's your name?' I said, 'What a fucking awful line. You must be able to do better – that's really corny.' So of course we started pushing and shoving each other. We were just messing around, really, nothing serious, but it led to me picking up a pint and pouring it over Robbie's head. Then Teddy Sheringham arrived. I poured a pint over his head as well. Steve McManaman came over and he, too, ended up wearing a pint. At the same time, I somehow managed to rip his T-shirt. The evening's game then became that everyone had to have a pint poured over them and their shirt ripped. Just a simple little intellectual game.

Bryan Robson was now on the England coaching

staff, no longer a player or one of us, so he was standing around, staying cool. The lads said, 'Go on, Gazza, rip his shirt and pour a pint over him. You said that was this evening's game.' I was a bit worried about involving him, as he was looking cool in his best clothes, whereas the rest of us were in T-shirts and tracksuit bottoms. I was afraid he might thump me. I decided I would rip his shirt, but only a little bit. But when I did it, for some reason the whole of his shirt came away, leaving him with only his collar on. It was very weird. And very funny. He took it in good humour.

I went and hid in a little telephone booth, and when I came out, Dennis Wise and Teddy Sheringham had taken down some boxing gloves that were hanging in the bar and were pretending to have a boxing match. As I stepped out of the booth, Dennis hit me with a real upper-cut.

Then someone said, 'How about the dentist's chair?' I thought, that's handy, I could do with some fillings. I didn't know what it was at first. It was explained to me that what you had to do was sit back on this big chair and the barmen would pour different spirits down your throat from the bottles. I think there was tequila and Drambuie. Obviously, most of it got spilt, as you were lying back, with your mouth open, just like at the dentist's

– hence the name. It was all a laugh, no more than us letting our hair down before the Euro finals. Nothing bad happened. Nobody got attacked, no girls were assaulted, the place didn't get wrecked. I went home quite early, in fact, sharing a taxi with Bryan Robson in his shirt collar, thinking it had been OK – a quiet night, really, nothing wild. Till we all saw the next day's papers.

I should think about eight of the England team had stepped into that dentist's chair, but most of the photographs that were published afterwards were of me. They had been taken by some punter who just happened to be in the bar and decided to make himself a few bob. But really, it wasn't all that bad. It just looked bad when the reporters put their own interpretation on it in the papers.

A couple of days later it was my birthday. I got some flowers from Regan, which was very touching. So I had to celebrate that, even if we were supposed to stay indoors and be sensible after all the bad publicity. I went out on my own for a quiet drink. Yes, I was wearing my England tracksuit and a big pair of Doc Martens, so I suppose you could say I was drawing attention to myself, but I didn't think of it that way. I just wanted to go out and have a bit of fun – I wasn't thinking about my clothes.

I found a little hotel and went to the bar, where

there was a load of locals, all smoking big cigars. I joined in, and some of them gave me a few cigars. I went back to the England hotel smoking a big cigar, strode into the dining room, where the FA officials were all eating, and ordered champagne all round. That was one occasion when Terry did tell me to calm down.

On the plane home, we were all knackered. I had a few drinks and soon fell into a very deep sleep – until some bastard gave me a hard slap on the face. I woke up with a start, really furious. I went round trying to make somebody tell me who had slapped me, but nobody would. 'Right,' I said. 'Welcome to hell. Unless yous tell me who did it, no one is going to sleep on this plane.'

I went up and down the aisles, kicking all the seats, throwing cushions around. We were on the top deck of a Cathay Pacific plane, in the first-class cabin, which had been reserved for the England squad. Dennis Wise climbed into one of the overhead lockers to try to get some sleep and escape my attentions. Jamie Redknapp got down under two of the seats. I suspected it was Steve McManaman who had slapped me, so I gave his seat and his TV screen a good punch. His screen did go a bit blurry, but it seemed to still be working, after a fashion. Then I did the same to Les Ferdinand's.

While I was going around shouting at everyone, an FA official came up the stairs from their seats on the lower deck, and told me to stop all the noise, sit down and go to sleep. I told him to fuck off. 'Don't you dare tell any England player what to do,' I shouted at him. 'We do the playing, you do fuck all.' It was a bit out of order, I admit, but then, I was a bit tipsy.

During the ten days or so we had been away, I had only actually been drunk on two nights. I didn't think that was so bad. Plus, of course, the plane home. So I suppose that makes three times. Still, it wasn't a lot in a ten-day period.

It wasn't till much later that I was told it was Alan Shearer who had slapped my face on the plane. He denied it when I asked him. Not that I would hold it against him. I would probably have done the same myself, seeing some mate fast asleep. It's what you do. A bit of harmless fun. But it wasn't so funny when the bill appeared for two broken TVs. It turned out they were new models and cost a fortune. And as I said, I didn't think I'd actually broken them, just made them go a bit fuzzy.

Tony Adams, as captain, decided that the whole squad should share the bill, as quite a few of the lads had been, shall we say, a bit boisterous on the plane, even though it was me who had damaged the TVs. We had to pay £500 each. I thought that was good of Tony. When you're in a team, you should all stick together. I gather that in his autobiography, *Psycho*, Stuart Pearce wrote that he didn't think it was fair. He went along with it for the sake of harmony, but his wife didn't agree with it. He didn't name me as the culprit, which was very decent of him, though he added: 'I had a good idea who caused the damage.' Oooh.

When I got home, I decided to have a really abstemious, sensible week at a health farm to get ready for the finals. I was told about this place in Wales, which was supposed to be very remote. No press people would ever find you there, or the public, they said. The word was that Hugh Grant had gone there, after his sex scandal in the USA, to get away from people. But when I arrived, I found sixteen cameramen and pressmen waiting for me. So I immediately turned round and went home to Newcastle instead, and had a quiet time there. I can, when I put my mind to it. I quite enjoy being on my own, if I'm tucked away, and no one bothers me.

By the time Euro 96 was due to start, I was feeling very fit. I remember hearing the Euro 96 theme song, 'Three

Lions', the first time. 'It's coming home, it's coming home, football's coming home,' we used to sing on the team coach, and I would play it in my room all the time.

Our first match was against Switzerland, on 8 June at Wembley. I hadn't slept well for a couple of nights beforehand. A silly worry had got into my head about my form, and I was scared that I might not get picked, which I knew was daft, since my form was so good. I asked Terry, privately, if I would be in the team, and he told me, privately, that I was. I said, 'In that case, I'm up for it.' I immediately felt so much better.

We didn't actually play very well against Switzerland, but we managed a 1–1 draw. I was taken off about fifteen minutes before the end. Against Scotland, I was much better, and I got our second goal, the one that is often still shown on TV. I remember it came just after Scotland had missed a penalty – well, more like David Seaman had saved their penalty. We'd gone one up in the second half but the Scots were fighting back. I suppose the penalty miss knocked them a bit but they were definitely coming back into the game. Playing well. Anyway, Darren Anderton had the ball out on the wing and passed it through to me. I was about on the corner of the Scotland box. In between two defenders. When the ball came through to me Colin

Hendry was moving over to close me down. I just knew where he'd be, when he'd commit himself, so I knew what to do. It felt brilliant when it all worked. I went to look like I'd knock it past him and try and go round the outside, but I changed direction and flicked it over his head with my left foot. Hendry tried to get back to me, but ended up on the deck, and I volleyed the ball with my right, into the corner of the goal, past Andy Goram, my Rangers team-mate. I think Hendry was still on his knees when the ball hit the back of the net.

Before the match, I suggested that if someone scored the winner, we would celebrate by taking the piss out of the dentist's chair incident, as it had been in all the papers. I would have done it to whoever scored the vital goal, but it happened to be me. So I lay down on the Wembley turf and Alan Shearer and the others poured drink down my gob. It was Lucozade, of course. Nothing stronger.

For the previous few months, I'd taken so much stick in the Rangers dressing room. They told me all the time how they were going to stuff England. So that made me relish the result even more, though I have to admit we depended on a few of Seaman's saves to keep us in the game. Afterwards, I cut out all the reports and headlines, and when we got back to pre-season training,

I sneaked early into the Rangers dressing room and pinned them all up on the noticeboard.

That goal against Scotland was rated the Goal of the Century in a television poll. The third choice was mine as well: my free kick against Seaman and Arsenal in the FA Cup semi-final of 1991. I was pretty pleased by that.

Before we played Holland, Terry gave us the most brilliant team talk. He made it clear this was going to be one of the biggest games in any of our lives. To get any result against Holland we would need to be on our best form, because, of course, they had some brilliant, world-class players. After we all got off the coach at Wembley, I got back on again, on my own, just to hear the 'Coming home' song being belted out one more time.

We thrashed them 4–1, one of England's best-ever victories. It was just a shame Holland got their one goal, otherwise Scotland would have gone through instead of them. I might have been rubbishing the Scottish boys, taking the piss, but I loved them, and the Scottish people. So I really wanted them to do well and go through – as long as it wasn't at our expense – and I was very disappointed for them when they didn't make it.

Throughout the Holland game I could hear the whole Wembley crowd singing, 'There's only one Paul

Gascoigne.' Towards the end, David Platt said to me, as he was passing to me, 'Here's the ball – it's your game.' And yet none of our four goals came from me.

We met Spain in the quarter-finals. It was still 0–0 after extra time, so the game went to penalties. Seaman made some brilliant saves – Old Beaver Face, I used to call him, because of his big 'tache. I got my penalty, and so did Stuart Pearce, which was great as it helped him get rid of the demons that had plagued him after missing that penalty in the 1990 World Cup semi-final. When I scored with mine, I remember looking up into the stands, searching for Shel. I couldn't see her, of course, though I knew she was there.

In the semi-final, we were drawn against Germany, once again. I seemed to have spent my whole life playing them. I had a good game, we all did, but we were level at 1–1 after 90 minutes. Shearer had scored for us, after Tony Adams flicked on my corner. Then it went to the golden goal – the first team to score in extra time would take the match.

I so nearly got a winner. A cross from Shearer went across the box, to the spot where Alan was usually to be found. I ran forward to try and get it, but checked myself when I saw the keeper coming out for it. Because I hesitated, I missed it by inches. I was really sick. If I'd been a proper striker, like Shearer, I would have gone for it without thinking, regardless of what the goalkeeper was doing.

Instead, with no further scoring, it was penalties again. I scored mine, even though I changed my mind at the last moment. It was Gareth Southgate who missed this time, poor sod. I couldn't believe it. Yet again we had been beaten by Germany on penalties. It all seemed so unfair. I was choked.

Back at the England hotel at Burnham Beeches, I drank to drown my sorrows, along with Robbie Fowler. We started squirting tomato ketchup over each other. We'd found a couple of tubes on a table and soon finished them off. I went into the kitchens and found a monster carton of ketchup, which I emptied all over Robbie. Then I ran to my room and had a good cry.

Next day, when we were all packing to go home, I found that someone had put a lump of shit in my washbag. I tried to find out who it was, without success. Some time later, Trevor Steven told me he'd heard it was Steve Stone. When I confronted him, he denied it, but he smiled and said, 'Divvent give us it back.'

Germany met Czechoslovakia in the final on 30 June and they were dead jammy yet again, winning with a golden goal in extra time. We'd really believed it would be us playing for the trophy at our national stadium. We had such a good team, and such a good manager, we felt we could go all the way. 'It's coming home, it's coming home, football's coming home . . .' We were just devastated.

I think we could have won Euro 96 – and we could have won Italy 90. England had a terrific team both times. One wasn't better than the other. I thought those two England teams were excellent. The team spirit was brilliant each time and in Venables we had a world-class coach, very experienced, and so was Bobby Robson.

Germany were the eventual winners of each competition and were no better than us. It was the luck of the penalty shoot-outs, that's what ruined it for us.

I have been a big fan of Paul Gascoigne since he started playing for England in the late eighties. His skill level has always been impressive and he is an intelligent player. Gascoigne is one of the few world-class players around and he is also very much a character.
Franz Beckenbauer, on eve of Euro 96

Gazza is no longer a fat, drunken imbecile. He is, in fact, a football genius.
Mirror *editorial headed 'Mr Paul Gascoigne: An Apology', after his solo goal against Scotland, 1996*

19

MARITAL MADNESS

At least I had something nice to look forward to after the disappointment of once again being knocked out of the semi-finals of an international tournament by Germany: my wedding to Sheryl, and our honeymoon.

We'd decided to get married after Shel and the children moved up to Scotland and we were all happy at last. Why did I decide to get married? Because I loved her. That's enough of a reason, isn't it? I always have loved her, despite everything. I promised to be good from then onwards, on my best behaviour. And she believed me. I believed myself.

The marriage took place on 1 July. We hadn't been

able to have it any earlier because we'd thought I'd be otherwise engaged in the Euro 96 final. Some hope. I was offered £150,000 by *Hello!* magazine for the exclusive rights to cover our wedding, so I accepted it. I spent the whole lot on the wedding – the clothes, food and drink, the honeymoon. Many of the England team came: David Seaman, Ian Wright, Chris Waddle and Paul Ince, and friends like Chris Evans and Danny Baker. Chris had said he'd be the DJ, but he got drunk and forgot about it.

It was a great day. Euro 96, and the season, were over, so we could all relax and enjoy ourselves. The reception was held at Hanbury Manor near Ware in Hertfordshire, a very posh Jacobean-style mansion set in huge grounds. We had the full treatment; the best of everything.

We set off for our honeymoon in Maui, Hawaii – somewhere I'd always wanted to go – on a real high. But the best part of it was the flight there. After that, for the whole of the holiday, we argued all the time. Don't ask me why, we just did. I was pleased to get home.

Back in Scotland, we settled down for a while, friends again. We were a proper little family, Mum and

Dad and three kids. Shel made our house in Renfrewshire very attractive. I later bought a lodge on Loch Lomond as well, for weekends and holidays for us and the bairns.

Everything was rosy – till I began to turn into a bastard again. Oh, for various reasons, most of them stupid. Sometimes I think I don't know how to be good. That next season, my second at Rangers, was not as great as the first. The other teams knew more about me, so I was marked man-to-man, and I was also drinking quite heavily, because of all my problems returning.

Walter discovered I'd been on the shandies the night before a game, and, in the dressing room, he ordered me to put on my suit and leave, which I did. I went straight through the gates and drove home. Some of the fans saw me and wondered what was going on. Why was I leaving just as they were arriving? Luckily, the lads won. If they had lost, it would have been worse for me, I would have felt responsible for the defeat.

I was starting to let Walter and assistant manager Archie Knox down on a regular basis. I would promise not to go drinking and break my promise. One Friday night I was sitting in my lodge on Loch Lomond when the phone went. It was Walter. 'What are you doing?' he asked.

'Nothing.'

I thought he was just checking up on me, making sure I was at home resting, as I was supposed to be.

'Right, if you're doing nothing, we'll pick you up in ten minutes.'

He and Archie appeared and took me to a Chinese restaurant with their wives. They offered me red wine, so I had a glass. 'You've failed the test,' they said, 'but don't worry, you'll play better tomorrow.' We won 5–0 against Motherwell, and I scored a hat-trick.

But I was drinking a lot. During one game, I had a row with Ally McCoist, so at half-time I had a brandy. In the second half I scored two goals and we won. I could see Walter and Archie in the dugout, shaking their heads in disbelief. I realise now that they were trying everything they could to help me, stop me being stupid. But they didn't know which way worked best, the carrot or the stick.

I came to training drunk one day after I'd been out boozing the night before. When Walter realised, he came across, picked me up by the scruff of the neck and said, 'Get out, go home, and never come back.' But that wasn't the first time it had happened.

All the rows and fights with Shel made everything

worse. It just seemed to go on and on. We were fine one minute, at each other's throats the next, she'd leave, or I'd leave, then whoever had left would come back. The drink relaxed me and dulled the stress.

In October 1996, as we were preparing to play Ajax in the Champions League, I took Shel and the kids to Gleneagles for a bit of a break. We had good fun. I took the kids swimming and we played with these amazing hawks. But later, over dinner in the hotel, we started arguing. It was partly about my family, and it was mainly my fault. I was mixing my drinks, champagne on top of whisky, which was stupid. The whole dining room could hear us. In the end, Shel left the table and went back to our room. I followed her and attacked her. I headbutted her and threw her to the floor. Her finger was broken, so she was screaming in agony. I tried to click the finger back into place, and that made her really shriek.

Bianca and Mason, aged about ten and seven, were in the next room with the nanny, listening to it all. I found out later that Bianca was so upset she wanted to take a kettle of boiling water and come and pour it all over me. Fortunately, the nanny calmed her down.

The next day, Shel took the kids and left, telling

me she wasn't coming back. I did nothing to stop her. I just accepted it. And yes, I had pushed her around a bit before, but nothing as bad as this. What I had done the previous night was terrible, and at the time I didn't even say sorry. I knew I'd done wrong, but I couldn't bring myself to apologise.

The day after that, I flew off with Rangers for the Ajax match. I was in a dreadful state, worked up, wracked with guilt, but just not able to say sorry. I was played up front. After ten minutes, I was sent off.

At half-time in the dressing room, Richard Gough, our captain, lashed out at me. He was mad with me for getting myself sent off so early in the game. I told him I was in a terrible state. I'd beaten up my wife and by now I knew that the press had found out and were waiting for me, and that they'd really tear me apart. Which they did, quite rightly.

Perhaps I had done a bit more in the past than just pushing her. I had twisted her arm once and yeah, there was the time I banged her head on the floor in Italy. I don't know what happens, except that when I get in a state, I take it out on the one I love most. But I paid dearly because it all came out and Shel and I separated, and I lost my wife.

One thing that really upset her was a story going around that the argument had started because she had been attacking my family and that I'd flipped because I love them so much. It was true that we had been arguing about my family, but Shel hadn't been criticising them. She knew how much I loved them, and that I would never say anything against my mother and father, or allow anyone else to do so.

I've always defended them, always loved them, even when I quarrelled with them when I was young, even when my mother gave me a right hiding. I love them because they worked desperately hard, especially my mam, to bring me up. They had things tough, and they had terrible rows themselves, but I will have nothing said against them. I know some people think that my family background is a cause of many of my problems, but I don't agree. I love me mam and dad, and I always will. I used to say I hoped I'd die before they do, and I meant that. I still do. I don't want to be in this life without them.

I should have had counselling. Years ago, when I was young, I had had my first chance to get help, but I didn't go back. During my marriage to Shel, after some of our bigger rows and my worst behaviour, she had persuaded me to go to marriage guidance counselling.

I only stood it for a short while and gave up quickly, but Shel stuck at it longer.

After the beating-up, I felt numb inside. I began to take Zimovane tablets, which I stole from Rangers after I found out where they were kept. I had had morphine several times over the years, before my operations, when I was in terrible pain, so I knew how it made you feel good and deadened the agony.

Neither Walter nor Archie Knox knew about the stolen pills. Walter was always the best counsellor I ever had. He took such time and trouble with me, put up with so much. I can never be grateful enough for what he did for me. Not long ago, I admitted to him that when I was at Rangers I had stolen those tablets. 'Ya wee bastard,' he said. 'If I'd known that at the time, you would have been straight out of the club.'

It was lucky for me, especially at this time with Rangers, when I was feeling so depressed, that I never got mixed up with any real drugs, I mean hard drugs. I did have a joint once, at a wedding, which someone gave me. I puffed away at it till I fell on the floor, laughing, but when the effect wore off, I was really scared. I vowed never to try a joint again, and I never have done. One of the things that put me off cannabis when

I was young, and just starting out as a professional, was someone telling me that it could be detected in your body up to twenty-eight days after you'd smoked a joint. I didn't want to fail a random drugs test and then get banned from football, which was what I lived for. Drinking was different. I didn't start all that till quite late anyway, but I always felt that I could sweat alcohol off. Besides, it's not illegal.

Until I had that joint, which wasn't till I was at Rangers, I'd never been a smoker. Afterwards, I kept off joints but took up cigarettes. That was a bad mistake. I'm still smoking today, though I tell myself all the time I will give up. But I also tell myself that at least it's better than cannabis.

After the incident with Shel, everywhere I went, on the pitch or off it, rival fans would shout 'wife-beater' at me. During that second season with Rangers, 1996–7, I also got another leg injury and was out for three months. People were saying I shouldn't be picked for Rangers or England any more as I was a wife-beater. Offers were coming in for me, so it was reported, from places like Aston Villa – even Spurs were rumoured to want me back – because it was thought Rangers might want to get rid of me.

But we had a great run in the middle of the season, with seven wins in a row, and I was back on good form. Despite everything, I still managed thirty-four games, scoring seventeen goals. We ended up winning the league again, and the League Cup as well this time – another Double. In the League Cup final against Hearts I scored two goals. So, as far as the diehard Rangers fans were concerned, I was a hero again.

> If he were ordinary, he would play ordinary football. Paul Gascoigne is an extraordinary footballer – it is hardly surprising then that he is an extraordinary man.
> *Simon Barnes*, The Times, *20 May 1998*

> I don't want to be rude, but I think when God gave him this enormous footballing talent, he took his brain out at the same time to sort of equalise it a bit.
> *Tony Banks, Minister for Sport, on BBC Radio 5 Live, 1997*

> Gazza was never truly the Great which his talent argued he ought to have become. There is immense sadness about Gascoigne's failure to master the demon drink. It is sad for all the football men who knew him to be brushed with rare brilliance as well as that incurable daftness.
> *Jeff Powell*, Daily Mail, *2 December 1999*

20

IRA DEATH THREAT

During my three seasons at Rangers, Walter Smith sacked me at least three times. I tried his patience so often. I remember rabbiting on in his team talk once, not paying much attention, and he got so mad with me he picked me up by the neck. I was wearing one of my daft suits, a brand new Armani outfit in some garish colour. I don't think he actually sacked me that time, but he was well pissed off.

One occasion when he did give me the bullet was that day he sent me home just before kick-off, when he discovered I'd been drinking the night before a vital match. He shouted after me that I'd never play for

Rangers again. And he kicked me out again for arriving at training half-cut. He threw my boots at me and said, 'That's it. Piss off and never come back, ever again.'

I was very upset that time. I thought that was it, I really was out. I stayed indoors at Loch Lomond for three days, and then one of my team-mates, Alan McLaren, came to see me. Alan told me Walter wanted me to ring him, so I did. Walter said: 'I'll tell you when you can have a drink, and when you can't have a drink. I'm the manager.' Then he got me picked up and we flew to Glasgow in a helicopter. We hovered over the Rangers ground, just to take in the wonder of it all.

Archie Knox once came to my house to see me the night before a match. We sat drinking and talking till the early hours and I was thinking, what's going on? What's he going to tell me? But, fuck me, he was still there an hour later, still rabbiting on. 'I bet you wish I'd go soon,' he said.

'No, no problems,' I told him. 'I like having you here.'

Which I did. And yet I was the one who would have been fined or sacked by Walter for drinking the night before a game.

When he finally left, he said, 'Sleep well,' and I

thought, no fucking chance now. I only got about an hour. Next day, he never mentioned it, as if he had no memory of coming to see me. I didn't mention it, either. Anyway, we won that game 3–1. Managers have strange ways of getting the best out of you.

My third season with Rangers began well. At the end of the previous one, Walter had signed a new three-year contract. He'd also bought some very good new foreign players, like Marco Negri and Lorenzo Amoruso. Amoruso got injured before the season properly began, but Negri started off brilliantly, scoring an amazing twenty-three goals in his first ten games for Rangers. But then they seemed to dry up: in the whole of the rest of that season he managed only another nine league goals.

Now that Shel had moved out, I spent a lot of my time off in London with Chris Evans and Danny Baker. I'd appeared on some of Chris's television programmes and, as I said, I'd met Danny when he worked on one of my videos, and the three of us had become good drinking mates and had a lot of laughs.

Sometimes they came up to see me in Scotland, too. Chris and I set off from near Glasgow one day to drive the twenty or so miles to my timeshare lodge at

Loch Lomond. Later, we were due to meet some of the players, along with Jimmy Gardner, at a restaurant on the loch.

We left my house in Renfrewshire in a brand-new Mercedes I'd just bought and Chris was saying what a flash car it was. 'But then, you're a flash git,' he added. I replied that so was he.

'Who would ever know we were both brought up in council houses with nothing?' I said. That gave us the bright idea of getting rid of the Merc and driving something beat-up instead. I flashed my lights at the car in front of us. It stopped, and a couple got out.

'Do you know where Loch Lomond is?' I asked them.

They said they did.

'If I give you my keys, could one of you drive my car there?'

If I'd been anyone else, I'm sure they would have been bloody suspicious, but they had recognised me, and they just thought it was funny. I didn't offer them any money or anything, but they agreed to take my car. So Chris and I got out of my new Merc, gave them the keys, and let the bloke drive it away while the woman followed in their car.

'What if I never see my new Merc again?' I yelled after them.

'Don't worry,' said Chris. 'I'll buy you another one.'

We found a garage and Chris bought an old banger for £300. We then bought some paint, and painted the windows black. Along the side of the car, Chris wrote the letters 'TFI', after his TV show.

We drove this heap on to Loch Lomond and made our way to the restaurant, which was on a sort of marina beside the loch. We could see the diners in the restaurant looking at our old banger approaching. As they watched, Chris drove straight on. And on, and on, and into the loch. When the water reached our waists, we got out and swam to the shore. By this time Jimmy had realised it was us and was standing on the balcony, pissing himself.

That incident didn't make the press, but a lot did, and they made me look far worse than I was. Newspaper readers must have thought I was permanently drunk.

Jimmy was rather less amused when I rang Chris Evans' radio programme once to say I was worried about him as he had decided at last to come out of the closet, but the trouble was, he didn't have any gay friends in Gateshead. He was lonely and needed to meet some gay people. I gave out his mobile phone number on the radio, appealing for any gay people out there to ring Jimmy. Hundreds of them did. For weeks afterwards, I could hear Jimmy picking up his mobile and shouting: 'I'M NOT FUCKING GAY!'

Walter Smith gave me a week off once and allowed me to go to London, on condition that I stayed out of the papers. So I went to stay with Chris Evans and Danny Baker, which probably wasn't the best way of keeping a low profile.

On the first evening, I said I felt like doing something daft. I suggested we went into town. So we got into Chris's chauffeur-driven Bentley and drove into the West End. Near Marble Arch, we stopped in front of a double-decker bus, forcing the bus to stop as well. I got out, climbed in beside the bus driver and persuaded him to let me take the wheel. I got the whole bus singing 'We're all going on a summer holiday'.

Along Oxford Street, after I'd given the bus driver his bus back, I saw some workmen mending the road, with pneumatic drills and all the gear. I thought, I've never done that – I wonder what it's like? So I asked one of them to let me have a go. I put on his hard hat and his earphones and had a good go with his drill. I hadn't realised they were so heavy.

I then stopped a taxi driver and told him I'd give him a signed England shirt if he'd let me have a drive of his cab. He agreed and got into the back with Chris. I drove the taxi down the street a little way before stopping to ask someone on the pavement for directions.

'You won't believe who I've got in the back of my cab,' I said to this pedestrian. Of course, he leaned forward to have a look in the back of the cab.

'It's Chris Evans!' I shouted.

The bloke stared hard into the cab. 'Nah, it fucking isn't,' he said. 'It's a wind-up.' And he just walked away.

The next evening we went out again in Chris's chauffeur-driven car. Chris was in shorts and slippers and a T-shirt and I was wearing a dressing gown and nothing else.

We were driving around, drinking in the back seat and shouting at passers-by through the windows. As we went through Hampstead I recognised the pop star Noel Gallagher's house. I told Chris I'd met him somewhere and had once been to his place for a few drinks.

'If you know him so well,' said Chris, 'go and knock on his front door and ask him to come out to play.'

I was hardly out of the car before it drove off at

speed. Chris had left me on my own to knock on Noel Gallagher's front door in my dressing gown. I banged and banged and nobody answered. I was starting to get cold and Chris had totally disappeared.

Someone came out of a house two doors along and I stopped him and asked if I could come into his house for a bit to warm up. 'Certainly not,' he said.

'I'm Paul Gascoigne,' I explained. 'You know, Gazza.'

'Never heard of him,' said the bloke, walking away.

There was a guy watching me from an upstairs window of a house across the road. I waved at him and tried to indicate in sign language that I wanted to come in for a cup of tea. I was miming pouring out a cup of tea from a teapot and sipping it. But the man just laughed and waved back, and didn't come to his front door.

I was beginning to get worried. I was bloody cold now, and I had no money on me for a taxi.

Just as desperation set in, Chris cruised back into the street in his Bentley, pissing himself. I discovered later that the house from which the man had been watching me belonged to the actor Bob Hoskins. But I don't know whether it was him or not.

I got a bollocking from Walter when I returned to

Rangers. Someone had rung Sky TV about the pneumatic drill business and driving the bus and they'd sent a crew out to follow me. Some of the papers had found out as well.

I had so many great times with Chris and Danny, but it wasn't just a matter of getting drunk. We didn't really do that as much as people imagined. A lot of our dafter tricks were played at 11.30 in the morning, when we were bored, and hadn't even thought of having a drink. Much of the time I just stayed in their houses, relaxing, lolling around.

It was all just a laugh, a game of daring each other to do mad things. And of course, when you've got money, and your face is well known, you can get away with a lot more than other people can.

Perhaps the stupidest thing I ever did was while I was at Rangers, during the Old Firm's New Year league game at Parkhead on 2 January 1998. In the previous Celtic league game, I'd been sent off, and this time I was only sub. When I was warming up, all the Celtic fans were giving me a load of stick, most of them shouting variations on the 'wife-beater' theme. They wound me up so much that to annoy them in return, I pretended to play the flute again. Mad? It was suicidal. I was just so furious with them for shouting abuse at me that I did the only thing I could think of that would shut them up.

The first time I had done it, in that friendly at home to Steaua Bucharest when I'd first arrived, I honestly hadn't appreciated its significance, as I've said. This time I did – and I had done it in the heartland of Celtic, in front of all their supporters. Worse still, the game was being shown live, nationwide, on Sky TV. So there was a hell of a stink. Celtic were raging, and so were Rangers. They fined me £20,000.

The next day I was in my car and a bloke drove up beside me, wound down his window, pulled out a knife, and said: 'Gascoigne, I'm going to slit your fucking throat.' I was shit-scared. Then death threats started arriving in the post.

One letter was from someone claiming to be writing on behalf of the IRA, and said they would get me. I was so terrified that I reported it to the police. They took it very seriously and tracked down the bloke who had written it. He was living in Dublin, and apparently wasn't a proper member of the IRA. They couldn't do anything about his threat to kill me as he was living in another country, but they said if he ever came over to Scotland or England, they could do him the moment he set foot on these shores for making death threats.

The police came to my house and showed me how to open letters and packages, in case there might be a letter bomb. I was taught how to look under my car before getting into it, in case someone had attached an explosive. I was worried, and sometimes scared, and then suddenly, after about six months, the police came to see me one day. They said they'd had a call from the bloke – and they were sure it was him – who now said I could forget it, they weren't going to get me after all. So that was a relief.

I've got no interest in religion either way, and I've never taken sides. I've certainly never hated Celtic or their fans. Once, when I was off injured, I was in New York and went into a bar there to watch a Celtic v Rangers game wearing a Celtic scarf. Does that sound like someone who's prejudiced? And of course my own father was born a Catholic, so I am half Catholic myself. But that's not to say the flute-playing thing wasn't really stupid. I wish I'd never done it.

At Christmas, I'd bought Chris Evans a special massage chair which cost me £5,000. For Danny Baker, I'd bought the biggest possible hamper from Harrods, at £3,500. Guess what they then bought me? A T-shirt that cost about a quid. It had a target on the front for the IRA to shoot at. Mean bastards. I spent a fortune on their presents. But it was a funny T-shirt all the same.

Shel had started divorce proceedings, but we spent that Christmas together, with all the kids. She also came to see me a couple of times, and turned up to a game to watch me play. It looked for a while as if we might get back together, but then, as ever, we fell out again.

Rangers' season was starting to collapse. In the Champions League we had once again failed to get past the qualifying round. New rules meant we were able to go on into the UEFA Cup, but we were beaten there, home and away, by Strasbourg. So by the beginning of October 1997, we were out of Europe. We'd also been knocked out of the League Cup in the quarter-finals by Dundee United.

In February 1998, with quite a way still to go, Walter Smith told us he would be packing it in as manager at the end of the season. He was already a director of the club, so he was effectively kicking himself upstairs. We then found out that Dick Advocaat, the former coach of Holland, was the man who would be taking over.

Walter told me there had been interest from several

clubs for me, including Crystal Palace. Then Middles-brough came in with what Walter thought was a good offer, for me and for Rangers. He felt it was likely I wouldn't be a part of Advocaat's plans, so it seemed the right opportunity at the right time. Rangers' officials had probably had enough of me anyway, after the wife-beating and now the flute incident.

When the deal was finally done, in March 1998, the Rangers chairman, David Murray, at first said I had to return the club Range Rover or pay them £24,000, which is what it was then worth. Then he suggested we could toss a coin for it. In the end, though, he said I could keep it.

The rest of the season turned out badly for Rangers, with Celtic winning the league and then Hearts beating them in the final of the Cup. But by the time all that happened, I had left Glasgow.

As I've said, I'll always be grateful to Walter Smith for everything he did for me. I remember one Christmas time, I was on my own, having fallen out with Shel. Walter must have found out because he rang me up on Christmas morning and invited me round to his place for Christmas dinner with all his family. His wife just set another place for me. That was typical of Walter.

I left the club on good terms with everyone, officials, players and fans. My excellent and very fluent Italian had come in handy when Gattuso joined us and I was able to assist in translating things for him, and help him get to know his way around the club.

I also, on one occasion, tried to be a big help to one of Scotland's better-known referees. In December 1995, when we were playing Hibs, and were coasting 2–0, Dougie Smith, the ref, happened to drop his yellow card from his pocket. I picked it up and pretended to book myself, holding it up in the air.

That seemed to go down well with the fans, so I then held it up over Mr Smith's head, looking very severe and serious, indicating that I was now booking him for having dropped his yellow card. The crowd loved it, but he didn't think it was quite so funny. He immediately booked me for real. Even the Hibs fans jeered him when he did that. And the Hibs players.

During those two full seasons with Rangers, we won so much. Looking back, from a playing point of view, they were some of my happiest times ever in football. But in my third season at Rangers, things weren't so good, especially the last few months. I didn't score as many goals. I wasn't playing as well. Oh, for lots of reasons, mainly to do with Shel. What I'd done to her, what had happened, and all the rows and problems over the divorce. My head wasn't right. I also got worried about the IRA and other things. So I was trying to escape from all my problems in drink.

Looking back, it was really at Rangers that my drinking became serious. I can see that now. And even at Spurs, going out on the piss with the lads, messing about, it hadn't really been a problem, just the normal thing, the sort of thing lots of young lads, and young lasses, do on the occasional night out. In Italy, of course, there wasn't a drink culture and for three months, sometimes six, I hardly got drunk at all. It was binge-eating rather than binge-drinking in Italy, when I was injured or not playing. But towards the end of my third season at Rangers, it all seemed to come together and get me down. My head seemed to be about to explode with all the things nagging me. I just wanted to forget everything, as quickly and as often as possible.

I never drank in the mornings, didn't hide bottles of vodka in kitchen drawers the way alcoholics are supposed to. I never touched a drop till training was over for the day. Then at about six o'clock each evening, I would start drinking, carrying on till I passed out. Not on the two days before a game, which usually meant not on Thursday or Friday evenings. But it meant I got into the habit of getting drunk on five nights a week – Saturday, Sunday, Monday, Tuesday and Wednesday.

I drank mostly at home. I only went now and again to a pub, usually the Duck Bay near my lodge on Loch Lomond, which I returned to after Shel had left Scotland. I might start there with a few drinks, and then go home. It wasn't really social drinking. I never went out much with the other Rangers lads. I mainly drank on my own. Jimmy would often be with me, but he wasn't drinking much. It was just me. He didn't try to stop me. He knew he couldn't. He knew why I was doing it. I would drink two bottles of wine on my own, red or white, it didn't matter which, then about nine or ten o'clock, I'd pass out. Jimmy would put me to bed. But I wouldn't be able to sleep, so I'd take sleeping pills.

I didn't realise at the time, but alcohol is a depressant. It might make you feel good for a while, get you out of yourself, but it doesn't help in the long run. Drink can actually make you more depressed, so I've since been told. But at the time, it was all I wanted to do. Anything to stop my head going round and round.

It was also at Rangers that my pill-popping got

worse. Because I couldn't sleep, which has been a problem my whole life, I was on sleeping pills. This is when I discovered Zimovane which seemed to be good at first, then I needed more and more to have any effect. So I went up from one to two to three a night and became addicted to them.

So, while I loved Rangers, and those first two years were probably about my best ever for football, the last few months were about the worst in my life personally. The worst up until then, anyway. So I was quite pleased to get away.

If you read the papers, people think Gascoigne and I have a father-and-son relationship. Well, I've got two sons and I have never felt like hitting them, but I have certainly felt like smacking Gascoigne a couple of times.
Walter Smith, *his manager at Everton and Rangers, 2000*

It is almost as if he gets into scrapes in order to extort forgiveness from the people he has let down.
Simon Barnes, The Times, *16 February 2000*

21

BORO AND FAMILY AFFAIRS

I arrived at Middlesbrough in March 1998, just in time to get fitted for my Cup final suit. Good timing, eh? This was for the League Cup final, or the Coca-Cola Cup final as it was called that year, or that week. I do find it hard to keep up with all the name changes. Boro had beaten Liverpool in the semi-finals and were due to meet Chelsea at Wembley on 29 March.

Boro were lying in third position in the First Division when I turned out for my first league game for them. I had joined to help them get into the Premiership, and also because of Bryan Robson, their manager. It was strange to be calling him Gaffer after all those years of playing alongside him. I was also attracted by the thought of playing with Paul Merson, another friend from the England team, and Andy Townsend. The transfer fee was pretty good as well. Middlesbrough paid Rangers £3.45 million for me, which meant that Rangers got most of their money back. I was on a basic wage of £16,000 per week but if we did well and got promoted I was on course to make a million a year.

In my last three months at Rangers, I'd had ankle and groin problems and had only played one full game, so I was still recovering and getting fully fit again. Bryan Robson told me it was a perfect opportunity for me, having a new challenge, at a new club, to get back to my best form. I should then be able to secure my place in the England squad for the 1998 World Cup in France. When people asked him about my record off the pitch, he said he expected I would give him a bit of grief, but he was sure it would be worth it, which was good of him.

It was exciting going to Wembley again for a Cup final, my first since 1991 with Spurs, which we don't talk about any more, but I felt a bit of a fraud being in the Boro squad. I hadn't played any part in getting the lads there, and on the day I only came on as sub, for Ricard. Chelsea beat us 2–0 in extra time. I got a medal, as a member of the losing team, but I gave it away to Craig Hignett. He deserved it more than I did. He'd made all the games and yet hadn't even been named as sub for the final.

My first league game for Boro was away to West Brom on 4 April. Their crowd gave me some abuse, of course, and it didn't help when I fell over with my first touch of the ball, and then, with my second touch, gave the ball away. I came into it more later, but I didn't do that much and we lost 2–1. Not a good start. Presumably some Boro supporters were wondering why they'd bought me.

After that, though, I played in six of the last seven league games of the season, missing one through injury. We won five of the last six and drew one, finishing runners-up in the league to Nottingham Forest. So Boro were back in the Premiership. I'd achieved what I'd set out to do. help Boro win promotion.

It was nice to be back in the north-east again after ten years away. Middlesbrough was very handy for Dunston, so I could see the family, and it was very easy for Jimmy to come and see me. I went back to my old school several times and gave them some kit and stuff.

I'd first returned there after the 1990 World Cup. I

happened to be in Gateshead, having a drink with some friends, and realised we were near my old school, Heathfield High. 'Keep an eye on my pint, man,' I said to my mates. 'I'm just going out for a bit.' I didn't tell anyone where I was going. I went into my old school, found the old classrooms where I'd sat, and tracked down Mr Hepworth, still giving his geography lessons. I marched into his class and said, 'Mr Hepworth. Remember me?'

'Yes, I remember you, Gascoigne,' he said.

'And do you remember what you said to me?'

'Yes, Gascoigne. And you were the one in a million who did make it.'

I made another unannounced visit after that, just to mess around and give the kids a bit of excitement. I walked along each corridor, sticking my face against the window of each classroom, making silly expressions till everyone in the class had seen me – except the teacher. Once I'd reduced the whole class to uproar, I moved on to the next classroom and did the same thing, till the whole school was in uproar. Then I went out and stood in the main playground and waved to the entire school, all watching me through their class-room windows.

After I moved to Boro I became friends with many

of the staff, and used to pop in for a game of five-a-side football with the teachers.

When I first arrived at Middlesbrough, while a house was being found for me, I stayed in a hotel. One of the tabloids sent a reporter and photographer, posing as a real couple, to book into the same hotel and keep an eye on me. They were convinced I would be binge-drinking, shagging all the chambermaids, wrecking every bedroom, and they tried hard to get something on me. They got fuck all, and left after three weeks, empty-handed. I didn't, of course, know they were there until they had gone. If I'd realised they were spying on me, I would have thumped them.

I eventually moved from the hotel into a big, six-bedroomed mansion at Seaham, on the coast, along with Jimmy. My team-mate Andy Townsend moved in as well. We didn't have any staff and that, we just looked after worselves. And no, we didn't wreck anything.

I had already bought my parents the house of their dreams in Dunston, best part, of course, which cost about £120,000. Then I bought a house each for my two sisters and my brother, all in the same area – in fact two were in the same street. Keep it nice and cosy.

I gave them cars as well. I bought a Rolls-Royce,

which I gave to me dad. He put on his personalised
number plate – JG 369 – which he'd had on the new
Jaguar. It wasn't a brand-new model, but only a few years
old, a Silver Sprite, and me dad, the daft sod, drove it
to the dole office when he went to pick up his money
and left it parked outside, for all to see. No wonder he
got his dole money stopped. He had remained unem-
ployed ever since he collapsed and nearly died when I
was young, but he wasn't ill all the time. He was usually
fit enough to hold up a pint or two, smoke a few ciggies,
kiss a few lasses and come and see me in London, Italy
and Glasgow. I wanted him to enjoy himself, after what
he'd been through.

He'd had another dodgy time when his eyesight
started to go. They said he had varicose veins in his head
– at least, that's what I was told – or it could even be a
brain tumour. He had to have an emergency operation,
and it was life or death. I was terrified he was going to
die. As he went under for the op, I promised I would
get him a brand-new Range Rover if he recovered.

When I heard he was OK, while he was still in
hospital, I went out, traded in his Rolls and bought him
a top-of-the-range Range Rover. But I forgot all about
his personalised number plate. I didn't save it, or get

anything extra for it, when I sold his old car. He tells me all the time it's now worth £10,000, and I let it go for nothing.

Another time I went to see my dad and he told me he'd bought this new boat. He said it was a smasher, a right belter. I asked him how much it was worth and he said £8,000. I said I'd give him £5,000 for it. He told me he didn't really want to sell it, as it was so brilliant for going out deep-water fishing, but in the end he said, 'Oh, all right then, as it's you.' But he insisted I had to give him the cheque there and then. And he wouldn't let me have the boat, or tell me where it was, until the cheque had cleared. So I gave him the cheque – and he rushed straight off to the bank.

The first time I saw the boat I went with my mates Cyril, Vinny and Hazy and a few others to watch it arrive at Whitley Bay. They saw it before I did, this little orange tub, and were pissing themselves laughing. I said, 'That's not it. My dad told me it was a belter, perfect for deep-sea fishing.' Of course, it did turn out to be the fucking little orange tub. One of the lads got on the dock tannoy and announced for everyone to hear: 'Class boat now coming into the harbour.' The first time I took it out to sea, the steering wheel fell off. It was hardly worth a packet of fish and chips, let alone £5,000. In the end, I gave it away.

Just after I joined Boro, in 1998, my parents split up for good. They'd had rows in the past, and had separated before, and me dad had lived away for various spells, but now they decided, finally, to get divorced. I suppose they got on each other's nerves so much that in the end they couldn't stand it any longer. Me dad's a good-looking man and there had always been girls hanging round him, but in the past me mam had been able to just laugh it off. They both enjoyed life and I always thought they enjoyed being with each other, despite everything. So I was very upset about the divorce. But one good thing is that at least they're still pals.

As if that wasn't enough, stories reached me that not only Anna and her husband, John-Paul, but also Lindsay and her husband, Tim, were going through difficulties in their marriages. I invited them all to have a pub lunch with me in Dunston, worried about what I was hearing. I knew from my own experience how emotionally destructive marital strife can be, and I wanted to help my sisters.

I invited John-Paul and Tim to the toilet, and locked the door. I said, 'What the fuck is going on? I'm not unlocking this door until you promise to try harder. If I find out you haven't, I'm going to smash both of yous.' They promised, of course, so I let them out.

Next I invited my sisters into the toilet – the same one, the men's. I said to them: 'You've got two weeks to get things sorted. And if not I want yous divorced.'

In the end, they both got divorced, like my mam and dad. And me. I paid for all their divorces, all the legal fees. Around the same time, Carl got married, and I paid for his wedding as well. I don't know why they chose to make that reality TV show about the Osbournes. I think the Gascoignes would have made much better television.

When my parents split up, they sold the big house I'd bought for them, divided the money between them and bought another house each, a bit smaller, round the corner from each other. Me mam recently moved even nearer to me dad, into the same street, in fact only a couple of doors away. I'm not sure if he's too thrilled by me mam being as close as that, and able to see everything he does. Apart from Anna, who lives a few streets away, they are in the same street now – Carl, me mam and me dad. Lindsay's just round the corner. They all get on fine. Mam still goes round to me dad's and makes the odd Sunday lunch for him. One of the things that has given me greatest pleasure in my life is having been able to provide nice homes for everyone in my family.

My own divorce came through later, in August 1998. I was heartbroken, even though I knew it was coming. I hadn't got married to get divorced. I'd thought it would last, despite everything; despite the horrible things I'd done. I sold the house in Renfrewshire and made a big settlement on Shel. I also agreed to generous regular maintenance payments, for her and all three kids. As I've said, I had always looked on Bianca and Mason as my own, and my responsibility, so I didn't moan or fight it.

At the end of the year, I then did something really daft. As a Christmas present, I gave Shel my timeshare lodge, the one on Loch Lomond. From then on I had no home or place to live of my own. I was staying either in rented houses or flats or in hotels.

But at least I was settled at my new club. That summer of 1998, Boro had got the promotion we were so desperate to achieve and, best of all, I had the World Cup of 1998 in France to look forward to.

I am sure he will give me a bit of grief from time
to time, but it will be worth it. Paul takes a few
pints now and again, but he is one of the hardest
trainers I have worked with.
Bryan Robson, manager of Middlesbrough,
Daily Mail, *March 1998*

There is a wildness about Gascoigne. On Monday,
he was talking about his life's ambition to be
picked up by UFOs. I have a suspicion he already
has been without knowing it for he is not really
like the rest of us Earthmen.
Simon Barnes, The Times, *20 May 1998*

At his peak, Gazza was phenomenal, the best
player I've seen in this country. Becks is a great
player but he isn't fit to lace Gazza's boots.
Paul Merson, 1999

22

WORLD CUP 98 AND TROUBLE WITH HODDLE

I was sick when Terry Venables parted company with England after Euro 96. Not just because he was my friend, and I admired him so much as a manager – the best in football, in my view – but because the whole thing was so unfair. All because he had business problems. What the hell did that have to do with his football work? He never mentioned any of his business ventures to us, never let us down at any time, for any event, and he wasn't neglecting his England duties. We knew nothing about his life outside the England camp. These days, players have many business interests, which can take up a lot of their time, but they don't get into trouble with England or their clubs if these go wrong, which some of them are bound to do. I don't see that it matters. All that matters is what happens on the pitch, and whether they are doing their job properly.

I was a bit worried when I heard that Glenn Hoddle had got the job. He was a legend, of course, but I'd never played alongside him – he'd recently left Spurs when I arrived – although I'd played against him when I was a youngster starting out at Newcastle. When he took over the England job in 1996, Walter Smith said to me, 'Be careful – Hoddle will want to make a name for himself.' I didn't know at the time what he meant by that. It would be two years before I understood.

I had no real complaints about Hoddle as he picked me regularly, as long as I was fit and well and playing OK. But there were irritating elements to his management. In England training sessions, I didn't like the way he told us how to do stretches. As professionals, we had all done stretching exercises for years and had long since worked out what suited our individual bodies best. Hoddle always thought he knew much better than anyone else. But of course, you do what he says – he's the manager. And his sidekick, John Gorman, I suspect, reported back any little bit of gossip to his boss.

When Hoddle heard stories about me drinking at

Rangers, and going out on the town in London with Chris Evans, he got it into his head that I needed some special treatment to sort myself out. He said to me one day, 'Would you like to go and see Eileen Drewery?' I thought he'd said, 'Would you like to go and see a brewery?' so naturally, I said yeah, good idea, boss, count me in.

Anyway, I went to see Eileen Drewery, who the press called his faith-healer. He thought she was marvellous. An England car was arranged to drive me to her home. She put her hand on my head, gave it a lot of soft chat, and then announced that I had bad spirits in my head. She said demons were coming out of my head and into her house. I couldn't see them – and you'd have thought I would have noticed them. She opened the window, to let my demons out, which was thoughtful of her.

I was there for about forty-five minutes, with Eileen feeling my head and mumbling away. When she had finished, she told me that that night, I mustn't have a cigarette, or a glass of beer, as it would let all my bad spirits in again.

When I was walking downstairs on my way out, I noticed her sitting in another room – having a fag. Just what she had told me not to do. Later on, at an England do, I spotted her in the players' lounge with a bottle of beer. Things she'd told me not to do, she was doing herself. Fucking cheek! I'd played in a World Cup, a European Championship and in Italy, and I'd won two Doubles with Rangers, and here she was, telling me how to behave and how to live my life.

Darren Anderton came back from Eileen's and said she had healed his ankle, or whatever it was that was wrong with him, I forget. Others, too, claimed she had really helped them. Don't get me wrong, I never rubbished her. I said nothing against her to the press or in public then, and I'm not going to start now. But I could not say she had helped me, either, when I honestly didn't think she had. All I'm saying is that her methods were not for me. I don't believe in all that spiritualism stuff. I'm not dismissing it as nonsense. I just don't go along with it myself.

Glenn sent me three times to see Eileen. What could I do? You can't refuse the England manager, can you? But personally, I thought all the visits were a waste of time.

In May 1997, in an England game against South Africa at Old Trafford, I had a bit of an argument with a linesman whose decisions I wasn't happy with. While I was reasoning with him, I noticed he was chewing that nicotine gum, which I'd heard about and wanted to try. It's supposed to make you relax.

At half-time, Hoddle said he wanted a word with me in a few minutes, and could I step into the other room? I knew which room he meant, but I deliberately went into the wrong room. When the manager didn't appear, I went off to try to find the linesman and ask him where he got his special tobacco gum. I got a bollocking from Hoddle for disappearing, for not going into the room he had told me to meet him in. I shouted at him, 'Stop treating me like a fucking schoolkid!' Which, of course, I should not have done.

There was somebody else Hoddle lined up to help us before the 98 World Cup. One day this French bloke arrived, a dietician I suppose, who talked to us all and told us there was something very important we should do – we had to chew our food properly. He said if we did so, we would win. The phrase he kept on repeating was 'chew to win'. So we went round saying it as well, shouting out to each other, 'Chew to win!' Taking the piss of course. I asked him one day, why, as he was French, he wasn't helping the French team, getting them to chew to win. He said the French team wasn't good enough. Showed how much he knew.

In June 1997, we went to France for Le Tournoi, a four-nation friendly tournament involving the hosts, England, Italy and Brazil, which gave us the chance to test ourselves against our rival challengers for the World Cup the following year. We beat Italy and France but lost 1–0 to Brazil. I played in all three of our games. In the second, against France in Montpellier – which we won 1–0 with a goal from Alan Shearer – I received my fiftieth England cap.

That autumn we played our two remaining World Cup qualifiers. I scored one of the goals in our 4–0 defeat of Moldova at Wembley in September. Then came the crunch match, the return fixture against Italy in Rome on 11 October. To make sure of qualification we needed at least a draw.

It was one of the most tense games I ever played for England. There were over 80,000 people in the Olympic Stadium, where I had appeared many times with Lazio. It held memories, too, of the 1990 World Cup. I so wanted to do well in front of the Italian crowds, to let them see what I was still capable of. From the beginning Italy had been the favourites to win the group, which, as well as England and Moldova, included Poland and Georgia, so they were pretty confident, especially at home. And they had already beaten us at Wembley, 1–0 in February, a match I hadn't played in.

On the night, we managed to play the Italians at their own game, being solid and defensive when we had to, giving nothing away. I knew I had to be mature and sensible and hold the midfield. This was my fifty-third cap, which made me the most-capped player in the team, ahead of Tony Adams who was on 48, Dave Seaman with 38 and Paul Ince with 34. I felt that, at the age of thirty, I had to use my experience to help the younger lads who had not been all that long in the side, such as David Beckham. When I'd first played for England almost ten years earlier, older players like Bryan Robson and Terry Butcher had been very good with me. Now it was my turn to do the same.

We got a 0–0 draw, which on paper seems nothing, pretty boring, but we played excellently. It was probably one of the most satisfying internationals of my career. The Italians are very good at diving and wasting time when they want to, so I did a bit of that, too, kicking the ball away and making them chase for it. It was great to see them running after it for a change. Afterwards, I felt I could walk round Italy for ever afterwards with my chest stuck out.

The papers next day were very complimentary. 'Gascoigne produced one of the most controlled performances of his career,' said *The Times*, 'and played with a sustained quality and maturity, illuminated by flashes of technical brilliance.' Doesn't quite sound like me, does it?

The draw put us at the top of our group, one point ahead of Italy, and we were through to the 1998 World Cup finals while Italy had to go to the play-offs. Ha, ha. If Hoddle doesn't pick me for his World Cup squad, I'll kill him, I thought afterwards. But at the same time, I knew I'd done my job well so far, and was content to see what the next year would bring.

At the end of the season, while waiting to depart with the World Cup squad for our warm-up camp, La Manga in Spain, I got a call from Chris Evans asking me to appear on his TV programme. I did the show and we went out for a few drinks afterwards. At 11.30 we stopped and had a chicken kebab. I was back in Chris's house by midnight. But in that half-hour someone had taken a photo of us, and once again I was all over the papers. I know for a fact that six England players were out in Soho that night till four in the morning, but none of them appeared in the press, just me. It seemed the media were determined to crucify me.

It wasn't even as if it was the eve of a big game. There were still a few days to go before we left for Spain. But Glenn Hoddle was furious. He said he was worried about my condition. Was I in a fit state to play for England any more? Following the Italy game, he had shaken my hand and told me I'd done brilliantly and was vital to his future plans. And now this. It was very depressing. After the kebab incident was blown up out of all proportion, I was seen out one evening with Rod Stewart and Chris Evans. Again Hoddle was quoted as saying he was worried about my behaviour but he didn't know the truth about either incident.

He had still been picking me, though, so that was something. After the Italy draw, I had played against Cameroon and then, in May 1998, in World Cup warm-up games with Saudi Arabia, Morocco and Belgium. I wasn't totally fit in the Belgium game, and had got a dead leg which meant I had to come off, to be substituted by Beckham. But we weren't beaten in any of those games except that one against Belgium, on penalties.

*　　　*　　　*

Twenty-eight players were taken out to La Manga, from which Hoddle would need to select his final squad of twenty-two for the World Cup. I was pleased, naturally, but not surprised, to be told I was on my way to Spain. Given my form for England, everyone expected me to be picked.

It was all light-hearted at first, a bit of training, bit of fun. We had karaoke one evening and I got drunk, but so did several others. Dave Seaman took me to my room and tucked me in while the others carried on drinking. At least eight of them were still up at four in the morning.

Next day, we were left to play golf, swim or just hang around the pool. It was then that I heard that Hoddle was calling in every player, one by one, at a set time, to tell them who would be in the final twenty-two.

This is fucking stupid, I thought; he's treating us like schoolkids. The idea of keeping us all sitting around doing nothing for several hours, waiting for our appointment, was petty. The more I thought about it, the more I thought, I'm not having this. I don't do waiting.

I wasn't drunk. Not at all. I might have had a couple of beers earlier that morning on the golf course, but I certainly wasn't drunk. Perhaps a bit hung over from the night before, but that was all. I was just so annoyed and irritated. I barged into a room where Ray Clemence, Glenn Roeder and John Gorman, the England coaches, were sitting. I glared at all of them, daring them to tell me whether I was in, to give me some sort of clue. I could see in Glenn Roeder's eyes what Hoddle had decided. There might even have been a tear there. It was clear to me that they all knew the score.

I couldn't control myself any longer. I burst straight into Hoddle's room, where he was talking to Phil Neville, and I went ballistic.

'What the fucking hell are you doing? You know what it means to me, you fucking bastard.'

'Let me explain,' Hoddle began.

'I don't want to hear any fucking explanations. I don't care what your reasons are. You know what you're doing to me? You are a fucking bastard . . .'

I went over to his wardrobe and kicked in the door. Then I overturned his table, smashing a pottery vase and sending it crashing to the floor. In the process I managed to cut my leg, so now there was blood all over the place as well. I didn't attempt to hit Hoddle, though I would have liked to. I suppose, deep down, I still respected him, as a player, if not as a manager. And perhaps I also had an inbuilt respect for the position of manager, if not for the man in it. I didn't lay a finger on him, but I was in a complete fury. It wasn't long before that he had led me to believe I would be in the final twenty-two, telling the world that we had not seen the best of Gazza yet.

But now I didn't want to hear any of his rubbish. I was hell-bent on trashing the whole room, and not listening to one word he was saying.

'Gazza, just calm down and I'll tell you why I've had to do it.'

'Just fucking shut up, you bastard.'

'The thing is, Gazza, your head isn't right.'

'I got you to France. I saved your skin, your fucking job, and now look what you're fucking doing to me.'

I was about to start smashing all his windows, when David Seaman and Paul Ince burst in and managed to restrain me. Then they called for the doctor, who gave me a valium tablet to quieten me down.

I was taken to my room. All I wanted now was to leave La Manga at once and never see Hoddle again. Walter Smith's words echoed in my mind. 'Hoddle will want to make a name for himself . . .'

I rang my dad and told him to cancel his French holiday. He wouldn't be going there any longer. None of our family would be going, not now. Then I got the first plane out of Spain, along with Phil Neville, Ian Walker and Dion Dublin, who had been chucked out with me. Six of us in all had been given the boot. The other two were Nicky Butt and Andy Hinchcliffe. I found out later that most of the squad were surprised, and some were stunned, that I'd been excluded.

From Luton Airport, I shared a car into London with Ian Walker. I rang Shel and asked if I could stay with her for a while. She was brilliant. The first thing she did when I arrived was to give me a big hug. I stayed with her for five days.

I didn't watch any of the 1998 World Cup, not even any of England's games. I don't like watching football at the best of times, as I'd always rather be playing. In these circumstances I really couldn't face it. I was too sick and gutted.

The press were stalking me, trying to catch me exploding, or doing something else daft. They doorstepped Shel's house and hid in the garden. One bastard of a photographer managed to creep up on little Regan and the flash went off in his face. Poor little sod. It hurt his eyes. He was in tears with the shock and the pain. For several minutes he couldn't see and we seriously wondered whether his eyesight might be affected.

I rang the newspaper this photographer worked for, sounding all calm and reasonable, but I was seething. Why didn't their photographer, the one who had just snatched a photo of Regan, come back and take a really nice photograph? I suggested. We would give him proper time so that he could do Regan justice.

The prat fell for it. The moment he arrived in his car, I drove mine behind it so that he couldn't get out again. Then I smashed his door handles. When he got out his camera, I smashed that as well. Some neighbours appeared, having heard me screaming that I was going to kill him. I let him go in the end without actually hitting him. Well, not very hard.

I went inside and told Shel the police would be here soon. 'I'll probably get arrested for assault, but fuck it, I don't care.'

The police did come, and took a statement from me. I just told them the truth: what the photographer had done to my son. I fully expected to have to go to court, but nothing ever happened. I presume the newspaper decided to withdraw charges. No doubt they could see I had a case; that they had caused all the trouble by invading private property and hurting my son. They must have realised that if it went to court, it wouldn't make them look very good.

I went on holiday to Florida with Shel and the kids to try to get over it all. But I was in a terrible state for about a year after that, which probably explains a lot of the stupid things I did during that year.

What really pissed me off was when, almost immediately after the tournament was over, Hoddle published his World Cup diary. In it, he described how I trashed his room. I might have spoken to the press about some of it at the time, but it is only now, at six years' distance, when he is no longer England manager and it doesn't matter any more, that I am giving my full story of what happened. I'm not denying what I did, but Hoddle should not have written about it while he was still the England manager. He was just cashing in on his position, making money out of my misery. I thought that was disgusting. I was not the only one who thought that, as he was widely criticised for producing that book.

I can't help wondering why Hoddle didn't realise when he dropped me that I might cause a scene; that I wouldn't be able to wait for his poxy appointment; that

I would not be able to control myself and would go mad and cause trouble. After all, he could have dropped the six of us quietly in England, ringing us privately at home, and then announcing the final squad to the papers the next day. But instead he dramatically dropped the axe while we were away in La Manga, all warming up together for the World Cup, being with the lads. I don't know what the reason for Hoddle's decision was, but clearly his mind had been made up before I lost it in his room. Yes, as I've admitted, I had been drinking the night before, but, as I've also said, I wasn't the only one. And it wasn't the first time I'd had a drink while with the England squad and gone on to play a blinder.

I still hate what Hoddle did to me, but I don't bear personal grudges. Never have done. Not for ever, anyway.

I met Hoddle by chance not long ago, in a hotel lift. I shook his hand and he said, how's it going Gazza? and I said fine, and he smiled, and I smiled, and that was it. It's all over now. But it will never be forgotten, at least not by me.

I wondered, of course, whether this would be the end of my England career, which was what everybody was suggesting at the time. It was obvious that Hoddle would never pick me again, after what I did to his lousy bedroom. I just had to hope that Hoddle himself would not be in the job for too long.

I was pleased when David Beckham wrote in his autobiography in 2003 that he felt Hoddle went about things the wrong way. England got through their first group, but were knocked out by Argentina in the quarter-finals, so they didn't get as far as we did in 1990. David clearly thinks I might have helped. 'I still wonder if that wasn't what we were missing in France '98,' he wrote. 'I think we'd have been better with Gazza there. Paul could bring something to the team nobody else could. He could change a game on his own. And I know we'd all have liked him to be around as part of the squad.'

Thanks, David.

Gascoigne, at his best, remains the pivotal player for England's World Cup chances in June.
Rob Hughes, The Times, 11 March 1998

He should have been the greatest player of his generation but wasn't. Why? He simply lacked the dedication that distinguished the truly outstanding sportsmen. His attitude throughout his career has been 'It's my life and I'll live it how I like.'
Michael Hart, Evening Standard, 20 May 1998

If Gazza had been given the right antidepressants or
decent therapy I do not doubt that he would have
been in the starting line-up against Tunisia on 15 June,
playing to the full of his creative capacity.
Oliver James, Prospect, *July 1998*

After all I had seen of him physically and mentally, I
knew deep down he had run out of time.
At the airport, it kept coming to me that I couldn't
take Gazza to France.
Glenn Hoddle in his World Cup diary

Once you've played in the same side as Gazza,
you fall in love with him because of the sort of
person and player he is.
David Beckham, England colleague, 1998

23

A VISIT TO THE PRIORY

One day after training at Boro, I noticed that the team coach was standing there empty, with the doors open and the key in the ignition. I thought, I'd like to drive that. I know, I'll drive it into town, take some of the lads to the bookie's so they can put a few bets on. I jumped in and started it up. It all seemed easy enough at first, till I came to this narrow gate on the perimeter of the training ground. I didn't see the big breeze block. And it slipped my mind that I was driving a huge coach, not a car. As a result, I took the bloody thing with me. I heard this horrible scraping noise and realised I must have done a bit of damage. Then I reversed, which made things even worse.

There was a security man on the gate, and I threw him the keys of the coach and said, 'Quick, you take it.' My team-mate Phil Stamp was driving up in his car and stopped, seeing what the coach had done, but not who had been driving it. I jumped into his car and said, 'Hurry up, get the fuck out of here.'

Bryan Robson rang me in town. 'I know you are mad, but this is fucking too much.' The team coach was so bashed up it couldn't be used for the next away game and the club had to borrow another one. And I had to stump up £14,000 for the damage I'd caused.

I thought Bryan Robson was an excellent manager. I had no problems with him, though he might have had a few problems with me. It was good having club football to look forward to again after the humiliation of La Manga, and great to be in the Premiership. During the close season, I had worked really hard on my fitness and agility, which is how I came to play the drums so well at David Seaman's wedding in July 1998. And I tested my reflexes by setting fire to Jimmy's nose. I then bet him £500 he couldn't hold a red-hot lighter to his nose for more than three seconds. He did it twice, so I had to pay him £1,000. But it left him with a scorched conk for weeks, and he claims you can still see the burn marks.

So I was, honestly, fit and slim by the beginning of the new season, and Bryan Robson was really pleased with me. But just before the first game, at the end of August, I had a lot on my mind. As well as the divorce from Shel, Glenn Hoddle's book was being serialised in one newspaper and picked over by all the rest, so the press were after me all the time, on both topics. In the middle of all this came a sudden blow which knocked me for six.

I was over in Gateshead, staying in a hotel with Jimmy and some friends, including David Cheek, who was Jimmy's uncle. I'd known him for many years, and he was a good lad. I sometimes took him training with me. He always called me The Boss.

We began the evening drinking cocktails, then went for an Italian meal, came back to the hotel, had some more drinks and crashed into bed. I woke at four in the morning and, as I usually do when I wake up early, wanted someone to play with. I rang Jimmy, who was of course still asleep, and he told me groggily to fuck off. I rang the others, but they all either hung up on me or didn't answer.

Not long afterwards, there was a call from Jimmy. I thought, good, he's getting up now so we can go and do something, but all he said was, 'Davey's dead.' He'd died in the night, just like that. I rushed out of my room and down the stairs to see his body being taken away in an ambulance.

Davey was only thirty-eight and had four bairns. I was shattered. He had been a heavy drinker for many years, but I'd never expected this to happen. He went so suddenly. Once again, I felt it was my fault, for taking him out drinking. All I could do now was act as pall-bearer at his funeral. I wondered if the same thing would happen to me, whether I'd go out like that, out of the blue.

After Davey died, I started having blackouts. I took tablets for depression and heaps of other pills, anything to numb my mind. Or I just got drunk.

I didn't feel much like playing after the funeral. Bryan Robson said I didn't have to, but I wanted to turn out for Boro's first game back in the Premiership. It was against Leeds at home. It ended in a goalless draw, but I lasted the full ninety minutes and most reports said I was Boro's best player on the day. I managed to get the better of Lee Bowyer, who was snapping at my heels, and gave Paul Merson a forty-yard pass which he nearly converted, but he got bundled over.

I was substituted in our next match, when we were

beaten 3–1 by Villa, but I played the whole of the home game against Derby, which we drew 1–1. I was getting fitter with every match. We beat Leicester away, 1–0, our first win back in the Premiership, and I scored our goal. Paul Merson had left for Villa by then, complaining that there was a drinking culture at the club. I don't know who he was referring to. Did he mean me?

Actually, Merson was teetotal when I knew him at Boro, so we all tried to help. I remember him coming to my house once and hiding two bottles of wine in the kitchen so he couldn't see them and wouldn't be tempted. I deny that I was part of any drinking culture among the players at Boro. Since my Spurs days, and that was just odd nights out when I was young, I hardly ever went out drinking with team-mates. In fact, on the whole I've not socialised with other players after a game or after training. I've kept myself to myself. Having seen them all day in training, at work so to speak, I preferred to be with other people in the evening, such as Jimmy and my other old friends. That's always been my style.

In the middle of September, we were due to meet Spurs at White Hart Lane, so I was looking forward to that. It would be my first league game there since 1991. David Pleat was now caretaker manager at Tottenham, in the wake of the departure of Christian Gross. I was given a good ovation by the Spurs crowd. Glenn Hoddle was in the stands, still England manager, but I don't think he'd come to see me. Probably he was checking out Sol Campbell, who didn't have a very good game and didn't look fit. We stuffed them 3–0. I was brought off four minutes before the end, as I was knackered, but I got probably the biggest cheer of the afternoon from the Tottenham supporters.

In the next game, against Wycombe Wanderers in the Worthington Cup, Bryan made me captain as Andy Townsend, our normal skipper, was injured. We won that one 2–0. At that stage, we were sixth in the league.

In October the Premiership clubs had a week off because of England's vital Euro 2000 qualifier against Bulgaria. Needless to say, Hoddle had not picked me for that. So instead of a visit to Wembley, it was a four-day break in Dublin for me with Middlesbrough.

I was sleeping very badly, far worse than normal, thinking about Davey and death and that his was my fault and that I would be next. I'd started taking sleeping pills at the end of my time at Rangers, in the hope that they would make me sleep and blank everything out. But all they did was make me feel really terrible when I woke up and go on feeling like shit all day. So I'd just dive into the booze to cheer myself up, stop myself thinking about death and dying.

Those four days in Dublin turned into a four-day drinking session. Jimmy and my friend Hazy had come over to join us, as my guests in our hotel, with Bryan Robson's permission.

When the time came to catch the plane back to England, I got myself into a state about flying and started drinking before we even boarded. I knew I shouldn't be doing it, because I was due to go direct from Newcastle Airport to Hertfordshire, ready to pick up my son Regan the next morning and spend a day with him as part of the access arrangements in the divorce agreement.

To get myself fit to fly, I drank sixteen hot toddies. That's about thirty-two whiskies (they were very strong hot toddies). I reeled off the plane at Newcastle and somehow got myself to the railway station and on to the train to Stevenage. I have no memory of getting off the plane or of catching the train. All I can remember is standing on the platform at Stevenage, crying my eyes out. I felt so miserable and depressed, and being drunk just magnified those feelings. I'd made such a mess of things, wrecking my marriage, ruining Shel's life and the children's. That row with Hoddle, then David Cheek dying. Everything seemed so bleak, and most of it was my own fault. It seemed to me that Shel and Regan would cope much better if I wasn't around.

So I decided, in this emotional state, to throw myself in front of the next train. I waited and waited, but no train came. A railwayman saw me staggering around and came over. I asked where the fuck the train was and he said there wasn't another one. The last train had gone. That's when I really started crying. Even when I was trying to kill myself I couldn't get it right.

I somehow managed to ring Shel, sobbing down the line, saying, 'Please help. Please come and get me.' She'd heard this sort of talk from me before, and she'd been taken in by it enough times already, she said. She refused to let me come and stay at her place, not in the state I was in. It would just upset the children. However, she agreed to come and pick me up from Stevenage Station and take me to Hanbury Manor. The hotel where we'd had our famous wedding.

About one in the morning, the phone rang in my hotel room. It was Reception. They said a Mr Robson was there to see me. I said fuck off, and hung up. Then there was a knock on the door. I opened it, and there stood Bryan. He really was there.

Unbeknown to me, Shel had rung him and told him about the state I was in and where I was. Bryan had immediately jumped in his car and driven all the way from Middlesbrough to Hertfordshire to rescue me. I'm so grateful to him for doing that. And grateful to Shel for making that call.

Not that I knew much about what was happening at the time. I didn't really take in what Bryan was saying to me, or what he was explaining about what he was going to do. I wasn't aware of anything, really. I was out of it. He dragged me into his car and we drove off. The next thing I remember was arriving at a big white building. It was the Priory, in south-west London – one of the country's leading private psychiatric hospitals, famous for treating celebrities for eating disorders, alcoholism and drug abuse, among other things – though I didn't know that till several days later.

They knocked me out for about four days, gave me tablets, tried to detox me. When I returned to some level of consciousness, they put me on a twenty-four-hour watch, fearing I might still be suicidal, that I might jump out of the window. I still didn't know what was going on, or quite where I was, or why. When I eventually sobered up, I asked what was happening. It was then that I was told I was in the Priory, suffering from alcoholism and depression, and that they were going to make me better.

Shel came to visit me. Of course, as I always did when I was at a low point, I asked if there was a chance she'd have me back, if I could come and live with her. She said no. She said I was an alcoholic, and I had to be cured before we could even discuss it.

I shouted at her, 'I'm not a fucking alcoholic!' I refused to admit it to myself or to anyone else. For the next few days, I just stayed in my room.

One day there was a loud knock on my door, and someone was shouting that I had a visitor. I called out, 'Fuck off. I don't want to see anybody. Go away.' But the hammering and banging went on and eventually I opened the door. The visitor was none other than the rock legend Eric Clapton. A real fucking legend. Not like me. And he'd come to see me? He said he'd heard I was here and that he'd been through a similar thing himself. I was so touched that he'd bothered to come and talk to me, and it helped a lot, just listening to his own experiences.

While I was in the Priory, one of the things they did was get me to answer about fifty questions about my life and habits. I thought I'd just lie, make it all up, that they wouldn't catch me out. I reckoned I knew what

COME ON ENGLAND!
Left: my debut for England (*below*) was against Denmark in September 1988. Before the game, with Bobby Robson and the other new lads in the squad: back row – Alan Smith, Michael Thomas, Des Walker, David Rocastle, Paul Davis; front – Mel Sterland, Bobby Robson and me. Walker and Rocastle also made their debuts in that match.

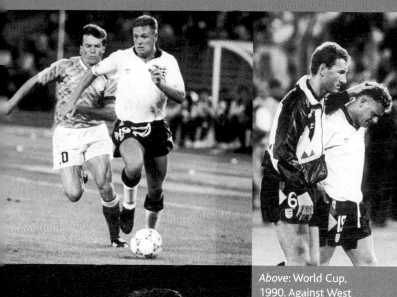

Above: World Cup, 1990. Against West Germany in the semi-finals I marked Lothar Matthäus out of the game, so I like to think, then I got booked and it ended in tears, despite being comforted by Terry Butcher. We lost on penalties and West Germany went on to win the World Cup.

Left: don't let the bairns see this. Scary. I was wearing a mask against Poland in May 1993, as I'd broken my cheekbone — just one of the 27 operations which lost me over four years of my playing career.

GOAL!

One of my all-time fab goals, as seen on TV, over and over again. It was in the Euro 96 game against Scotland at Wembley. I flicked the ball over Colin Hendry with my left foot and smashed it past Andy Goram with my right. Andy was my colleague at Rangers at the time. Did I enjoy the dressing room at Ibrox after that . . .

EURO 96

We drew Germany in the semi-finals. Again. In extra time I nearly got the golden goal which would have taken us straight into the final. A cross came over and I lunged for it, missing by inches . . .

It went to penalties. I scored mine, and was congratulated by David Seaman, but poor old Gareth Southgate missed. Germany went through – and won the final. Again.

. . . As I lay there on the goal line I couldn't believe I'd come so close to putting us into a major final after 30 years of hurt.

Glenn Hoddle then took over as England manager, although I did try to give him his marching orders, early doors . . .

I played one of my best, most mature games for England in our crucial 1998 World Cup qualifier against Italy, along with young Beckham and Paul Ince. It was an exciting 0–0 draw, enough for us to go through to the finals in France.

England about to play Belgium, 29 May 1998. I got my 57th cap that day – but didn't know at the time it would be my last . . .

they were trying to do. If you answered half the questions in a certain way, it would prove something or other. I responded to about thirty-five of the questions, making things up or hiding the truth, but it didn't seem to make much difference. They still said the answers proved I was an alcoholic.

I continued to deny it. I felt I could control my drinking. I only did it when I got depressed, to give myself a nice buzz, to blot out all the bad things in my head. I didn't call that being an alcoholic. I didn't even like alcohol much.

As I began to feel a bit better, I took part in various activities. I organised five-a-side football games and quite enjoyed myself. I felt safe in the Priory. But at the same time, I still did not believe I was an alcoholic, so I did not accept what they said about me or the ways they were trying to help me.

I should have stayed there longer. Everyone told me that, Bryan as well as all the experts, but I was fed up with it. I didn't think it was doing much for me. They didn't seem to really understand my problems. Or perhaps I wasn't giving them a proper chance.

It costs a fortune to stay in the Priory, about £20,000 a month, but that wasn't the reason I wanted out quickly.

You're supposed to stay in for twenty-eight days, and Robbo had said I had to finish the whole course, that was the point of it. But after three weeks I was begging to be let out, and I left before I had had the full benefit of the course. I was determined to show that I was not an alcoholic, that I could stay off the booze if I really wanted to. I could do it all by myself.

I should have been going regularly to meetings of Alcoholics Anonymous. I managed only about three. I wouldn't admit I was an alcoholic; instead I vowed to stay off the drink, never again to touch another drop. I know that when I put my mind to something, I can do it. It's just another form of excess, after all. I was resolute about staying sober, even over the Christmas period, whatever happened.

But I'd left the Priory still full of anger. I was angry at what they were telling me, that I was an alcoholic. I was saying no, no, I'm not, that's not my problem, and they were saying yes, I was now an alcoholic.

Genius alone does not make for the Gazza Factor. The Gazza Factor is something strange and capricious and delightful. It cannot be contrived and it cannot be controlled. Any sport that has a Gazza Factor must revel in it and hope that the effect lasts.
Simon Barnes, The Times, 24 September 1997

24

BINGES AND BREAKS
AT BORO

I missed only two games during my stay in the Priory, far fewer than Tony Adams and Paul Merson were absent for when they had had treatment for alcoholism. I suppose I looked upon football as the best cure, the one aspect of my life that has always kept me focused, cleared my head of all my worries and phobias, allowed me to escape from my worst self.

I returned at least half a stone lighter, in time for the game at home on 1 November against Nottingham Forest. I was given a thunderous reception from the Boro fans. The match was being shown live on TV and the commentators made me Man of the Match. I could sense the crowd wanting me to play well, out of sympathy as much as anything else, and I think I did. We managed a 1–1 draw. When I came off, ten minutes before the end, I shook hands with Chris Bart-Williams of Forest, embraced his team-mate Scot Gemmill and even went to the Forest bench to shake hands with them. I was just so relieved to be playing football again – when I might well have thrown myself under a train on Stevenage Station, though of course no one in the crowd, or anyone else for that matter, knew about that.

In the next game we were away to Southampton. The team was due to fly down from Teesside Airport. I wanted to drive, but it wasn't possible. I hated the idea of flying without a drink to steady my nerves, so it was tough for me, but I managed it.

I scored from a twenty-five-yard free kick and then, from another of my free kicks, Southampton headed in an own goal. I also set up our equalising goal and it finished 3–3. Afterwards, Bryan Robson said I had been fantastic, that it had been the best game I had played for Boro so far.

In early December we met Newcastle at home. I'd been seeing Shel again, and we'd spent a weekend in a hotel in Glasgow. We were getting on well and, of course, the fact that I was staying sober helped enormously. Mason and Regan were mascots for that game. Regan was about two at the time. He wore a number 8 shirt with 'Regan' on the back and scored a goal when we were warming up (Middlesbrough goalie Mark Schwarzer kindly moved aside to give him a helping hand). We got another draw, 2–2, but I had another good game and the papers were starting to speculate that Hoddle was thinking of bringing me back into the England squad.

For our next game, in which we beat West Ham 1–0, John Gorman turned up, which seemed a good sign. By Christmas, Boro were lying fourth in the league after an eleven-match unbeaten run, about the highest they'd ever been. I spent that Christmas at a Loch Lomond hotel with Shel and the children. I was beginning to think she might take me back again.

Middlesbrough had a poor run in January and February, getting stuffed 5–0 by Everton only a couple of months after we'd beaten Man United at Old Trafford. But I was still sober, and so was Jimmy. He'd come off the booze as well and had lost four stone. We looked everywhere for it. He was now so gorgeous and attractive that the *Daily Star* fixed him up with a Star Bird for the weekend. She was a stunner, though no more gorgeous than Jimmy.

In February 1999, Kevin Keegan took over as England manager, initially just for four games. Everyone said that was good news for me, that I would be back in the squad. I had played with Kevin years back at Newcastle, but I knew that would not make any difference, or make him fancy me more. Still, I was quietly hopeful. Especially as Keegan was saying publicly that he was having trouble finding a creative midfield player apart from me. And the team wasn't doing so well, either.

Boro improved towards the end of the season and we finished ninth in the league, which was pretty good, considering we had only come up that season and there had been talk at one time of relegation. I made twenty-six league appearances and scored three goals, which wasn't bad, given that I'd had a few injuries as well as a spell in the Priory.

As the end of the season approached, I started drinking again. I stuck to soft drinks when I was out in public but at home on my own I was drinking vodka, which I hoped no one would smell on my breath. I had been taking antidepressants and other pills to calm me down, but they were beginning to make me feel worse, not better, and I thought maybe a quiet drink of vodka would help.

The relationship with Shel was all off again so in the summer I went off with Jimmy and some other pals to Portugal, which was not exactly the best way of staying off the booze. But it was summer, it was holiday time, and I had managed to stay completely sober for nine long months, which showed I could do it.

In August, in London, I met up with Hugh Grant, Liz Hurley and Liam Gallagher and various other stars at a film premiere, and that led to a few drinks. I did have several nights on the binge, which upset Bryan Robson when it made the press. And it didn't impress Kevin Keegan, either. Then yet another kiss-and-tell story appeared. Some Newcastle waitress gave me 11 out of 10 for my performance in bed, which was much better than Ruud Gullit's, apparently. She gave him only 7 out of 10. It was mostly bollocks, but of course all the papers started hounding me again, to see what I was up to and find out if I was seeing any girls.

The new season started well enough, for me anyway, but poor Jimmy got into some bother. Like me, he'd been off the booze for over six months, but one evening he fell out with his girlfriend and had six pints. On the way home, these kids started shouting 'fat bastard' at him, and it really upset him. He went home, got his gun and ran at them with it, just to frighten them. It wasn't even loaded. Next thing he knows, there's a helicopter overhead and the police are looking for this mad gunman running wild. Jimmy legged it, throwing the gun in a hedge. When they cordoned off the area and caught him, he showed them where the gun was.

He went to the magistrates' court and it was chaos. About thirty press and TV people turned up. Then he had to go to the crown court. We had lots of character witnesses lined up for him, including Chris Evans. In spite of their support, he was sentenced to six months for threatening behaviour and possessing a firearm without a licence. I helped with his legal costs and he appealed and got his sentence reduced to three months. He spent eight weeks in Pentonville Prison. He says he made some good mates inside, who knew all about him, but no, he wouldn't like to go through it again.

The next thing was Shel deciding to tell her story in the *Sun*, all about how I beat her up, threw things at her in Italy, tried to control her. 'I know people think I stayed with Paul because of the money,' she wrote.

'But I can honestly say I kept trying to make it work because I loved him and because I thought I could be the woman who would save him.' She also said I didn't like myself and would probably never be happy. That might be true.

But I was furious about all the personal details she was revealing about me. I would never have done that to her. We had divorced, and I had given her a fortune, and was still paying her a fortune, but even so I was trying to see her at regular intervals, for Regan's sake. I didn't want him harmed by all this, and I didn't want Bianca and Mason to read all this private stuff about me and Shel. Even if they didn't, I knew what would happen at school when the other kids read it.

She wasn't doing it for personal gain. All the money was going to Refuge, the organisation to help battered women. That was all very well, but I was still extremely upset. I got my lawyers to try to stop the rest of the serialisation. At one point she was also planning to be interviewed on TV by Martin Bashir, who did that notorious interview with Princess Diana. The judge agreed that she had to stop revealing details in the *Sun* of my personal relationships with her and her children. They did print more, but with some paragraphs blanked out.

No wonder I was tempted to have a drink or three, with all that going on. And no wonder I wasn't playing so well. And taking more antidepressants. Once again, I had to put up with rival fans shouting at me, 'Gazza beats his wife.' I was tempted to pack it all in and emigrate to the USA, get away from everything. Forget Shel and the family for ever.

But I knew that football was my only hope, so I had to keep going. I was doing well enough, in patches, for Fulham to come in and make an offer for me, to help their bid for promotion to the Premiership just as I had helped Boro.

Before our home game in February 2000 against Aston Villa, which Kevin Keegan was coming to watch, Villa's George Boateng was quoted as saying he was going to mark me out of the match. I knew this was just the papers stirring things, to wind me up. Towards half-time, I was in a tussle with Boateng near the centre circle, and I flung out my arm at him, hitting him on the head. I apologised, as of course I hadn't meant to actually injure him. But I was just over-eager after two months out and what I'd done, once again, was hurt myself. I felt my arm go and feared I'd broken it. I was stretchered off and went to hospital for tests.

They gave me oxygen in the ambulance, I was in such a state. I remember counting the bumps in the road. At the hospital, one of the nurses looking after me chatted to me about how she was fundraising for this hospice. I thought that was amazing, helping sick people in her work time, and in her spare time as well. I somehow managed to get my Boro shirt off my back, despite my damaged arm, and signed it for her, to be auctioned for the hospice.

From the hospital, I got a call through to Paul Merson. I worked out that he would probably be on the Villa coach by that time, and so he was. After he'd asked me how I was, I said it was George Boateng I wanted to talk to. I apologised again to George for what I'd done, explaining that I hadn't wanted to hurt him, and that anyway it had been my arm that had caught him, not my elbow. He told me not to worry. He understood. It had been an accident, and I'd come off worst.

After a lot of tests, I was allowed home. But all night I was in agony. I just lay there in my big, rented house, and in the middle of the night I was in such pain that I dialled 999 and asked for an ambulance to come and take me back to hospital. They said they didn't have any. I dialled 999 again and asked for the police this time, begging them to take me to hospital. They said it wasn't their job, I should get a taxi. But there were no taxis available locally at that time of night. In the end I just took a load of painkillers and suffered all night.

Next morning when I went into the club, Gordon McQueen asked me how I was. I said fine – apart from a broken arm.

It was broken, too. I had to have an operation to have a pin put in and I was out for over six weeks.

Idiots in the papers who knew nothing about football, or me, like David Mellor, slagged me off, taking the opportunity to lay into what they considered an easy target. It's not brilliant journalism to do that to people when they're down. We can all do that. I was much more upset when several players were quoted as saying it was one of the worst fouls they had seen, even Gary Mabbutt, whom I'd always thought of as such a fair person. More than that, he was a friend, and I'd done a lot for his testimonial. But I know exactly how it happens. A reporter rings you up and asks a slanted question, and you grunt some sort of reply, or even just half-listen while they grind on. If you don't clearly disagree, you immediately have words put into your mouth that you never actually said.

But the worst consequence was the fact that I was hauled up before the FA, given a three-match suspension for misconduct and fined £5,000.

After a few weeks with the plaster on, I couldn't stand it any longer and I took it off myself, with a bread knife in the kitchen. I made such a thorough job of it that I also took off some of my skin, and had to have stitches.

When I got back to full training, it wasn't long before I collided with Curtis Fleming and thought I'd broken something again. I went to hospital for an X-ray, but this time all was OK. Phew. All the same, my season ended in a bit of a mess, as I'd missed so much, what with the broken arm and all the aggravation and legal worries over Shel's outpourings in the *Sun*.

In spite of the *Sun* business, in the close season, I took Shel and all three children to Dubai for a holiday. How could I do that, after what she had done to me? Yeah, it made my advisers despair. I just so wanted to have a happy family, and I was desperate to keep in touch with Regan. And I never like being on my own, especially on holiday.

You tell me where you can find any really adventurous midfield players who can change a game in a moment or make a goal out of nothing? After Gazza, it is difficult to come up with another name.
Kevin Keegan, England manager, The Sunday Times, 13 June 1999

I was sorry to see Gazza go. He is probably the kindest man I've ever met in football. I had a golf day and he gave me his putter to auction, which he'd had since he was in the 1990 World Cup squad. Everton won't change him – he'll do things that will wind them up, but deep down there's a heart of gold.
Robbie Mustoe, Middlesbrough player, 2000

25

EVERTON AND ARIZONA

My time at Boro wasn't wasted. I got to meet Tony Blair when he came to open the club's new training ground. We all had to be there at a certain time to meet him. I was put to work on the treadmill, ready for his arrival, so he could see how it worked.

He was late and I'd been on this treadmill for fucking hours, so when he eventually turned up, I said to him, 'Where have you been, Tony? I'm knackered.'

'Sorry, Paul,' he replied. He seemed a nice enough bloke.

I was also contacted by Elton John, when I was at a low ebb after I'd come out of the Priory. He rang to offer me one of his houses to stay in. He said he would make sure it was kept secret and I would be looked after, away from everyone. I could stay till I felt better. I didn't take up his offer because it didn't fit in with my plans at the time – I just wanted to get back to playing football as quickly as possible – but it was very good of him.

I'd first met Elton at Watford when I was seventeen, and playing in Newcastle's youth team, and he was chairman of Watford. We beat them in the Youth Cup final and I was lying in the bath with the lads, holding up the cup. Elton came in to congratulate us on our win. I shouted out, 'Elton, Elton, give us a song,' but he didn't. I ran into him some years later, at a charity do, and he seemed another nice bloke.

But overall, my memories of Boro are not very good, I'm afraid, because they are tarnished by all the injuries and drinking, drinking and injuries – the two demons that have dogged me throughout my life.

I began to realise that I needed a fresh start. It looked, anyway, as though Boro were keen to release me from my contract. There were reports of offers coming in from Australia and other exciting places. I could have stayed, held them to my contract, which had another year to run, so they would have been forced to pay me up to another million or buy me out of it. But I've never been motivated by money – except when I've needed it to pay Shel's maintenance. I just wanted to play football, at the top if possible. I was determined to stay in England and in the Premiership if I could. Boro were very good in the end. We did a deal and they agreed I could leave on a free transfer, if I found a club I wanted to go to.

Bryan Robson was having a tough time with his critics who believed the players were allowed to be too free and easy in the dressing room. Perhaps that was my fault. He had been so good and kind to me during all my problems, knocking himself out for me, bending over backwards to help, that maybe some of the others saw this and tried it on, and he didn't quite get the respect he deserved. Perhaps he was too young for the job, having only recently ceased to be one of the lads in the dressing room himself. Perhaps he didn't have enough experience at the time for such a big job. But as far as I was concerned, he was an excellent manager.

I went to Henlow Grange health farm and got myself really fit, and then I made contact with Walter Smith, who was now at Everton, along with Archie Knox.

It was clear Everton could do with some experience in their midfield. John Collins and Don Hutchison had gone, and they were about to lose Nick Barmby to Liverpool, which, of course, upset all their supporters. I thought I could do a good job for them, but it was quite possible Walter might not want me again, after some of the things that happened at Rangers. On the other hand, I'd played some of my best-ever football there under Walter and Archie.

'Please, Walter,' I said to him over the phone. 'Will you help me? Take me back?' I told him I needed to sort myself out, get back on the road again, but I was fit and wouldn't let him down, honest, honest.

I could sense him and Archie at the other end, shaking their heads, saying, 'No, not him again.' I respected both of them so much. I was promising to be good, and meaning it, partly because I was scared of them – they are both very hard men – but also because it was what I wanted.

I have always tended to lose a bit of spark after two seasons or so at a new club. I don't think it's ever been down to a lack of motivation, or not trying. I've always tried hard, in every game. Too hard, very often, which is why I get injured or booked. I put it down mainly to the long lay-offs because of injuries. Walter and Archie knew I had done it for them at Rangers, winning four medals in three years, and they believed – or hoped – I could do it again.

They gave me the biggest grilling I'd ever had. It went on for hours while they checked everything and spoke to other people. Eventually they agreed, provided I passed the medical. So I had the medical, but there was something wrong with one of the test results. Something had shown up. They wanted to sack me there and then, before I'd even begun. I explained to them that I'd just taken a few sleepers, and told them about Davey's death, and how it had affected me. I hadn't been able to sleep, so I was on strong sleeping pills. They believed me and I was given a two-week trial to prove myself, to show I was fit and right in the head. Then I signed for two years. Because I was on a free transfer, Everton didn't have to pay for me. My basic wage was to be £12,000 a week and £5,000 appearance money.

I saw playing for Everton for two years as a perfect way to finish my career in England. To end it at the top, aged thirty-five, still playing in the Premier League: that was what I wanted. I wasn't thinking any further ahead than that. Perhaps afterwards I might go abroad

– I didn't know. I just wanted to concentrate on giving my all for Everton.

I deliberately chose to live in an out-of-town hotel, in Woolton, so I wouldn't get mixed up with any boozers or have too heavy a social life. Or have the press following me round all the time, waiting for an eruption. I was having the odd drink, but not getting drunk.

I know I have only myself to blame for a lot of the attention I have attracted, but it was starting to get me down. But for ten years they had been looking out for me, ignoring other players out on the town. Punters with £1.99 disposable cameras would snap me with a beer or a kebab, and make themselves a fortune. And on the pitch it was turning into the same story. I would get picked on if I wasn't playing well, and blamed by the press when the rest of the team wasn't playing well, either, or even worse than I was.

It was about this time that I fell out with Mel and Len, who had been my advisers for many years. I decided they were proving too expensive. What brought it to a head was a small thing, a mobile phone. I wanted my phone changed, because too many reporters had got hold of my number, so I asked for a new one – a pretty simple thing, you'd have thought. I didn't actually realise how much it had cost me for some time, till I happened to be looking at a list of old expenses and charges. Getting another mobile had cost me several hundred pounds. I couldn't believe it. I was told that somebody had had to wait for four hours for the new number to come through. Perhaps that was how they worked out the cost, by the hour. Whatever, I felt enough was enough.

I also hadn't realised just how much money was being made out of my transfer to Lazio that I didn't know about.

According to documents I have now got, at least £300,000 was paid to my advisers and their various firms and companies during the period of the Lazio transfer. Personally, I think they would have been extremely well paid if they'd got around a third of that.

The 2000–01 season started very well for me at Everton. I scored a spectacular half-volley goal in a pre-season game against Plymouth Argyle. In the next friendly, against Tranmere Rovers, I lost my temper, so we won't go into that.

My league debut for the club came in an away match at Leeds on 19 August. I started on the bench, coming on for the last sixteen minutes or so. We lost 2–0. But the next game, at home to Charlton, I was on from the beginning and we beat them 3–0. It turned out to be Everton's biggest win that season. I played well and made a goal for Franny Jeffers. Walter said afterwards that he was very pleased with me. There was even talk of Kevin Keegan having another look at me.

I wasn't quite back to full fitness, but I felt I was getting better all the time. I knew I was likely to be a sub, or be subbed, a lot. Walter had given me number 18, not my usual number 8, so that was a clue to his thinking.

We were due to play Boro, away, on 9 September and I sent Bryan a text message saying: 'I'm coming to get you. Love Gazza.' I bore him no grudge for letting me go. I would have done the same if I'd been the manager. I played for all ninety minutes. We won 2–1 and I set up the winner for Jeffers.

I was on the pitch for the whole game away to Leicester, too, and had a good tussle in midfield with Robbie Savage. We drew 1–1 and I was Man of the Match, turning in my best performance so far for Everton. I lasted for the full ninety minutes for the next five or six games. At Newcastle, where we won 1–0, I was applauded off the pitch by the Newcastle fans.

And then I got a succession of niggling injuries and

everything seemed to go wrong. I was depressed about not being able to play, and the team started doing badly as well, failing to win seven league games in a row in December and January. I began to get terrible headaches. I was scared that my brain was going, that I was going to have a breakdown. Once again I had a brain scan; once again it showed nothing untoward. And of course, that old vicious circle was cranking up: the more depressed I became, the more I started to drink. When I've been injured, I've tended to keep myself to myself. You are out of things anyway, the club seems to forget you, carrying on without you. I didn't really want to be visited anyway, people trying to cheer you up. But of course keeping yourself to yourself, and without a wife and family to support you, or put up with you, you get more and more depressed. Football is all I know, all I've ever known, so being out of it was utter misery. I drank to pass the time, to make the days go quickly. That was the point of drinking.

In that game against Leicester, they brought on Stan Collymore. He didn't really look interested and got some stick afterwards, but I felt sorry for him. It seemed to me he was a genuine depressive, a condition most people can't understand. They think that people like

Stan, and me, I suppose, say we are depressed as some kind of excuse. I've been down there, I know what's it like. It's an illness. You do think the whole world is against you, that life isn't worth it. I like to think that I also have a sunny side, that I am willing and able to get on with things, pick myself up, get focused again. Often I can do that. But I can usually only concentrate on one thing at a time. So when I have a worry, a problem, that's all I can think about. I can't take in anything else. But when I am doing something positive, like training, getting fit or, above all, playing football, I can focus on that and my depression recedes into the background. It's off the pitch, when I'm alone, with only something bad like an injury to worry about, that I get really low.

I had more hernia trouble and was out for about two months. During that time there was more about me in the papers beating up Shel. No, this was no new outburst – she was helping to launch some police campaign against domestic violence, and they trotted out the same old stuff. It was in a good cause, I suppose, but it all ended up concentrating on me. That was all people took in, not the reason for the campaign. So all the headlines were about Gazza the Wife-Beater. '"I beat you up because I love you so much," Gazza told Sheryl.'

It was so depressing. It had all happened five years before, and I was a different person now, or so I hoped. Life had moved on. It seemed I was destined to be convicted over and over again for the same offence, when I'd already admitted my guilt, paid the penalties and lost my wife and family, not to mention a huge amount of money. No wonder Bianca and Mason didn't think much of me, having to put up with all that again.

I was drinking a lot while I was on the injury list, so I wasn't all that fit when I got back. Then there was another upset: the death of David Rocastle, who had lost his fight against cancer. He was my age, my generation. I'd played alongside him in the England Under-21s and probably did him out of his place in the 1990 World Cup. He was gone, yet I was still alive and going strong, in theory, anyway; still playing in the Premiership at thirty-three. It certainly put things into perspective, and made me wonder why I was moaning so much.

But of course that feeling of being grateful for what I'd got didn't last long, and the depression soon took hold of me again. And so did the drinking. Walter called me into his office and read me the riot act, saying I was getting out of control. I promised, as always, to stop.

I was driving all my friends mad. I was desperate

for their help, but at the same time I would turn on them, accusing them of all sorts. I'd send text messages all day long to Shel, and blamed Mel for all my troubles, which were not his fault at all.

At Everton, the players didn't go out and socialise in the same way as they had at Boro. Most of the lads were genuinely scared of Walter and Archie and didn't dare break any of the rules or curfews. So the last thing they wanted was a night out on the town with me. I became aware that a lot of them were beginning to steer clear of me.

I was very lonely in my hotel on my own. One night I picked up a total stranger and invited him to come out and have a meal with me. He agreed and was very nice. The evening ended with me slumped over a table. He was a good bloke. Evidently he was the soul of discretion, because the incident never appeared in any of the papers. Instead of rushing off and telling tales, he rang the club and got hold of someone who arranged for a taxi to come and pick me up.

I would have one drink, to make up for my miserable life, when I was injured and couldn't play, feeling sorry for myself. Then immediately I needed another to reinforce the effect.

One night I fell over, drunk, and hurt myself. Somehow I developed an infection. I woke up in the night with a huge lump on my leg filled with blood. That meant another trip to hospital, another operation, another set of lies given out to present the problem as a training injury.

I missed Regan's fifth birthday party. I meant to go, but I didn't make it. There was no real reason, so I felt a right sod. I sent a card and £500. Pathetic, really. I still feel ashamed about that.

Bill Kenwright, the chairman of Everton, was brilliant, just as good as Walter. He listened to me moaning on for hours and tried so hard to help me, or at least accommodate me.

Towards the end of the season, Walter began to insist I went into a clinic. I was hoping my latest injury would clear up soon and I would get some games in before the season was over. I had managed only fourteen games so far. I said, 'Please, please – anything but that. A month out of football, while the season is still going on, will destroy me. The only thing that makes my life worth living is football. I can't do it.' I put it off for a while, then they gave me an ultimatum.

'If you respect me,' said Walter, 'you will go to the

clinic. If not, we'll shake hands now and you can walk away from Everton.'

While I was mulling that over, Archie chipped in. 'Surely, Gazza, you want to fight. You can beat twenty-eight days, can't you?'

'You bastards,' I said, and walked out of the room, returning almost immediately. 'OK, you've won – I'll do the clinic.'

I didn't want to go back into the Priory, as it hadn't done me much good last time. I'd heard about this place in Arizona, Cottonwood, so I booked in there.

I talked to Shel and she said she'd help me through it. She said if I got through the treatment successfully, she'd consider taking me back, so that was another incentive.

I went for my twenty-eight days in Arizona in June 2001. I had to pay for it myself, with the help of an advance on my wages from Everton. I still had some money saved from my signing-on fee, but altogether it cost me £21,000. After that month spent in the middle of the desert, miles from anywhere, I arranged for Shel and the kids to travel to Florida and join me for a holiday. I was calm and sober and enjoyed playing with the kids, but even though I wasn't drinking, Shel and I still argued quite a bit. Cottonwood was stricter than the Priory, and I took it more seriously. I suppose it did help me a bit more, but I was too busy helping others to really help myself. I just went round talking to other people. They didn't know me, I wasn't a name to any of the Americans there, so I could just be myself. And, as you know, I'm a lovely fella, always willing to help others.

The fact that I argued with Shel so soon afterwards shows it hadn't really worked. One of the things I got upset about was that I stupidly got it into my head she had been seeing another guy. I was still angry when I came out – angry because I'd had to go there in the first place. And also angry because I got angry. I divvent know why.

We returned to Shel's place in Hertfordshire, and I drove myself back up north from there in Shel's car, a Jaguar which I'd bought for her. I fell asleep at the wheel. I was still tired after the long journey back from Arizona, and I careered into the side of a lorry and went off the road. The lorry was hardly scratched, but Shel's car was really smashed up. The lorry driver came over to see if I was OK and recognised me. 'Been drinking, have you, Gazza?'

'Fuck off,' I said. 'I've just been in a fucking clinic.'

I stayed sober for about nine months after that, and

got the fittest I'd been for years. Once again, the season started well enough for me. I got my first Everton goal, away to Bolton, in November 2001, and was playing well – and then it started all over again. My hernia came back. I could feel the pain, so I rested it for two weeks, but it wasn't enough. It went again. I had another op and was out for a month. Then I ripped a muscle, trying as always to come back too soon, and had to have eighteen stitches. In all I had three ops in three months. I was really miserable. I managed to keep off the booze but I was back on sleeping pills. Then Maureen died – Maureen the mother of my childhood friend Keith Spraggon and little Steven, the boy I'd seen run over all those years ago. I'd remained very close her, so that affected me badly.

In January 2002, before a home game against Sunderland, all my Sunderland friends were telling me that Gavin McCann was going to get the better of me. He would really play me out of the match, they said. I didn't sleep the night before. Nothing unusual there – except that I decided to take eleven sleeping tablets to get me off. And then I drank two bottles of wine.

Next day, just before kick-off, I had a double brandy. We won 1–0 and I was voted Man of the Match. I had, of course, been off the booze for about six months before that, so probably my body was in good enough shape to take it at that stage.

In March we were beaten by Boro in the sixth round of the FA Cup. None of us distinguished ourselves, including me. It turned out to be my last game for Everton. It was also that defeat that finished off Walter.

Walter had done his best for Everton, and I had done my best to help him. My injuries had buggered everything up, and then the drinking made it worse, so I was never able to contribute as much as I would have liked, or as much as I felt capable of.

David Moyes took over as manager, stepping up from First Division Preston North End. He was another Scotsman, and I've always got on well with them. However . . . he didn't say he wanted me to leave, but I could see the writing on the wall. Besides, with Walter gone, I felt it was time to move on again.

> Good for Gazza, but not quite good enough. Paul
> Gascoigne, that immensely talented maverick, not
> only started the game but finished it in style, doing
> an abundance of skilled, original, intelligent things.
> *Brian Glanville, on the Blackburn–Everton game,*
> The Sunday Times, *23 September 2001*

26

RECOVERY

A LOST YEAR

After I left Everton, I got myself a new agent, Ian Elliott, and he fixed me up with Burnley.

It was a bit of a culture shock, joining a club struggling in a lower division. I had played in the First Division before, during that first season at Boro, till we got promoted, but Boro were really a Premiership club, in terms of wealth and facilities. Apart from that year, I had spent sixteen of my seventeen years as a professional, since making it into Newcastle's first team in 1985, playing in the top league with a top club.

After my first proper training session, I saw that my dirty kit was still lying around in the dressing room.

I asked this apprentice to take it away to wherever it got cleaned. In seventeen years, I had never thought twice about where it went. It had always been dealt with automatically.

'It'll cost you,' he replied.

'You what?' I said.

It turned out you had to pay an apprentice to clean your stuff, or else do it yourself. The club didn't do it for you. This lad charged me £5 a week to clean my boots and £20 a month for my kit.

One day I arrived for training and there was no kit laid out for me. I sat there for a while, waiting for my clean stuff, before I got hold of the lad. He said he was sorry, his washing machine at home had broken down. I had to borrow someone's old kit to train in.

The deal with Stan Ternent, the manager, was that he would use me when necessary in vital games, bringing me on to change things if the team were getting nowhere. My basic wage was £5,000 a week, quite a drop from Everton's £12,000, but I was also on £5,000 a game appearance money and a big bonus if Burnley reached the play-offs and got into the Premiership. I was also promised a share of the gate money, if it went up, and a percentage on the sale of all shirts with my name on them.

There was one week when I had just got over an injury and wanted to rest, so Stan said fine, go off and have a break, and I went off to Dubai for a few days. When I got back, Stan said there was no need to train, as I would be jet-lagged. Come Saturday, he didn't pick me. 'What's the problem?' I said. 'I'm fit.'

'Ah, but you haven't trained.'

I stayed in a hotel during all my time at Burnley – I was only there about two months and made only six appearances. My last was as a sub, coming on for the final ten minutes against Coventry. We had to get at least as good a result as Norwich did to get in the play-offs as we went into the last game level on points and goal difference, though we'd scored more goals. We won 1–0 but just missed out on the final play-off spot as Norwich beat Stockport 2–0. I had two free kicks, which went near, but we didn't make it, and that was it.

I didn't really enjoy my football at Burnley. I found the First Division very tough. The lads were fine; it wasn't them, it was me. Their sort of football wasn't my style. It was all kick and rush. Perhaps I'd lost a bit of the necessary pace for it, but whatever the case, I wasn't comfortable with it.

Gates had shot up by about 6,000 when I played,

so my presence did give them a boost. And they sold hundreds of extra shirts. I remember standing in the chairman's office and signing 150 of them. Yet later, when I got the figures, they said only seventy had been sold all season. Funny, that.

The rest of that year, 2002, is a bit of a blur, even though it wasn't that long ago. I was depressed, as ever, about the usual things: about not playing football, about my stupid behaviour, about all my worries and obsessions, but also about not seeing Regan. I'd always put football and drinking before my family, which was wrong. By this time, Shel had washed her hands of me yet again. I was getting more and more blackouts with the drinking and desperate to find more ways to numb my misery. I experimented with a line of coke, just the once. It did give me a high, but afterwards I was left even more down.

I went back to the north-east, where I was living in hotels or rented flats, which didn't help. I took more cocaine. So that made it twice I used it. Except the second time I took it for three weeks, solidly, every day. I didn't pay for it. It was given to me by someone – not someone in the north-east.

Ian Elliott fixed me up with a trial in the USA with

Washington DC. I knew it had been a bad move to take cocaine, and that it would show up in the blood tests, so I drank water for ten days to try to disguise it before going out to the US.

But all Washington DC offered me was $1,500 a week, which was a disgrace. I couldn't afford to accept that, even if I'd wanted to. Not only would I have had to live in a hotel in Washington, but there was the small matter of the £10,000 a month I had to give Sheryl. I would have been paying out far more than I was earning, so it was impossible.

I might have got the order of events wrong here. Perhaps it was after the US trip that I spent those three weeks on cocaine. I was in such a state that I can't remember all this clearly. My dad suspected I was taking the stuff. He asked Jimmy about it, and Jimmy confirmed his suspicions. My dad gave me a right bollocking. He said he couldn't believe I'd been so stupid.

It began to frighten me, and I became really paranoid. I had another head scan, in September, I think. I was down to eleven stone by then, the lightest I'd ever been as a grown-up. If I actually was a grown-up. You wouldn't have said so if you had seen me fighting with my own brother. Both Carl and I were drunk, and had some argument over our family. We both ended up having to go to hospital with cuts and bruises. We weren't angry with each other for long: the next day, we were laughing about it.

During one of these hospital visits, the cocaine showed up in my bloodstream. I thought, fucking hell, this could ruin my football career for ever, if it gets out. So I stopped, just like that. Luckily, I hadn't been using it for long, and I hadn't got hooked. I don't know why I tried it. I suppose because I'd tried almost everything else in life. I thought I'd see what it was like. Until then, I'd never seen anyone taking cocaine. I'd mixed with showbiz celebs, but they hadn't been on it, as far as I knew. Nor had any players. There had been rumours about Paul Merson, about a couple of years previously, but I didn't know if they were true or not. So you can't say it was because of the circles I'd moved in. It wasn't until this person came along and offered it to me.

For a while, I had fallen out of love with football. I couldn't watch or go to a match – not that I've ever really been able to do that anyway, not when I wasn't playing. It was thinking about Alan Shearer that brought me back to football; thinking of how he had organised his life. My dad gave me a kick up the backside, too.

'Do fucking something!' he shouted at me one day when I went to see him.

I felt I needed a helping hand from someone I knew well. So I parted company with my latest agent, Ian Elliott, and asked Dave McCreery if he'd work with me. I'd played with Dave at Newcastle, and he had always been a good friend to me, on and off the pitch.

I wanted to start training again. I thought, I'll show them I'm not finished. At thirty-five, I realised I couldn't give up football just like that. From the age of five, it had been all I had known, all I could do. What would I do with myself? Football had been my saviour, and without it, I'd probably just collapse, unless something else that challenged me in the same way came along, which looked unlikely. I was aware that I wasn't the player I had once been, and wouldn't be again, but I couldn't suddenly turn it off, bring it to an end, while I still had plenty left to give.

I was living in a hotel near Morpeth, and Dave arranged for me to train up there under Steve Black, the fitness coach to the Newcastle Falcons Rugby Club. I was banging on the gym door at five in the morning, trying to get in and start my training and exercises. In six weeks, I got myself really fit, thanks to Blacky. Offers began to come in from all sorts of places – the USA, Russia and Malta, as well as some English First Division clubs.

I was training like buggery. After the gym work, I'd do an eight-mile run and feel absolutely knackered. I trained so hard it was painful, made me ill. Stupid, I know. It led to the panic attacks starting again. But I have so much energy I sometimes imagine I'm going to burst. I have to let off steam somehow, otherwise I feel I will explode.

When the panic attacks returned, I began having a few drinks again, though nothing mad, and I did a few daft things, such as me arms. I now have these two tattoos. On my left arm is a panther and on the right one I've got 'Gazza' in a sort of Celtic script. I hope it's not something that's going to insult the Bhoys again. It's all right, I'm only joking. I've learned my lesson. Last time I teased Celtic Football Club, I got a death threat.

As well as the panic, all my old obsessions came back again. My face started twitching down one side. It was in spasm all the time – I couldn't control it. I kept asking myself why I was worrying when I had nothing to worry about. I was getting offers from various clubs, so I was confident that my career wasn't quite over. Why had I had those tattoos? Why did I do all these stupid things? Why did I train so hard and make myself ill when I was back to full fitness already? People were saying to me, 'You look so well!' because I was so thin, but I didn't feel well. I felt terrible. I was sleeping no more than three hours a night and going for walks in the early hours, trying to shake off my anxieties.

Then one morning I woke up with my face in spasm and I could feel a tingle down my arm as well. I thought, fuck it, I'm having a seizure. My dad had been about the same age as I was now when he'd had that seizure and then his haemorrhage. I went to the Queen Elizabeth in Gateshead, my original home from home, where my endless run of operations had begun. At first it looked as if I might have had a stroke. My dad tried to reassure me, reminding me that when he'd had his blood clot he'd been given only a fifty-fifty chance of survival. 'And now look at me.'

In the end, the doctors couldn't find anything physically wrong with me. They didn't seem to know what was causing the spasms. Probably, they said, I was suffering from stress as a result of doing too much training. When I came out I had a few drinks – and immediately my arm felt better.

Nevertheless, I knew I wasn't right. Even at really brilliant times in my life, there have always been bad thoughts going round and round my head. I can't escape them, so I start crying or screaming. I seem to be saddest when I'm happiest. I didn't understand it. I went off and checked myself into the Priory. Not for alcohol problems this time, for head problems. I only stayed there a few days.

Therapists and counsellors and people like that are like anybody else. After all, you get good footballers and bad footballers, good bricklayers and bad bricklayers, good book writers and bad book writers. I've now met a lot of therapists in my life and some of them don't seem to care. They just stare out of the window and say nothing, waiting for the next patient.

But that, of course, is negative thinking, and I've been told often enough that all of life is good and bad, and I must stop dwelling on the negative things in my mind and wanting to smash up the place and instead concentrate on the positive, good things. It's easier said than done.

I think the year 2002 must have been one of the worst of my life. It's a period I don't really like looking back on now.

I came back from the Priory and returned to my training schedule, fixated on getting as fit as possible, doing twice as much as I needed, all day, round the clock. I was determined to have at least one more year playing for some club, somewhere.

I felt I would prefer to go abroad, make a fresh start. After all, there was nothing much to keep me in England. There seemed no future in my relationship with Shel. I also thought that, by going abroad, anywhere, I could remove myself from the spotlight a bit. I wouldn't be quite as famous – or notorious. I could make mistakes, or learn new things, without my every move being followed.

I signed up with another new agent, a professional one, Wes Saunders, who was working with a well-known national football agency. He was based in Sunderland, his home town, which was handy. I had played with Wes at Newcastle when I was young and he had always been helpful to me. In fact, I used to clean his boots at one time.

So Wes got working on a deal to take me abroad, away from everything. What he came up with turned out to be a lot further abroad, and further away from everything, than I had expected.

Some people cry through pain but I don't think that's the case. I think Gascoigne was crying because he was in despair with himself. Many of his problems and his injuries have been self-induced. Gascoigne has cried regularly for years. That tells you something: that nobody in football has done anything about it. I find that incredible. If a snooker player or a golfer cried during a game, I think people in that sport may realise there was a problem. Gascoigne could have been helped a long time ago.

Dr Raj Persaud, psychiatrist, Daily Mail,
16 February 2000

27

CHINA AND BACK TO ARIZONA

At the end of 2002, I flew out to China. It wasn't my first visit. I had been there, you'll remember, before Euro 96 with England, when we had a warm-up game in Beijing. I scored in that game and was Man of the Match. 'He comes, he sees, he conquers' was one of the headlines. All bollocks, of course.

This time I was to have a two-week trial with a First Division club – the name escapes me now – to see if I liked them and they liked me. Wes came with me. I hated it at first, especially the food. We had duck's head, duck's eyes, chicken feet, and a lot of bat. I didn't realise it was bat to begin with. It was not bad, as it happens.

When I turned up for training on the first day I was greeted by a lot of reporters and photographers, Chinese and British. I'd been filmed stepping off the plane and appeared on the main Chinese news. People were following me in the streets. The press all said that Gazza looked unfit, Gazza was knackered, which was true enough. I'd been travelling for about three days without sleep.

I was soon feeling bored and restless. When I wasn't training, there was nothing to do except hang around all day. I couldn't speak the language and none of the hotel staff could speak English. When I wanted more water, I had to point at the fridge and try to indicate it was water I was after, but couldn't make myself understood. It was like being locked in a cave. China is eight hours ahead of England, so whenever I rang home I always seemed to wake up my friends and they'd say 'Piss off, why are you waking me up?'

Out walking, I came across this video shop run by a woman who spoke brilliant English, really good. She said yes, they had a James Bond film, so I bought it, took it back to my room and put it on. Fucking hell, it was in Chinese. James Bond speaking Chinese.

From what I saw of it, China was very beautiful,

very colourful. It wasn't like I imagined it would be, what you'd expect of a grey, boring, dull communist place. That was the image I'd had from what I'd seen on the telly. But there were so many poor people, kids running around in bare feet. I looked at them all and wondered why I was worrying about my trivial problems. I could be living here, like them. And then I thought, yeah, perhaps it wouldn't be so bad. If I could earn myself £5 a week here, I would manage.

I trained hard, because I was on trial, proving my fitness. It was 86 degrees and I was doing laps for an hour with Wes timing me. Every time I went past him I asked 'How long?' and he'd say 'Fifty-seven minutes to go.'

'Fucking hell, stop messing around.'

At team meetings, they had to translate everything for me. So the manager would start talking, then stop and turn to me, while someone repeated what he'd said in English. Then he'd be off again, in Chinese, while the bloke was still translating. I sat there thinking, what am I missing? What's he on about now?

I was reaching the stage where I was getting really wound up, wanting nothing more than just to go home. Then we had a proper practice match and, suddenly, everything seemed to click into place. I felt really good, scored three goals and made some others. My fitness was OK.

I knuckled down to the training, but I was still lonely when I went back to the hotel. At a loose end one day, I noticed a pool at the front of the hotel, an ornamental thing with koi carp in it. I said to Wes, 'Let's go fishing.'

'Don't be daft. You've no rod, no tackle.'

'Just you watch.'

I went to my hotel room and fetched that little packet of needles and thread that hotels provide for you and you never ever use. Not me, anyway. Why would I want to be doing any sewing?

I then got Wes to go outside and find a bamboo cane while I went off to a shop and bought a Jammy Dodger. Obviously, it wasn't an actual Jammy Dodger, but the nearest biscuit-type thing to a Jammy Dodger the Chinese have. I tied the thread to the bamboo cane, bent a needle at the end to make a hook, put a lump of Chinese Jammy Dodger at the end, and I was off to the pool to do some fishing. 'We'll be stopped,' said Wes. 'They'll send security.'

'Never you mind. Just look at this.'

I started fishing, and I caught one, I really did. I blew a kiss to the heavens and fell to me knees. It made my day. After that, China began to grow on me. It always takes me time to acclimatise. When I moved to Italy, I spent the first week crying in my hotel room. Then I loved it.

After the two weeks were up, the club said they were still not sure about me and asked me to stay on for another week. I said, 'Piss off. It's yes or no now, or yous can forget it.'

There happened to be another club, in the B League, the Chinese second division, who were also after me. They had been monitoring my progress at the First Division club, showing real interest. They were offering me the same money, but what really appealed to me was that they wanted to give me the chance to do some coaching.

First, though, I had to do three days' training with them. It was knackering. When I tried to have a rest, they kept on passing the ball to me. I said, 'Don't keep passing to me. What's happening?' Then I remembered. I was supposed to be becoming one of their new coaches. They were passing to me all the time so that I would show them what to do with the ball.

After the three days, they offered me a contract. Meanwhile, the first team came back and said they'd take me after all. I said, 'It's too late, I'm accepting another offer.' The British press gave the impression I'd been turned down by the first team, that I had somehow failed, but that wasn't the case. Wes and I agreed a deal for one year, and I came back to England to sort out various things. Then, in February 2003, I set off for China again, this time to start a new career as player and coach.

The club was called Gansu Tianma, and it was owned by a multimillionaire who lived in Hong Kong, so my first stop was there, to meet him. I flew out with me dad, Jimmy and Wes. We had three first-class tickets and one club class, so Jimmy had to take that. At the Marriott Hotel at Heathrow, where we stayed overnight after coming down from Newcastle to catch the plane to Hong Kong, I had a few glasses of wine, and a brandy, and a few ciggies, just to pass the time. But if I'm scared of flying, my dad is worse. He was in a right state.

An Italian barman from the hotel came across to speak to me in Italian. I replied in Italian. He turned out to be a Lazio fan. They're everywhere. He asked me to fill in the hotel's Guest Satisfaction Survey – giving him top marks, of course. So I filled it all in, both sides, even though he'd said he was going to frame it and stick it above his bar, so there wasn't much point in writing on the back. But I always complete things. It's part of the obsession I've got, having to have everything neat and tidy.

As my home address, I put China. It looked like a joke, but it wasn't really. I still didn't have a home. The survey asked for questions, so I wrote 'Do you take yuan?' It amused me, and kept me occupied till the plane took off.

I was really looking forward to getting to China after the Hong Kong meeting, and especially to getting away from the British press. I don't mind being followed in the street, people looking at me, Italian barmen coming up to talk to me – it's the lies and stupid tales in the papers that get me down.

The other week, for example, there was a piece headed 'Gazza wants to be a Girl', complete with a computer photo of me with boobs and a frock. God knows where they got that from, or why. Just stupid. There was another which really hurt. It said I'd only got three friends left in the world. I like to think I'm respected by all the people I've met in football – and loved by a lot of them.

Lanzhou, the home of my new club, turned out to

be the most polluted town in China, in the heart of a heavy industrial area. A bit like Gateshead used to be, but not as nice.

I didn't mind that too much, as I spent all my time either at the training ground or the hotel, but it wasn't much fun for my dad and Jimmy. Still, I hadn't brought them with me to give them a treat. It was for my sake. I wanted Jimmy for company and me dad to keep an eye on me. If I got out of order, or started drinking or misbehaving, I knew he would sort me out. I take more notice of my dad than of anybody else, even after all these years.

Wes left after a few days, once he'd sorted out the contract and various sponsorship matters. My wages depended on me agreeing to support Gansu Tianma in various ways. The deal was worth roughly £400,000 for the year. Jimmy and me dad stayed on for a week or so longer, just to settle me in.

The manager of the club was thirty-eight, so not far off my own age, and he spoke some English. I liked him. The standard of play was about the level of the Second or Third Division in England, but their technique was good, and they regularly got gates of 25,000. They just needed organising.

I was fit enough and I enjoyed trying to coach some

of the young lads. I like helping people. In games, I make a point of telling people when they have played well, or what they should be doing, even those playing for the other side. What was more difficult was trying to combine my bit of coaching with playing. I found it harder to concentrate on my own game.

I would like to be a coach one day. I must have picked up a lot of useful experience over all those years. I'm sure I would be able to rely on Walter Smith or Terry Venables if I needed help or advice at any time. Even Fergie. I could ring him. And there can't be many dodges the players get up to that I don't know about. I've tried most of them myself.

Going to China was the biggest challenge of my life, in many ways. I had to get to grips with a new and very foreign language, a new culture, a new lifestyle. But I had gone out there determined to do it, and to learn from it all.

What I began to learn was that I couldn't escape from myself, even all those thousands of miles away. Stuck in my hotel room all the time, when Wes, Dad and Jimmy had gone home, I started to worry, wondering what I was doing here. I was missing Regan, my family, everyone. And I started drinking again.

The football itself was fine. I played four league games and got two goals and the fans loved me. But of course it wasn't long before I began to feel unwell, what with all the antidepressant pills and the drinking. I still wasn't right in the head.

The panic attacks returned, and sleepers didn't help. I was shaking and becoming paranoid. I rang Shel in tears. She suggested I called the therapist I'd been put in touch with by the Priory. He said hang on till May, which was when I was due to have a break, and he'd see me then. I managed to stay sober for ten days, but I still couldn't sleep and my breathing was terrible. I felt I just wanted to die.

I talked to the club, and they could see I wasn't well. They agreed that I should fly home, have a break and get treatment. Before I left, I had eight days on the booze. I knew it would be the last time for a long while that I'd get the chance.

I returned to London and then flew on to Arizona and checked myself into Cottonwood. This time I took it all much more seriously. I told them about everything, including the cocaine.

By the time I came out, the Sars virus had started in China, all their football games were off and the season was in chaos. Then I had a row with Gansu Tianma about my contract. As far as I am concerned, they still owe me money. What with one thing and another, in the end, I never went back.

It was while I was in Arizona that I started writing out my life chart, confessing everything awful I'd ever done or that had happened to me. And it did make me feel better, getting it all down.

I also admitted this time that I did have an illness, which I had to work on if I was going to get better. I had never properly acknowledged that before. I even found myself praying, something I'd never done.

I stayed the full period in the Arizona clinic. In fact, a few days longer – I was actually there for thirty-three days in all. Yet it cost me less than my previous visit – only £16,000 this time. I got a discount for being a regular.

The reason I went to Arizona again, rather than back to the Priory, was partly because I found Arizona stricter, which I felt I needed. We were put in dormitories, sleeping alongside other people, not in single rooms, so it was a bit tougher, not as luxurious.

But the main reason was that I knew I would be a stranger there. None of the therapists or the experts or the ordinary workers at Cottonwood had ever heard of Gazza, or read stories about him. They didn't know beforehand about what sort of person he was.

It meant I was able to tell my life story as if I were telling it to a stranger, someone who knew nothing about me, just like everyone else. I found this easier. It freed me to talk about everything, keeping nothing back. That in turn enabled me to make my chart as complete as it can be.

I rang Shel from Cottonwood and asked if she would take me back now. She said I could come and stay, as long as I was sober and behaved myself. So that's what I did.

That was one good thing that came out of Arizona – that and my chart. I realise now, as I'm glancing through it, that it seems packed with awful things about me. But that was the main point: to own up to all those awful things, in the hope that I could then put them behind me.

But it might give the impression that my whole life, inside and outside football, has been all bad, which of course it hasn't. I honestly think I've had a brilliant career. I've met so many people, earned so much, achieved so much, seen so much.

Gazza's only gift is for sport and he grows old. He has never been able to bear being crossed, now life itself is crossing him. His ageing body can't do it like it used to. And so we no longer have any time for him. It is as terrible as any of the things he has inflicted on himself. He thought he was loved for himself. Now he learns that he was only loved for his football.

Gazza: whither now? What else is he good for? Gazza was born to trouble as the sparks fly upward. His alternation of scandal and sublime have given us deep pleasure, endless fascination. Should we really abandon him now he can no longer play football to our satisfaction? Didn't we all bring him to this pass?

It seems that Gazza, the glutton for forgiveness, has gone too far. He is running out of football and so the world is running out of sympathy. All the more reason, then, to be sympathetic.

Simon Barnes, The Times, *16 February 2000*

28

RECOVERY

SOME FAMOUS PLAYERS AND SOME TOP MONEY

For me, the best player among my contemporaries, the best I ever played alongside, was Bryan Robson. When he was captain of England, it always felt so good knowing he was there. He could do everything: he worked all over the park and was an inspiration. I admired him so much. I think he was the greatest in the world in his position.

I've always been a great admirer of Chris Waddle and Peter Beardsley, and not just because they are friends and former team-mates, but because they both had such natural talent. Beardsley was so clever. He could open up the hardest defence. Waddle was a brilliant person to have in your side. If you wanted a break, to give yourself or the team a little rest, and also to annoy the opposition, all you had to do was give the ball to Chris. He'd keep it and hold it for five minutes, driving the other side mad.

Gary Lineker was about the best striker I ever played with. You always knew, in every game, he was more than likely to score. Just as good was Alan Shearer. Like Lineker, it was great to have him in front of you, knowing he could always get us a goal. It gave us such confidence, having either of them up front. I probably had more laughs with Alan. In the dressing room, he would shout 'COME ON BOYS' and I would shout back 'COME ON ENGLAND'. It was a sort of daft routine we always had, which made us all laugh.

The greatest footballer of my generation still playing is Roy Keane. He's getting on now, and has had lots of injuries, but currently he remains the best in his position anywhere. I remember first encountering him when he was at Nottingham Forest. Quite a few people in football had been talking about him, so I gave him a roasting that day, dominating the midfield. Which, of course, he will deny. During that match, to wind him up, I said to him, 'I thought you were supposed to be the next Paul Gascoigne.'

The most professional was probably Gary Mabbutt,

the perfect pro, an example to us all. Kevin Campbell at Everton was also an excellent professional.

I never played against Johan Cruyff, but he's probably the footballer I have most admired from afar, along with Pele. As I've said, I did play against Maradona, but he wasn't at the top of his game then.

Of today's players, I admire Beckham, of course. And not just because he said so many nice things about me in his autobiography. In that book, he also tells a story of me sitting by the pool with him during the preparations for the 1998 World Cup, before I got chucked out, obviously. He recalls me saying to him: 'Do you know something, David? I love you. You're a great young player and you're a great lad. I love playing football with you.' It clearly made a big impression on him, and gave him a boost. I don't actually remember that but it sounds like something I would say. I always tried to encourage the younger players, reminding myself of how much it had mattered to me when I had first got in the England squad.

We all now know about his free kicks and passing. You could see that talent from a young age. He doesn't beat people by dribbling, and his speed is not amazing, but neither was mine. His vision, however, is incredible.

I also admire him for the way he's handled the press – despite various scandal stories. He's taken his share of stick and bad publicity, but he's used the media to his own advantage, which is something I never managed. I was always getting angry with them, or was rude, or belched or farted, which I thought was funny, but they didn't – especially in Italy. I grew to hate the press, and of course they were the winners. They got their own back.

Becks has also been excellent in his commercial dealings, keeping sponsors happy and stuff. I tended to fall out with mine, or say the wrong things, or fail to do what they wanted, like the time I buggered up the Brut campaign. I couldn't be bothered with them. Becks has made all that work for him. That's one reason why he is now so rich. I had the chances, the offers, but I wasted most of them. I did make money from deals with the *Sun* and *Hello!* and stuff, but at the same time I took several papers to court for writing lies about me, which did not of course make me popular with them. Becks has had enough going wrong in his life – especially the reaction to the incident for which he was sent off against Argentina in the 1998 World Cup – but his troubles have made him stronger. He coped with them the right way. Whatever his problems with Alex Ferguson at Man United, he never criticised or badmouthed the manager after he left.

He seems to plan his life so well, right down to what he will wear, what he will be doing in a week or a month's time. I could never do that. I didn't know what I'd be doing or what I'd think from one day to another, one moment to another. I just cancelled things if I couldn't be arsed. I feel David seems to like the publicity, and has learned to handle it. He's been very clever. I wasn't consistent. Some days I liked publicity and some days I didn't.

There are lots of excellent new young players coming through now, though perhaps not as many as there should be or used to be, especially in Scotland. I blame it on the influx of foreign players. There are just too many of them. Clubs today buy experienced players from abroad, who can go straight into the side, and the young lads don't get a chance of a decent run in the first team. They need the experience, to get used to it, to develop, to make mistakes, to learn, as I did, when I got into the Newcastle side. I was given time. Now youngsters might get one chance in the first team, for a minor game, or when there have been a lot of injuries, but they soon realise that if they are going to get regular first-team football, they have to leave, go elsewhere, down the leagues.

No wonder kids see their local team and think, well, it's not worth trying to join them, I'll never get in the first team. Look at Rangers and Celtic: loads of foreigners. We had quite a few when I was at Rangers, but not nearly as many as there are now. And when I started at Newcastle, back in the eighties, we didn't have any overseas players at all. Not one.

Of the new generation, Wayne Rooney is the outstanding player so far. People have described him as a younger version of me. I suppose he is, in a way, though fame and success have come to him at a younger age than they did to me. He became a household name at seventeen, playing for Everton and England. I first played for Newcastle at the same age, but didn't play for England till I was twenty-one, and wasn't well known nationally.

I first saw Rooney when he was fourteen, when I was at Everton, and this lad came on as a sub for the Under-17s. They were 1–0 down before Wayne was brought on, but he scored two goals, and they won 2–1. I said to Colin Harvey, who was running the youth academy, 'This is some player.' So I knew of his existence long before the general football public had got to hear about him.

He will have to be careful. There are snipers out there who have built him up and will be looking to knock him down. He must be wary about making too many celebrity appearances, or letting *Hello!* or *OK!* do features on him. The opportunities will be very tempting, and very lucrative, so he will need to learn how to pick and choose. There are good and bad celebrity events, like good and bad footballers.

I am hardly the one to give him advice, and God knows, I have had enough advice in my life and never taken it. I've always hated being preached at, so I would never preach at anyone else. The thing to remember in football is that there is always plenty of talent out there, coming through in every generation, all over the world. There are plenty of players who are capable of making it, of going far, but it's what is going on in your head, that matters most in the end.

I don't know how much money I have earned in my career. Twenty million, perhaps? I never kept track of it, even when it was pouring in. All I know is that I haven't got twenty million now.

Today, I haven't even got a car. I had nine Harley-Davidsons at one time, but I've only got two of them left, and I'm not sure where they are. At Shel's I think. I gave the other seven away.

For the last five years I've been homeless. By which I mean I haven't got a house. I've been living in either hotels or rented flats. Of course, I've owned quite a few good houses in my time, and over the years, I've bought enough for my parents, sisters and brother, but I've ended up without one for myself.

I've heard that Robbie Fowler has lots of properties. They might, of course, include a lot of places in Liverpool he bought cheaply to rent out, but he's obviously invested wisely and well. So have many other top footballers. It's the sensible thing to do. I wish I had done it.

I was fortunate enough to come into the Premiership at a time when wages were high, if not as huge as they later became. I've always considered myself to be rich, from the moment I left Newcastle for Spurs in 1988. I played in the Premiership till 2002, when I left Everton, so I did very well, and I was lucky. It's the players who played ten or twenty years before me who are the unlucky ones. They made very little in comparison. They didn't end up millionaires who could afford to retire when their careers were over and never needed to work again. But that's what every established player in the Premiership should be able to do today.

So where did all my money go? Well, a lot has gone to Sheryl over the years. The main divorce settlement was around £700,000, plus £120,000 a year in maintenance. I was paying out a huge amount of money when we were married, and before that, so for about thirteen years altogether. Then I gave her the Loch Lomond house. So let's say around £2 million in total has gone on Sheryl. I'm not moaning, or blaming her. I'm just trying to work out where the money has gone.

Another £2 million has probably gone on my own family, in houses and cars and presents and treats over the years, and £2 million more on presents for other people. Not just Jimmy, but friends, people I happened to meet, people begging for money, needy people, people who helped me. I have always given to charity as well, when I had the money and even when I hadn't. I was giving away between £50,000 to £100,000 to charitable causes every year. I haven't got as much now as I had, but I'd still give away my last 5p if I thought someone needed it more than I did.

I began getting begging letters, sacks of them every year, after the World Cup of 1990, and I still get them now. I read them all, and then tear up the ones that are rubbish. But I try to help if I can, if I think someone is genuine.

When I was at Rangers, I got a letter one day from a boy near Newcastle with leukaemia. He said I was his hero and that his dying wish was to go to Disneyland. I didn't know whether his story was true or not. The lads in the dressing room said it was obviously a total con, and they wouldn't fall for that. So, after training, I jumped straight in my car and drove to Newcastle. I found the boy's house from the address on the letter and knocked on the door. When his mother opened it, I asked her if her son had written it. She said he had. I asked if I could see him. It turned out it was all true. So I gave him money, enough for a trip to Disneyland, two or three thousand pounds, then jumped back in me car and drove home to Glasgow. It must have been a 200-mile round trip.

At Everton, I did something similar when an old woman wrote to me from Norwich, saying she had only two sausages for her Christmas dinner, to feed her and her dogs. I was really touched by her letter, but I wanted

SOME FAMOUS PLAYERS ... |

to check out whether it was true. It was. I gave her the cash for a turkey and all the trimmings.

When I've been feeling down, I often think, what a selfish bastard. What have I got to moan about? I'm so fucking lucky. That's when I try to help someone or go off and visit a local hospital.

I was walking down the street in New York once when I saw this tramp crouching in a cardboard box, begging. I got in beside him and gave him a can of lager and $25. He started crying. He said no one had ever done that before. I asked him how he'd ended up begging and he told me a long story about falling into debt, being made homeless and starving. I then took him to a hotel for a champagne breakfast and gave him $100.

Another tramp gave me a sob story about some terrible operation on his stomach. He took his shirt off to show me the scars. He said his wife had died of cancer and he'd gone to pieces. I gave him money as well.

The press reported both these incidents. They happened at a time when I'd gone off on a binge and was being followed around by the rat pack. They cross-examined both tramps after I had moved on, and discovered that the first one had been telling the truth, but the second had made it all up – his stomach wound had been self-inflicted and his wife hadn't died, but left him for another man. However, he did say that he was grateful to me, and that if he ever won the Lottery, he'd give me the money back. I liked that.

I've probably spent about a couple of million on myself. I don't mean on just living, but on daft things I didn't need to spend money on: mad luxury holidays, drinks, running up ridiculous bills in hotels. I must have donated a fortune to Disneyland over the years, taking all the family and the kids several times, treating them all. And also treating myself. I love Disneyland, being a big kid myself.

I don't know what Mel and Len made, but with hindsight I wish I'd parted company with them earlier. I appreciate that they made me a lot of money for many years, organising all my business, financial and legal affairs, which took the load off me. But charging me £200 or so an hour for advice, plus expenses, made it a costly service for me. If Mel and Len came out for the weekend to see me in Rome, for example, to discuss business matters, the bill could easily come to £5,000, what with the plane fares and hotel bills.

Their statements came in every month but often I

didn't really grasp them or even read them properly for up to six months, so it's my own fault.

In addition, I must have frittered or given away something like £8 million. All of which I would have now, if I had been sensible, or if things had been different. If, over the years, I'd put that sum into property, for example, it could have grown to about £30 million today, judging by some of the increases in house prices.

I haven't the energy to try to work out where it's all gone — or even where it came from. My best wages were at Lazio when I was eventually on over £24,000 a week, and then £17,000 at the end of Rangers. Boro's were also good, around £16,000. And those were only my basic weekly wages, don't forget. I was actually paid a lot more than that as there were always extras, appearance bonuses, bonuses when I played for England. I got £10,000 every time I pulled on an England shirt. And then there was all the commercial stuff. The best deal I got was £1.2 million over four years from adidas, but there were plenty of others.

I did invest in a little company once, in Newcastle, a clothing company. I met the two blokes who ran it and they seemed all right, so I put £120,000 into their firm. They had two shops, and some other ventures, like a café. After a year or so it became clear they weren't making any profits, or at least, if they were, I wasn't seeing any of them. I wasn't being ripped off – the business just wasn't making the money they had hoped it would. In the end, they offered me one of the shops, the café and some cars, so that at least I would get my investment back. But I thought, bugger it, it's my mistake. I shouldn't have got into something I didn't know anything about. So I just gave the shop and café and the cars away to friends. I couldn't be bothered with them any more.

Looking back, I've obviously been stupid, and I should have done things differently. But at the same time, I have no regrets about money. I suppose that doesn't quite make sense. I just know that, given my time again, I would probably do exactly the same.

One regret I suppose I do have is that I never could seem to get the right balance with the press. The media first became interested in me because I was seen by many as a genius on the pitch, but I didn't want them to follow me around all the time off the pitch, reporting everything I did. You could say that I drew attention to myself, doing daft things in public. But I would have done those things whether I was rich and famous or not.

That was just me. I'd always acted spontaneously, pulling stupid stunts and playing practical jokes. But I don't think they should have been reported and held against me.

From the beginning, when the press and TV were after me, Mel Stein always said I should charge them. He got a fee out of everyone, sometimes enormous fees; if they didn't pay, I didn't speak to them. He said I had to make the most of my position, earn money while I could, because I'd be a long time retired. And why, he argued, should they get things for free anyway? They were commercial people, trying to sell newspapers.

That all seemed fair enough, but what I didn't realise, not at the beginning, was, of course, that the papers that don't have an exclusive will try to get at you in some other way, to beat their rivals. And I realise now that I was hardly ever interviewed about football, or written about in the so-called serious papers, the big papers, as I call them. I haven't kept my own cuttings – I've got nowhere to keep them – but me mam has, piles of them, filling stacks of cases, all sitting in an outhouse in Dunston, covered in dust. But they are mainly tabloid scandal-type stories.

When I was in demand, being offered £100,000

for a story, it was always because of some personal drama: going on the booze, falling out with Shel. That was what they wanted. I agreed not only for the money, but also because I saw it as a chance to set the record straight. Whenever there was a nasty piece in a paper, people would come up to me all the time and say, 'Ooh, I read about you doing so and so – aren't you terrible?' So I thought if I told one of the rival tabloids the truth, put my point of view, at least some people would read an accurate version. The tabloids were, after all, the papers all my friends read, not the big papers. So why would I want to be in them? But if I were starting again today, perhaps I would do more with the big papers, and concern myself less with being paid for it.

I remember, at Spurs, seeing Gary Lineker giving interviews for free to kids' comics and fanzines when he could have earned a fortune for the same stuff and same amount of his time elsewhere. It was a sensible thing to do. He wanted to broaden his outlook, to see all sorts, as even then he was thinking of a career in the media.

I did once give an interview for free, to Brian Viner of the *Independent*, when I was at Everton, and that was, for a change, mainly about my football, not my personal life. I should have done more of that. The kiss-and-tell, booze and binges stories eventually became the only part of my life people read about, and it just led to them wanting more, or finding more, or making up more of the same, if they couldn't get it from me. It gave no insight into what I was really like, or into my dedication and passion for playing football.

> Gascoigne suffered more than anything from being Gazza, a showbiz character designed to keep his name before the public. The professional game turns over billions of pounds and it continues to produce woefully inadequate human beings. Some of these highly paid social misfits would struggle to sit on the toilet the right way, were their agents not on hand to show them. Gascoigne's story is not over yet. And don't kid yourself. It won't have a happy ending.
> *Michael Henderson,* Spectator, *25 January 2003*

> This is what I will be aiming to do. To show you how to do the best for your client and still earn enough money for yourself. Greed is not good, but making money for yourself isn't bad either.
> *Mel Stein,* How to Succeed as a Sports Agent, *2002*

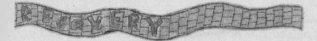

29

BACK TO MY ROOTS

It's December 2003 and I'm sitting in my hotel in Shropshire, Patshull Park Hotel, which has 280 acres, a golf course and a huge fishing lake. I've played some golf but I haven't done any fishing. They have trout and pike, but I don't like them mixed up in the same lake. The estate and the landscaped gardens and the original manor house date back to 1768, so it says in the information by my bedside. It was originally laid out by Capability Brown, it says. Dunno who he was. Perhaps a relation of Wes Brown.

For the last two months I've been playing for Wolverhampton Wanderers Reserves. This place has been handy for their training ground, where I've been going each morning, taking a taxi there and back. I haven't been getting paid, just training with them. It was my old England and Boro mate Paul Ince who suggested it. I told him I wanted to get fit, do some proper professional training, and he said, 'Why not come here?'

David Jones, the manager of Wolves, was very good, letting me join in. He told me when I arrived I was in too much of a hurry. 'You want to be fit yesterday,' he said.

In my first game, at home to Sunderland, I played the full ninety minutes, which pleased me, although we were beaten 3–1. It was at Telford United's ground. The gate was about 2,000, instead of the usual 200-odd. So I must have brought in a few interested spectators.

In the next game, against West Brom Reserves, I couldn't get back on to the team coach because of all the fans wanting autographs, hundreds of them. I hate turning people away, but I knew the lads on the coach would be getting pissed off waiting for me, and I just couldn't get through. In the end I borrowed a steward's orange jacket and was able to dodge between the media and the fans. The steward had to run after me to get his jacket back.

In the local evening paper next day, the *Express and*

Star, they said that putting on the steward's jacket was a 'classic Gazza prank'. They went on to say that my body 'will no longer obey the brain in time for English football to once again savour one of the most glorious and instinctive talents'. Bastards.

I played four games (we lost three and drew one), scoring one goal. Then I got a groin strain and had to come off in the last game. Wolves are bottom of the Reserves League, which was where they were when I arrived.

At the back of my mind, I suppose I was half-hoping that I might get a contract out of them. Not a big one, obviously; just a small, modest one, to last me for the rest of this season. I find it hard to let go of my old fantasy of finishing my British career in the Premiership. I had offers from several Third Division clubs, like Boston and Carlisle United, offering quite good money, around £5,000 a week and a share of the gates. Wes Saunders, my agent, thought I should have taken one of them, made some money and played competitively, rather than carrying on playing for no money in someone's reserve team. But at the time I didn't fancy the English Third Division. Mind you, things can change.

I have to admit that the training has been

knackering me. I'm fit enough, lean enough, but my whole body aches all the time. It's so much harder to recover from any knocks when you get to thirty-six. I can't remember feeling like this before, being in agony in training. Even three years ago, I don't remember twinges or pains or tiredness when I was in full training.

When you're young, you can play two and sometimes three proper games a week, but not at my age. One is more than enough. In the old days, I could train for hour after hour, no bother. As you know, I was often half-drunk. Perhaps the alcohol killed off or disguised the aches and agonies so that I couldn't feel them. Now, when I'm not drinking, I can feel every little twinge. Perhaps I should start drinking again. Only joking.

I never actually liked drinking. That's something people have never understood. I don't understand it myself, for that matter. I didn't even really like the taste. Stuff like Baileys I enjoyed, but that was because it was sweet. When I was with Chris Evans and Danny Baker, I very often poured my drink into a plant pot because I didn't like it. Ask them. They'll tell you.

The only reason I drank was to numb my brain. It was good fun at the time, drinking to feel numb, and

I enjoyed being daft with my mates. But my main aim was always oblivion.

Danny always says I'm not a mad drunk, just a mad risk-taker. And I did take crazy risks, like jumping in front of buses without thinking. I did that on the pitch as well, which was why I had so many injuries. And I did it as a boy, swinging between trees, to see if I could, then falling off and breaking my arm. At the time I didn't feel brave, or that I was taking a risk. I just didn't think ahead to what the consequences of my actions might be. Of course, drink does make you braver, so I suppose I was even more of a risk-taker when drunk. Today I like to think I'm more careful, more cautious.

Drinking also makes you dehydrated. With age, you're more likely to get injured, and dehydration makes it harder for the body to recover from the injuries. I've been told all that often enough. In training at Wolves, I was thinking all the time, what the fuck am I doing? Is this really worth it? What's the point of all this fucking training? Then I told myself I couldn't give in, not yet. I was still a winner. I could still do it. I could still help a team.

But now, sitting here in my hotel, I've had to admit to myself that it's not going to work. Wolves are not going to give me a contract, however titchy. It's heart-breaking, but I might as well acknowledge that that's it. I feel devastated.

I only hope I won't go into a deep depression. For the last two months, training has been all I've really been concentrating on. It's all I've done. I trained all morning, came back to the hotel and rested. Then I played a bit of solitaire on my mobile phone, or a chess game, playing against myself. I usually have the telly on as well.

I still quite like living in hotels. It doesn't depress me, thinking I haven't got a house of my own to go to. Even when I was married, or had my own house, I would move into a hotel for the odd week or so, on my own, just to have peace and quiet, get away from everyone. I don't eat in the dining room. I just stay in my room, order food from room service. I don't get bothered. Other guests have been asking for autographs, so I've arranged a system with the girls on Reception. People leave their autograph books there, and I sign when I next pass through.

I ring people a lot, talk for ages on the phone. Or people ring me, old friends like Archie Knox from Rangers and Everton. We have a laugh. Or I ring Jimmy, ask him to do little things for me. He came down from

Gateshead and drove me to Telford for my first game for Wolves. When we lost, of course I screamed and swore at him, and he screamed and swore back, saying it was my mistake. Jimmy has been there for every first game I have ever played in my career, from Newcastle to Lazio, Rangers to China, every one.

I don't feel lonely, not really. It's just nice and quiet. You don't have arguments when you're on your own. I like hotels the way I like hospitals. After all, I've spent years of my life in hotels and in hospitals. It's the sense of being looked after, and the comfort.

I especially like it in hospitals when they give you morphine. I could do with more of that, just to zonk me out, stop me thinking. I suppose it is part of my longing to escape, my fondness for hotels and hospitals; of wanting to cut myself off from the real world, from bills, the public, the media. In a hospital or a hotel, you are not aware of family worries or domestic aggravation.

I'm not missing the drink, but I don't know how long that will last. I've got lots of panic pills and anti-depressants which I take instead of getting drunk. They're supposed to settle me down. Before that first game for Wolves, I left them behind in my hotel room, so I got myself in a panic. Having Jimmy with me helped.

I don't suppose the lads at Wolves realise I've been taking these pills. But they're bound to have noticed how quiet and serious I've become, very different from the loud, daft Gazza they thought they knew. I've enjoyed their company, tried to help the young lads where I could, talked to everyone, but I can be very subdued with people I don't know. Wary, perhaps, rather than shy. Over the years, I've learned to be wary of new people, of what they might be trying to get out of me. But in dressing rooms, I'm not a stranger. I know how they work.

I would like to have some sort of final exhibition match, a testimonial for myself, perhaps at St James' Park in Newcastle. I've appeared in lots of testimonials for other people over the years – such as Alex Ferguson, Paul Merson, Matt Le Tissier, Peter Beardsley, Alan McLaren, David Busst. When you play in a testimonial, you do it for no money. I hope people will do the same for me. I'll give a good proportion to charity, of course. I've been invited to do some after-dinner speaking, and I quite fancy that. I need some income, after all.

So, have I ended up with nothing? Not quite. Fortunately, I did manage to do one very sensible thing. When I moved to Lazio, I put all of my £2 million signing-on fee into a bank in the Channel Islands. I've used bits of it, but it's still mostly intact, except it was put into US dollars. That was the advice I was given. Dollars have gone down in value, but I'm hoping it will be enough to keep me going. I probably won't be able to live on it, or on the interest, not these days, but at least I've something set aside. My plan is to put it into something which will give me an income and also perhaps a job, if I need it.

With my Channel Islands nest egg, I might buy an estate in Northumberland with a trout farm, and try to get an income from that. Or a little string of pubs which Jimmy could manage. We could call them Gazza's or Five Bellies. That's still an idea.

Or I might pack it all in and move to Australia or the US. I could open my own coaching school, like Bobby Charlton did.

I can't see myself pursuing a career as a football commentator or pundit. During the 2002 World Cup, I did a few weeks for ITV, but I wasn't comfortable with it. Sitting in a studio, I was nervous, and it showed. I was with people who are very good at the job, and very experienced, like Ally McCoist, which just emphasised that it wasn't for me. I know some people thought I was drunk in the studio, but I wasn't. In the hotel, perhaps, but not in the studio. I didn't drink in the studio. But

I was taking lots of sleeping pills to help me sleep, and having to get up early meant I was still a bit slurry in the mornings. I got on better when they sent me out in the streets to talk to fans. Being among ordinary people, on my own, suited me more.

There was a lot made about the hotel bills I ran up while I was working for ITV. Yeah, perhaps my bar bill was pretty big, around £9,000 for the three weeks. But it wasn't just me, as everyone imagined. Ally and Andy Townsend were coming back to my hotel with me, so it was for several of us . . .

I have a bit of jewellery, too, which Jimmy has put away safely in the bank for me. I did buy myself a few nice things when I had the money. I've got a limited edition Ayrton Senna watch, and a couple of other limited-edition racing-driver watches. And I have my medal from the Pope, and of course my football memorabilia, my England shirts and caps and football stuff. I gave a lot of it away, either to raise money for charity or just to friends as presents. Probably about a third of it. The remaining stuff is being kept safe for me. If and when I buy a house for myself again, I might display it there, to remind me of all the good times.

*   *   *

Now I'd better start packing up, getting ready to leave this hotel. I have to go to London, see my therapist, go to an AA meeting, and then head back to the north-east. See what turns up.

My plan at this moment is to go and stay at Jimmy's for a few months. I've got legal matters to sort out with Shel and I need to be near my Newcastle lawyer. I could go to my family, but I don't want to get in their way. Jimmy only has a small flat, but he has a spare bed I can use. It will be like going back to the past, to where it all began. Maybe I will end up being famous for being a friend of the well-known Jimmy Five Bellies. That would be a laugh.

For Jimmy has become a celebrity in his own right. The BBC in Newcastle recently devoted a whole documentary to him, he's been offered hundreds of thousands over the years by the tabloids for his story, and now he's thinking of doing a proper book about his own life. It's not a joke – several publishers are interested. It'll be X-rated, I reckon.

The BBC documentary about him was excellent. When I asked him why he agreed to do it, he said it was because he hoped it might lead to something else. 'Such as?' I asked. He said he'd quite fancy being a presenter of children's TV programmes. Well, it would be easier and warmer than being a roofer, which is what he's been doing recently.

Jimmy has been round the world with me, to Italy, America, everywhere. We went to New York once. It was his birthday treat and I took him on Concorde, just for one night.

We stayed overnight at the Peninsula Hotel, and as usual, I couldn't sleep. I was just lying there, waiting till it was morning and I could get up. At about five o'clock I heard noise outside, all this banging. It was the binmen, out on the sidewalk. I thought I'd get up and get dressed and go and help them. They let me join in, emptying the garbage into the truck, and I was enjoying myself so much, I forgot all about the time. When Jimmy surfaced he couldn't work out where the hell I'd gone. I got back to find we'd missed the Concorde flight, and we had to stay on another day.

I didn't often venture far without Jimmy in those days: he is the only person outside my family I feel I can really trust. He's always been there for me and I know he always will be. He's never let me down, or told any secrets, or revealed any awful things about me. That's my job.

We do argue, all the time, like an old married

couple, but I am relaxed and comfortable with him. He knows all my thoughts, all my secrets. I don't think Shel liked me going out with him, or going to stay with him. Some people think he is a bad influence. But he's not. He'd drop anything he was doing if I were in trouble and needed him.

He looks upon himself as my brother, and he's been through everything with me. He did have a long-term partner, Joanna, with whom he has two children, Liam and Sharnie. But they split up. He now has a new girl-friend. Well, he is very attractive.

I have given him lots of cars over the years, prob-ably about five, and other presents, and I pay his way in hotels when he travels with me, which is only fair, but he's never been on a salary. I did once, just to wind him up, say in a radio interview that he had a full-time job working with me and I was paying him £100 a week. When that got into the papers, Jimmy had his dole money taken away. He was furious. He works in the building trade, laying floors, mending roofs, but of course he is often out of work, so it's only right that he should be able to claim the dole.

I'm looking forward to going to stay with him now. With Jimmy, I can just be myself.

Those with a soft spot for him wait for the almost
inevitable news of the latest mischief to befall the
boy who once had the world at his dazzling feet.
Steven Howard, Sun, *4 April 2003*

30

SOBER THOUGHTS

It's now a few months on, May 2004, and I've just about finished writing this hardback edition. When I began the book, I was spending some time at Shel's after I'd returned from Arizona. I thought I would be staying there, perhaps for ever. She said I could stay as long as I wasn't drinking, and I didn't start drinking. As I write, I still haven't. It's now well over a year, a world record for me, since I was eighteen, anyway. But God knows how long it will last.

So drink was not the problem. I've been depressingly, boringly sober. And I honestly thought it might work out this time, if I behaved myself. But there again, I've thought that on many occasions in the past. This time, it does look as if it's the end. Money has been the main cause of the arguments. I haven't had any income from football for about a year now, and not much from anywhere else. I turned down a lot of money from *Hello!* last year. They wanted to do a piece on me living with Shel again. Good job I declined. When I started maintenance payments, I was making about £2 million a year while at Rangers, so I could afford it. Not now. But that's all in the hands of the lawyers.

My sister Anna thinks I have kept it going with Shel for so long because I can't admit defeat. Throughout my life, whenever I've really wanted to do something, to win something, whether it's been a football match or a game of tennis or snooker, I've gone for it, and refused to be beaten. Perhaps I have seen my relationship with Shel like that, too.

But I'll have to admit it now. Defeat, I mean. I'm forced to acknowledge that the relationship, like my football career, is over. I miss Regan, all the time; I think about him constantly. I will of course have some sort of access, perhaps have holidays and Christmas. But I worry that Regan might not respect me, nor Bianca and Mason. I have tried to do things for them, in the way of holidays and money and stuff. Obviously I've done wrong in the past. I know that. They know that. Perhaps one day, in the future, Regan will look upon me more kindly. It breaks me up, every time I think about it.

One thing I don't believe in is badmouthing other people. I didn't like Paul Merson talking about me in a recent TV programme, claiming I was swallowing all these sleepers. If he was going to say it on national television, he should have told me first. I'd never criticise a fellow player in public. I'm not saying everything said about me is untrue, but if you have no warning that someone is about to air your dirty linen for you, it can be very hurtful for your family. And I hated all those therapists and experts analysing me on TV when they'd never even met me.

There have been lots of stories about me in various other autobiographies, like Stuart Pearce's and Tony Adams'. I suppose publishers think it sells books if they can spice up their memoirs with some tales about me. I could tell some good stories about them, too, but I'm not revealing them. I hope in this book I haven't hurt anyone at all by what I've said about them. Except for myself. Over the last four years, I like to think I've done no harm to anybody, not in the way I may have done in the past.

But it's all my fault, the place I find myself now, and I know it. I threw away Shel's love. I put her through so much that she can't live with me any more. Yet other people I've been bad to in the past still love me. There must be some good in me, for them to be still there for me. My problem is mainly myself. When I play against myself all the time, I'm the loser.

And yet I've been so lucky. When I go into a corner and cry, there are still people around who will kiss and cuddle me, who ring me up, want to see me, want to cheer me up.

As I said earlier, I suppose many people in the world have experienced to some extent the same sorts of fears and silly worries that plague me. Most people learn to cope. The ones who don't can end up in the gutter, being kicked while they are down rather than being offered help. I have been lucky there, too. I have had the support of so many family and friends as well as the money to pay for the Priory and Cottonwood.

I know I'm a selfish, self-centred bastard. I go on about my own worries when there are kids out there with no money, no friends, no help, no hope. I am taking up the help they could be receiving. So what have I got to moan about?

When I take tablets for depression, I think how depressing, and feel more depressed. I know I should try to enjoy life, and not get depressed, because I'll be a long time dead. It's very hard for other people to understand my mentality. It's only those who have experienced the same kind of obsessions and compulsions who can really understand it. You look in the mirror when you're slumped in the middle of a depression or a panic attack and you don't see yourself. You see another person, someone you don't like. You hate him so much you want to try to get away from him.

I've been in enough clinics, from Arizona to the Priory, with countless people trying to help me, offering me therapy, counselling, medication, all sorts. It often works – for a while.

People are always trying to analyse me, explain why I'm like I am. They go on TV or write in the papers about what's wrong with me without knowing me. They often say I'm suffering from ADD – attention deficit disorder. That's bollocks. They all seem like idiots to me. I might be hyperactive, always wanting to be doing something, unable to sleep properly, but I can concentrate when I want to. I always concentrated on training, doing more than was required rather than less. My attention never wandered and I never gave up. Doing this book, I was able to concentrate and talk for three hours at a stretch – though I admit it did my head in at times.

OCD, those are the other letters they throw at me – obsessive compulsive disorder. That's probably true. All the clinics have told me that, so I have to agree. I've always been obsessive, about little things as well as big things. I still have to have everything in a certain order.

But why I'm like this, fuck knows. Perhaps it's the traumas I've been through, starting with the death of Steven. That still comes back to haunt me. The more I have been in therapy, or talked about myself, as in this book, the more I understand myself, but I still can't explain why I'm the way I am. Would I have been different without the traumas, the things going wrong in my life? I don't know. Or if my parents and childhood had been different? Fuck knows. All I know is that I still get obsessed and have panic attacks and my head feels like it's about to explode.

Not drinking for a year has helped. Drinking only made me more depressed, especially when I woke up. The pills are helping, ones which my psychiatrist has recommended, and I'm going to AA meetings. I'm on something called melatonin and also Zyprexa to help me relax, control the panic attacks. I could be on pills for some time. Perhaps years. We'll see.

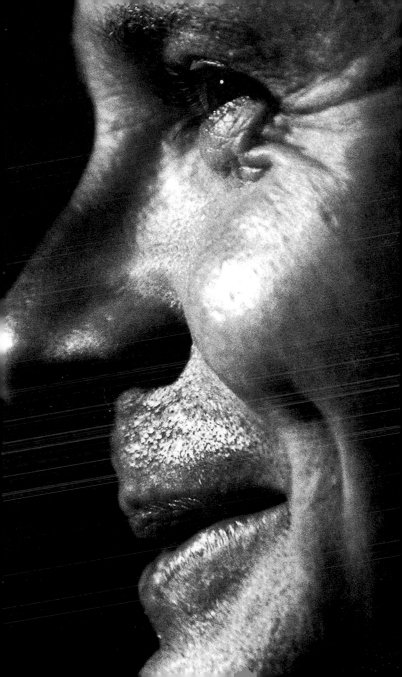

DODGY HAIRCUTS

Plus a very nice suit. I don't think my hairstyles won many prizes but I did win an award once for Best Dressed Man of the Year.

DODGY DECISIONS

Opposite top: me and Jimmy Five Bellies make guest appearances in Wes Saunders' 1997 testimonial. Jimmy's appearance was bigger than mine.

Below: while at Rangers, playing against Hibs, the ref dropped his card. I picked it up, pretended to book him – and he booked me instead. Cheek.

PRIVATE SNAPS

These are some of the photos I keep in my wallet, to remind me of happy times. With Chris Waddle and Chris Evans (*top left*), and Paul Stewart while at Spurs (*middle*).

Above: me and Jimmy in Florida, having a singsong.

Below: with Danny Baker and Chris Evans. Not a kebab in sight.

Marco Negri, left, my colleague at Rangers, with some hunting hawks in Scotland.

Left: with Peter Beardsley in my Newcastle days;
right: me and Chris Waddle, a couple of toffs at Spurs.

DAFT DAYS

Opposite, clockwise from top left: Newcastle's secret new midfield creator – luckily, I was not asked to mark anyone; I reveal Paul Ince's beautiful bot to a gasping world while we're watching England's Under-21s against Moldova; on arrival back from the 1990 World Cup I was presented with my own boobs and belly – Gazzamania began; my birthday cake was presented to me during Italia 90 – and tasted delicious.

Right, top to bottom: walking on the water at my villa in Italy; no, it's not Benny Hill, but me fishing; clutching Bell's Player of the Year and Scottish Football Writers awards, 1996.

MORE HAPPY MOMENTS
Winning BBC Sports Personality
of the Year, 1990.

With Sir Stanley Matthews at the
Football League centenary dinner,
1999.

Gone fishing, something I've always loved, as you can see from this
happy, smiley face while in Arizona at the Cottonwood clinic, May 2003.
Another snap from my wallet, just to cheer me up when I feel down.

I've often wished I was dead, but I just haven't got the balls to commit suicide. Then I think, if I did kill myself, what's that going to do to all those good people behind me who love me, who are constantly trying to help me? They would be devastated.

Then I think I'd quite fancy it. I'd like it all to be over, to be in heaven, or perhaps in hell. I'd like to be cremated and have my ashes scattered on St James' Park. I can just see myself going to heaven and God saying to me 'Hello Gazza, how're you doing?'

But for football, I know I would be in a far worse state than I am today. There are people who think I threw it all away, just as they think George Best did. They believe I could have done so much more with my talents if I hadn't been so self-indulgent and daft and drunk and stupid. I think the opposite. I think I have achieved far, far more than I ever expected to achieve, considering I'm me, stuck in this body and this head with all this going on. I would have done much less in life if it hadn't been for football.

I'm surprised myself how long I've kept going, given all my problems. I've now just turned thirty-seven, but I'm fit and slim and still able to play, if anyone wants me. Most of all, I'm still here. Everybody knows about my drinking, but few have been aware of the mental troubles and depressions that triggered it. If I'd taken advantage of the psychiatric help I was offered back when I was a child, it might have helped.

But you can't go back. Obviously, I do regret belching in Italy, and playing the flute in Glasgow. I sometimes feel I haven't put myself first enough, worrying about so many other people, like my family and Shel and her children. And of course my biggest regret of all is beating up Shel.

But I don't regret all the silly things I did, the years when I was as daft as a brush, playing childish tricks, firing air guns at Jimmy's arse. I never planned them, said to myself today I'll do this to Jimmy, or me and Chris Evans will try this. I just did them, off the cuff, for amusement.

I was younger and dafter then, but I would do them again if I had my time over. I wouldn't do them *now*. I don't do daft things any more. I haven't done anything daft for at least a year. Well, I've just dyed my hair silver, but I don't call that daft. It's fashion, innit.

I don't really regret drinking. Because I know I would do it again, so why regret it? You can't change things that have happened. That was me, that was then.

And I certainly don't regret anything in my football career. I think it's been brilliant, far more than I could ever have hoped for.

It goes without saying that I wish I hadn't been injured as much. I reckon I lost four and a half years of my career through injury. That's a huge slice of a first-team record of seventeen years, from when I got in the Newcastle first side to when I left Everton. That's over a quarter of my football life completely lost. In all I've had twenty-seven operations. Out of the four and a half years lost, ten months were spent in hospitals, the rest recovering from injuries.

Most of those injuries were my own fault, notably that disastrous FA Cup final injury when I was with Spurs. The elbow in the cheek at Lazio, though, wasn't my fault, and neither was being beaten up in that nightclub in Newcastle. But mostly my injuries were a result of my own recklessness, of being too eager and too worked up.

Still, seventeen years in the top divisions is more than many professionals achieve.

In my club career, I beat the transfer record at almost every club I moved to. At Spurs, we won the Cup final. I did well for Lazio, when I wasn't injured; I won everything in Scotland at Rangers. I helped Boro get promotion and they rose higher in the Premiership than they'd done before.

My unhappiest period in club football was at Boro, but that wasn't to do with football. It was to do with me. My happiest time was probably at Rangers. But I loved it at Spurs as well, and at Lazio. But of all my football, I'm probably proudest of my England career. I won fifty-seven caps for my country, and only four of those games go down in the record books as defeats – but of course there were also the two games we lost to Germany on penalties. If only I had not been injured so often, I would have been well on course to reach 100 caps.

I had no way of knowing, when Glenn Hoddle chucked me out in 1998, that I had played my last England game. I was pleased when Kevin Keegan became manager, as I had always admired him, but although the papers often predicted that he was going to pick me, I didn't believe it. I was going through a bad patch and not on my best form.

When Sven-Göran Eriksson came along, I had a fantasy about being selected when I was doing well at Everton. I would have loved one more game at Wembley, just to finish off my England career in style, instead of in humiliation at La Manga.

Of all the England managers I served under, two were brilliant for me. Bobby Robson was so experienced and wise and mature. He gave me my England debut, so I'll always be grateful to him. He is also still England's second-most successful manager, after Sir Alf Ramsey, having got us to a World Cup semi-final in 1990, which is further than any of his successors have reached.

I loved Terry Venables, perhaps even more. I thought he was the best coach in the world. He was so good at man-management, especially when the man was me. I looked upon him almost as a father.

Graham Taylor . . . well, I never liked his way of playing, though he was a nice enough man and good at man-management himself. Hoddle I didn't like, either him or his methods. He treated his players like schoolkids. It wasn't just me. Perhaps he got the England job too early, and could have done with some more experience.

When you look at the young crop of players coming through, you would expect one or two of them to get 100 caps. Wayne Rooney made his first appearance at such a young age, and Michael Owen seems certain to get the ton. I think Sol Campbell will as well, and, of course, David Beckham. Good luck to them. But football, like life, is unpredictable. Injuries can bugger up everything, or loss of form. Different England managers will come in, bringing different ideas. You might be good, and playing great football, but the team itself might not be playing great football and fail to make the finals of the big competitions. Your chances can then evaporate, and you might never get the sackful of caps you deserved and everyone expected.

So I think I did well. I had one whole World Cup, and a good Euro 96, when again we got to the semis. Quite an achievement, really, even if it could have been better.

Let's say I fulfilled my dreams, but I didn't fulfil my potential.

I look upon myself as two people: Gazza and Paul Gascoigne. Paul Gascoigne is the sensible, kind, generous, caring one, if a bit boring. Gazza has been daft as a brush, but could be very entertaining.

I think the Gazza stage in my life could be over. At least until I do something daft once again. What has helped me to feel that I have changed from the sort of person I have been in the past is getting it down on paper for the first time.

It's encouraged me to face myself. Now I can move on, I hope. Don't know where, though. I wish I did.

Now you can all fuck off. I'm fed up talking about myself. For now anyway. But you've been a lovely audience. Cheers.

Gary Lineker: When you're stuck with a bunch of lads for a month, you need people like Gazza, who'll give you a laugh. He drove you mad sometimes, but he was great for morale . . .
Sir Bobby Robson: He was brilliant for the group; he kept everyone laughing.
Terry Venables: He was a great trainer, great player, but off the pitch he was a riot!
Discussion on Gazza, FourFourTwo, April 2004

31

THE END OF MY CAREER

OK, perhaps I'm not quite done talking about myself after all. It's almost a year on from when I finished the hardback edition and I did say then that my football life was over, and I believed it, not expecting to be playing professionally ever again. But in the summer of 2004 I got an offer from Boston United of what is now League Two, an offer which seemed to be interesting and attractive. It would also, I thought, help me on my path to becoming a manager.

I was approached by the owner and chairman of Boston, Jon Sotnick, and the manager, Steve Evans, to come and help them out. I would play a bit but mainly I would be coaching. In fact I got the impression I would be as good as managing the team, with Steve and the other main coach, Paul Raynor, gradually moving into the background. That's how I saw it, but of course I might have allowed myself to believe this.

The deal, to play and coach, would roughly earn me about £15,000 a month, plus I would get extra money every time the gates went above 3,500. I wasn't really doing it for the money but to get experience and finish off my FA coaching badge. I had started to do the work for the B badge by then, but you have to be observed and tested on giving coaching sessions.

I moved into a hotel, the New England, in the middle of Boston, just to be at the heart of things, be part of the community which I tried hard to do. The public baths and fitness centre is near Boston's York Street ground and I spent a lot of time there – not just keeping myself fit but helping others. If I saw people struggling with their exercises, I'd give them a bit of personal fitness coaching, help them along. John Blackwell, Boston's secretary, says that local people were ringing the club all the time, thinking I was actually working at the baths.

Boston is in rural Lincolnshire and not exactly one of the heartlands of football, but Boston United has been going since 1934, though there was a football club in the town long before that. They were non-league for years but in 2002 they came up from the Conference as champions. They had spent just two seasons in League Two when I arrived. So it might have been a little club, historically, but it was on the up and up.

The first game I played in was a friendly against Newcastle United which of course I had helped to set up. This was on 27 July 2004, and we won 4–1. The gate wasn't huge, not as many as I'd expected, somewhere around 3,500. I played my first league game for Boston on 28 August, coming on as sub against Cheltenham. We lost 1–0. I started in the game against Chester on 30 August and we won 3–1. Against Cambridge, I played the whole game for the first time and we won 2–1. Then we had our big derby game on 11 September, away to Lincoln City in front of a crowd of 7,142. I came on as sub and made a goal from a free kick for Jason Lee which gave us a draw, 2–2.

In training, I got on well with the young kids. I think they liked working with me, but I never really did much coaching, far less acting as manager. I found myself sort of third coach, taking the apprentices. I never got to coach the first team. I didn't actually like their training methods, but then that's my opinion. If a player lost the ball in a training session, he got a bollocking and was made to run up and down. The lads had to take a load of stick. When I first heard it, I couldn't believe it. It was as if they were not trying hard enough. I imagine that's what life is like in the lower divisions. The coaches think they have to do it, I suppose, because their players don't have the natural ball skills of the higher leagues, but a great spirit. I began to realise that in my career, playing so long at the top, I perhaps had been a bit spoiled. I'd had some of the best coaches, best facilities and trained with the best players.

Funnily enough, in hospital today, where I happen to be at this moment, who should appear in my room but Ray Wilkins, come on a surprise visit. I played with him for England and he's now assistant manager at Millwall. He asked me what it was like at Boston – and asked me specifically about David Noble, the Boston midfielder. It turned out that Ray had him when he was with Luca Vialli at Watford. He thought very highly of him, but it didn't work out. They found it hard to motivate him.

That was interesting. I had similar difficulties with David Noble at Boston. He has such natural talent; I think he has the ability but he just needs to work that little bit harder. Coaches over the years have probably tried to push him. In the games I played with him at Boston, I used to say him, 'I want you to get a yellow card in this game.' What I meant was get stuck in, put yourself about, throw yourself into it, even if you get booked. Didn't seem to make much difference.

He was formerly at West Ham, so his talent had been recognised early on, but he hasn't really progressed as far as he should. He's still quite young, only twenty-three, so I suppose there's still time for him to develop and come good.

It just shows you that in football, determination is almost the most important element. Above a certain level in the game, you can take natural talent for granted. It's what you do with it that matters most. I remember as a boy at Newcastle there seemed so many lads with brilliant skills, yet they never made it, for lots of reasons. I always had that inner determination, that ambition to succeed, which was why I trained hard and played hard. OK, I might have done a lot of daft and stupid things as well, on and off the pitch, which showed I wasn't in fact very grown up, but I was always serious about football itself.

Anyway, it became clear that Boston wasn't quite working out in the way I'd hoped. It was hard to do three hours' coaching in the afternoon, and then play in the evening. But the coaching I was being given was mainly with the kids. We only had eight apprentices so I couldn't organise proper games or routines, which is what I needed for my B badge.

So the club wasn't helping me as I had hoped but I like to think I did a lot for them – signing sessions, appearances at various places. I must have got them about £100,000 of national publicity. But I began to feel unhappy. After three months, I decided to pack it in.

I told the lads the reasons why – that it wasn't what I wanted to do, that I wasn't doing enough proper coaching. They all understood. I left with no hard feelings.

In all, I played four league games for Boston, mainly as sub, plus that friendly against Newcastle. I also played in a County Cup game against Lincoln City. That was when I got my one and only goal for Boston – a free kick towards the final whistle which drew the game 3–3.

In the end, I didn't make much money. The crowds didn't increase by much, though odd blokes turned up from halfway round the world, like Australia, just to see me play. You'd have to be odd, to come all that way to see me. They were football nuts, or should I say Gazza nuts. Generally, the fans didn't flock in enough numbers to make me any extra money. By my reckoning, I'm still owed a bit. But that's football. You do these sorts of deals, late in your career, when clubs hope that just by signing you they'll make a bob or two. In this case, it wasn't just late in my career, it turned out to be the end of it. As a player, anyway.

After Boston, which had turned out very stressful, I decided just to chill out for a bit, relax and take it easy. Then another football opportunity came up which I was quite interested in. There was this consortium planning to take over a certain club. They had lots of money and if they succeeded, they wanted me to come in and be manager with another ex-player working alongside me. I went to lots of meetings, watched a lot of videos and it looked pretty good. But it all fell apart. They thought that the club's debts were only something like two million, which they believed they could cope with, but they were more like six million. So that fell through.

Over the last year, I have been invited to appear in various charity games. I did one at St James', Newcastle, called 'The Match' which was Celebrities versus the Legends. The Celebs were managed by Graham

Taylor and the Legends by Bobby Robson. I was in the Legends. I played OK, and enjoyed it.

Then I was going to be in a big charity game in Madrid, with Zidane and Figo and Becks and the rest. It was all arranged, but come that weekend, I wasn't well enough to play. I went out anyway, as there were various events connected to the match, and my dad came with me. He had a good time at least. He always does. I mentioned earlier in the book how at one time I had a load of Harley-Davidsons, nine in all. I gave most of them away, or left them at Shel's. I told my dad he could have my last one. Then I decided I wanted to keep it and guess what the cheeky sod said? I had to buy it off him. So I did. Bastard. I'm now going to trade it for the very latest model.

Now that my playing career is over, I've realised one important thing: I'll have to work for a living from now on. It's a strange feeling, one that most people have experienced long before they're thirty-seven.

I hate it when the papers say I'm skint, which a lot of them have been saying this last year. I might have lost or wasted millions, but I'm not bust. I've got myself a new agent, Jane Morgan, and she's started working on various things for me. I've recently been offered my own show on Channel 4, interviewing people, anyone I like. I think I might decide just to interview children. That's about my level, being one myself . . .

I got approached about all those 'I'm a Celebrity' things, to go into the jungle or to the Arctic. I was offered £250,000 to go into the jungle, and I agreed, but then they came back and said I was 'too famous'. I also wonder whether it had anything to do with stories a few years ago about me dating Vic Reeves' wife Nancy, who was suddenly brought in. Who knows?

One thing I was really looking forward to was the BBC TV Christmas show, *Strictly Ice Dancing*. This was when a so-called celeb learns to skate along with a proper ice skater. They dance as a couple, against other pro-am couples.

I worked really hard on that as I wanted not just to do it well, but win it. My partner Zoia was great, a lovely girl. I thoroughly enjoyed it – till I had my accident. One of the papers said I fell and injured myself while practising at home with Jimmy Five Bellies. We were arguing about who was Dean and who was Torvill. That was the story in the papers. Quite funny, really, but total bollocks. I fell on the ice, while practising, and hurt myself. So I had to pack it in, which was such a shame after all that work. Dave Seaman took my place – and he won, the bastard.

During the year I've also set up a company, along with Chris Evans and some others, and we are going to start our own chain of restaurants and bars. In fact, we have set up our own website and an office in London. It's called G8. Which is what I decided would be my new name.

The plan was to call the new business G8 and all the restaurants and bars the world over would have the same name. Quite trendy really. The design plans looked great. But we now think it might be simpler and easier if we just call them Gascoigne's. So that's the present situation. But we're still bashing on with it. I'm sure it will happen. They'll be really high-class places. None of this phoney sporting memorabilia tat all over the place.

I did say that I was going to be called G8 from now on. It was partly a joke – but also serious. I was fed up being called Gazza, wanting to be Paul Gascoigne in future, a different sort of person. I am going to sign myself with G8 from now on. The 8 comes from the team number I usually had. And I also used to eat a lot. Neat, eh?

I've worked out a way of signing myself with my

new name. I do the G with a sort of O beneath it, so it turns into an 8. Well, it amuses me. What I do now is sign myself in the old way – 'Paul "Gazza" Gascoigne' – plus the new 'G8'. I've done a deal with a memorabilia firm so that from now on, that will be my only authorised signature. That's what will appear on official merchandising and autographed material

I know it sounds mad, as if I'm getting carried away with myself, but it's not me – this whole football memorabilia business has gone wild, with people being ripped off, dealers making thousands. And yet a lot of the stuff is fake.

What the dealers do is use little kids to get the autographs, which is why Manchester United have stopped their players signing autographs at the training ground. They found that it was the same kids, coming day after day – not for themselves but for the dealers who were sending them. They paid the kids a few quid then they sold the stuff on the Internet for hundreds of pounds.

You might have seen during this last year that my 1990 England shirt, from Italia 90, the one in which I cried, was up for sale at Christie's, signed by members of the England team. The estimate was £20,000 – but it went for £30,000 so everyone was pretty surprised by the high price. What people didn't realise was that I sold that shirt in 2002 – for £90,000. It went to the *Observer* newspaper, who were running a competition in their sports magazine, as a sort of special promotion. The bloke who won it eventually decided to sell it. That's how it ended up at Christie's. So I was the winner, on that occasion, getting a better price than it fetched at auction.

I only wish now I had kept more of my England shirts and memorabilia. I gave most of them away – for charity events, or to friends. I probably wouldn't have so many money worries today if I'd kept everything. I read the other day that George Best now makes far more money than he ever did when he was playing football just by being George Best, not for actually doing anything but from merchandising, books and stuff.

People do seem to love legends. Judging by all the offers I'm now getting, I do seem to be considered a legend. It's nice, but I am surprised. I thought when my playing career was over, that would be it, end of my story. So despite the Boston United thing getting nowhere, which did depress me at the time, it's not been a bad year in some ways. My playing career might be over, but I'll probably do the odd charity game.

And I am still hoping to be a coach. I still have a fantasy about being a top manager one day. Me and Chris Waddle are going to do some coaching work together and I hope I'll pass my badge. There was a club in Newcastle, Australia, that asked if I was interested in a coaching job. I quite fancy that, going off somewhere I'm not known, getting my head down and learning the coaching trade. Or I might just concentrate on various business and media opportunities. I have found I can make some money, despite what some people predicted.

But I haven't mentioned yet the two other things that have obsessed and upset me this last year. One of them I can hardly bear to go into, as it's all been such a fucking mess, and buggered up my whole year, but the other is something I want to get off my chest, which I feel I have to, before I can move on.

The best of this year's blockbusters. The first half is hilarious, a litany of japes which underline the appeal of Gazza. Then the tale darkens as his psychological problems and alcohol take over. One fears for Gascoigne, but at least he faces up to his faults and spares those who came into contact with him.

Glenn Moore, Independent, *14 December 2004, on publication of the hardback edition of* Gazza: My Story

---

A moving book about a tragic figure in a wonderful if tainted game. Fuelled by anxiety and paranoia, on the field Gazza seemed like a gifted child, a kid of whom the other players rarely spoke unkindly.

Ray Connolly, Daily Mail, *17 December 2004*

Gazza: My Story is one of the scariest football books ever printed, so terrifying in its candour as to make you wonder if its subject knew what he was doing in signing off the proofs.

D.J. Taylor, New Statesman, *13 December 2004*

32

BODY BLOWS

I'm sitting in the Princess Grace Hospital in London. It's not far from King's Cross, I think. That's where I usually arrive when I come down from Newcastle. Quite near Madame Tussaud's, that's another focal point I can always remember. Strange, but I don't actually know the exact address. Yet I've been here so often they should give me a season ticket. Or at least my own key. It was here that I came after the Cup final of 1991 when it looked as if my career, not just my leg, had been ruined for ever.

This is the sixth time I have been ill and in hospital in the last year. What the fuck is wrong with me? Just when things seem to be going right, something comes along to bugger it up. Or is it me? Is it my own fault, after what I have done to my body over the last thirty-seven years?

The first problem happened when I was still at Boston United. I developed an ulcer. I've had this sort of problem previously, but this was hellish. I had an endoscopy – camera down my gob and that shit – then they poked around, did various things, put me on some medication.

Next, my knee went. I had left Boston and was just chilling out, going to watch England train, and then Liverpool train, trying to pick up a few tips, see how they did things, compare and contrast, in order to help my coaching career and get my coaching badge. I was getting out of the car one day and my knee just buckled under me. I went to see Mr Browett, who has operated on my legs over the years more times than he's had his own leg over – joke, I don't know anything about his private life. I had to have an operation on it and I came here, to the Princess Grace.

Then came the ice skating accident, when I slipped and hurt my back. It felt hellish at first, but then it began to feel a bit better. I hoped I'd get over it. But I was at East Midlands airport, about to fly to Dublin to do a chat show, when I suddenly found I hadn't got the strength to pick up my own bag. The moment I tried to grip the bag, or anything else, I could feel my neck was in agony. My dad was with me and I told him to pick up the bag for me. I carried on to Dublin, did the show, but felt terrible.

I then got Mr Browett, when he was still treating my knee, to have a look at my neck. I got in a panic when I was told I had intrusions on the discs at the top of the neck, where it joins on to the spine. They did a little operation on the neck, going into the side of it and into the spine. I felt sore for about ten days, but it seemed to have sorted it out.

While I was in hospital, Dave Seaman won the ice skating thing. I was lying here, in agony, when I got a text message from him saying he was at the airport stuffing his face with a bacon sandwich and about to fly off to Disneyland in Florida. The bastard. He didn't, of course, know that by that time I was back in hospital. After that, my stomach flared up again, with all the stress and worries, and I went to hospital for a while. Then I got pneumonia which turned out to be really serious.

I didn't want to know what the problem was at first. I just felt rotten, run down, no energy. Dave Seaman arranged for me to go to Arsenal, to see their physio,

Gary Lewin, and their doc. They did lots of checks, which was good of them, suggested various things. Then they said I'd better go and have some proper chest X-rays. So I went to the Wellington Hospital, had them done quickly for £180.

I had to be somewhere that day, a business arrangement I'd made, so I sent the X-rays to Arsenal in a taxi for them to look at, saying I couldn't make it myself, not in the flesh. When they saw the X-rays, they realised I was in a bad way. That's when I got rushed to hospital. My lung had collapsed, so I was told. I could hardly breathe. Literally. They put me on oxygen at once and filled me up with antibiotics, injecting me with them for speed.

So that was five times in hospital so far this year, which includes three operations. This is the sixth. Yeah, I'm now back in. My neck has been playing up again.

I am still arguing the money over some of the hospital bills. The knee problem was a football-related one, so the PFA have paid for that. I rang up Gordon Taylor and told him about it. Bloody hell, I paid into the PFA for fifteen years as a player, so I should get something out of them. They should still cover me for football-related problems, such as my knee. That's been buggered up, all because of football. With the neck, which happened doing the ice skating, I'm hoping the BBC will pay for that, though we are still in discussions.

During my playing career, I had to put up with away crowds shouting 'fat bastard' at me, which of course was true, on many occasions. I'm sure most people thought that once I stopped playing, I'd balloon up immediately. I'd be like a fucking pig and they'd all say, 'Told you so, he's still a fat bastard, only fatter.'

I was determined that wasn't going to happen. That's one of the reasons I've been so obsessed by keeping fit. I still go to the gym every day, working out. I do actually enjoy it. I like keeping my weight down.

But what happens is that some shite paper gets a photo of me looking really thin and they then have a story that I'm wasting away, that I'm a skeleton, down to eight stone, that I haven't got pneumonia but, aha, I've got something far worse and that I'm not long for this life. There are people who do want to see me wrecked. What one paper said was that I feared I might be HIV positive. I sued for that – and got £15,000 in damages.

But I'm not wrecked, as you can see. I'm 11 stone, which I consider the perfect weight for someone of my height. When I was playing I did like to be bulkier, around 12 stone. That was because I needed upper body strength to fend off all the thugs trying to clatter me.

So I'm fit enough, basically . . . well, apart from all the fucking things wrong with me. I mean I'm not overweight or run to seed. And I've been quite good for a while, mentally. I'm not taking as many pills as I was last year. I haven't been going to the shrink as often, though Johnny is still a friend. And at the moment I'm not as obsessed by things as I used to be, apart from my health, though I still want things neat and tidy, all lined up.

But it is true I haven't been looking after myself properly. I know you should have three proper meals a day, eat lots of greens and all that shit. I tend to live on a sandwich at lunch, then sweets in the evenings. And I have been rushing about, doing a lot of things.

When I was lying here, those first few days after I was rushed in with pneumonia, I felt like shit. I was all wired up, tubes sticking out everywhere, so I couldn't move, couldn't breathe. I started thinking about what lies before me, if and when I do get better and get myself out. I knew I still had to have more tests for my stomach. Then my neck and spine still had to be sorted. And my knee – I could still feel twinges, so how the fuck was I going to be a coach? You need to be able to kick a ball, run about, as a coach, otherwise you can't do it.

I've been told I should never head the ball again, not with my neck problems. Because I'm on warfarin, it could cause a blood clot and I could die, just by heading the ball. So how can I qualify as a coach, with all these things wrong with me? That's why my coaching career is on hold, for the moment.

Anyway, while lying here, I began to think what is the fucking point. I feel fucked, full stop. Fucked with life, fucked with myself. I'd be better off fucking dead.

I just couldn't think of anything to look forward to in life, except shitty, crappy, awful things. The press would be pleased I was a gonner. Oh yes they would, well a lot of them would. They would be able to say, 'I told you so . . . I always knew it would end in tears . . . he was always going to end up skint and a fucking wreck.' They'd love it if I topped myself. It would prove what they'd always predicted.

Yes, I know, don't tell me, it's not all the press. There have been some good things written about me – Gabby Logan did a nice piece in *The Times*, wishing me good luck and good health when I had pneumonia.

That was nice of her. But there are a lot of journalists who might say complimentary things to my face, but who are waiting for me to fall flat on my arse. They know that would make a good story, and it would sell papers.

The other crappy thing hanging over me was the thought that when I did get out, and felt well again, I'd still have to find the money for Shel. For years now, I've been having to find £10,000 each month, in cash, after I've paid tax. It hangs over me, every fucking month, wondering how I'll manage it. OK, I did say I was doing a few business and media deals, but I have no regular wage, not like when I was playing football and money was coming in, even when I was injured. Then I thought of Shel herself. Shel of course wouldn't care, either way, whether I lived or died – apart from the fact that her money would dry up. So if I did die, that would muck it up for her.

I got myself more and more depressed. Every way I looked, or everything I thought of, seemed to be full of problems. And they're just going to go on and on and on. All these times in hospitals, all these operations, that's me. I seemed fated. And it's never going to get any better.

So I decided I'd ask the next nurse who comes in to give me an injection for the pain – and then a bigger one, to finish me off, once and for all. And if she won't do it, I'll somehow nick the drugs and do it myself. I thought that would be the best way. It would solve all my problems. After all, I don't have a wife or kids at home waiting for me. Who would be really upset if I topped myself? Just my mum and dad and family.

So why didn't I do it? Well, I suppose I began to get a bit better. That helped. But the main thing was the support I began to get from my friends. When they heard I was in here with pneumonia, so many texted me or popped in to see me and wish me well. I thought, Fuck the press. They're always on my back, but I mustn't let them win. I'll keep going, just to show them. I decided I had to win the battle, on my own, and not give in.

My real friends know what I'm like, what the truth is. A lot of them happen to be quite famous themselves, so they know what it's like. It's happened to them, rubbish stories in the press which is all shite. So they never believed stories about me being down to eight stone, with half a lung, no stomach and two heads and that I was dying.

I got a text message today from Richard and Judy. I don't really know them, but they sent best wishes. Terry Venables came in to see me. We had a good laugh, going over all the daft things I did with England and with Spurs.

One day when I was really doped up because of the pneumonia, there was this little kid crept into my room one morning, about 7.30. I thought it really was a kid at first, as I wasn't concentrating and was feeling dopey. This kid stares at me and then starts pissing himself laughing. It was Dennis Wise. I liked him laughing at me. I wasn't hurt or offended. I'd rather have someone laugh at me than go on all sad and soppy. It was the sight of me, all tubed up, that's what amused him. He's a good lad, Dennis. I also had nice text messages from Alan Shearer and Chris Waddle.

While I've been in here, I read a story about Gary Charles, you know, that kid at Nottingham Forest I tried to clatter in the Cup final and ended up buggering myself. He was such a nice young lad, very talented. I did feel guilty at fouling him. But I never had any contact with him after that game, or since. Now I've found out that he had to retire at thirty-two, because of injuries. He took to the drink and has been in prison twice. Dear

God, I thought *I* had fucking problems. That was a lesson to me, not to feel self-pity. When I get out of here, I'm going to ring him. Perhaps I'll go and see him, help him if I can.

I also read a bit about that World Cup referee, the one who gave me a yellow card in the semi-final in 1990 against West Germany. A bloke called Jose Roberto Wright. Sounds English, eh, perhaps an Ian Wright love child, but no, turns out he's Brazilian. In reading this bit about him, I discovered something I never knew at the time – that he had been selected to referee the World Cup final, but the Germans had lodged a complaint. It was to do with superstitions. A Brazilian had refereed two previous World Cup finals, in 1982 and 1986, and the Germans had lost both, so they didn't want another. The German complaint had been upheld. The ref knew before that game that he wouldn't be in charge of the final if Germany won. It would have been to his benefit if England had won.

In this interview with him, he said he had always regarded me highly as a player and had been looking forward to seeing me in the final, with him as ref. So he was probably in tears as well, but for a different reason. Just shows you, eh? I don't know what it just shows. Something or other.

Hey, look, there's Julian Dicks on the telly. Haven't seen him for ages. Yeah, I have the TV on in my room all the time, tuned to Sky Sports. While I'm watching I'm also on the phone, talking, and at the same time, on my mobile phone texting while I'm talking. Clever bastard, eh. I like to be active, keep myself busy.

I had some good laughs with Dicksy when we were in the Under-21s together. One evening, he tried to get me to sneak out into town and go to a pub, but I didn't feel like it. He went on and on, wouldn't let me go to sleep. Next day, when he was asleep, I got my own back. I went out and bought some fireworks and went into his bathroom. I lit a big banger and set it off. The noise in the enclosed space was incredible. I rushed into his room shouting, 'Evacuate, evacuate, bomb blast, bomb blast!' Dicksy jumps up and runs naked out of the room into the corridor. The firework did a bit more damage than I had intended. In fact it blew off the lavatory seat. I had to pay for it. But it was a good laugh.

Yeah, I did have a wild time for about twenty years. I don't do that sort of thing any more. It's now almost two years since I had a drink and two and half years since I touched any substances. I haven't actually gone to an AA meeting for, let me see, two months. I should go every day. I did for a long time, but with being in and out of hospital so much, I haven't been able to, have I? But I'm determined to keep off the alcohol. I can't see myself ever going on the drink again. Life is so much easier, not drinking. I'm aware of that all the time.

I've also given up smoking. When I say given up, I mean I haven't had a fag since, well, since I came in here, yesterday. And when I had the pneumonia, I didn't smoke for, well, must have been eight days. My lungs were knackered and I was unable to breathe, that decided me. I won't go back to smoking. Not heavy smoking. That's what I tell myself. What I really like now is the odd cigar. So I'm leading a pretty healthy life, apart from the sweets. Last night I had a craving for popcorn so I asked for a big bag.

I know what will happen, though. In about ten years' time, when I have become a manager of a decent club, I'll lose my first game and the press will say, 'Oh what do you expect, he did cocaine fifteen years ago.' I know my dissolute past will always follow me around, for as long as I live.

For some of the first part of the year, I was living with Jimmy in his flat in Dunston, but it wasn't my home. Just where I stayed when I was in Newcastle. I got pissed off when the press made a big thing about it, said it showed what I'd come down to, living in an ex-council flat with Jimmy. It's actually a nice little place. It was handy for going to see Mam and Dad, my sisters and brother and their bairns. There's a fish shop at the end of the street, though I don't eat chips any more, or kebabs, well not very often, and also a fishing tackle shop. So it was convenient. But it was just a base, where I kept some clothes. All my real stuff is in store, or at me mam's, till I decide what I'm going to do next.

While I was at Boston those three months, I was in that hotel; then whenever I come to London, which has been quite a bit, I stay in a hotel. Or in a fucking hospital.

I've recently taken on an apartment in Newcastle – in Jesmond, in a new luxury block. A few of the Newcastle players live there. It's dead smart, two bathrooms, two bedrooms, all mod cons. The first day though, when I moved in, it felt so weird. For the last five years, since the move to Everton, I've either been in hotels, or hospitals or fucking clinics. I couldn't stand it, I felt sort of displaced, not having room service and that. So I moved out again and spent the next two nights in a hotel.

I don't mind living in hotels, or being in hospitals, never have done. I like the feeling of being cut off, yet looked after. But it would be sensible to have my own house. I've given enough houses away in my life. After two days, I moved back into the apartment. Before I came down here, I'd got it organised better, got my own telly and other things. I'm living there alone. I make my own food, such as it is. I do forget to eat and don't look after myself as well as I should do. If I had a proper home, and a proper wife and normal family life, then that might be different.

The apartment is only rented till the summer, then I'll decide. I haven't put much of my personal stuff in yet. That's mainly at my mam's or my dad's, all the bits from my career. They keep telling me to sort it all out, but I can't face it. I don't want to look back at my past. It'll be too sad. I might cry.

All this year, I haven't been able to make any big decisions about my life and the future because of all the money arguments with Shel. Now those are over, for the moment anyway, which is why I want to tell some of the things I've never talked about before, until now.

> Ally [McCoist] would regale us with stories about his generosity and compulsion. For example, on hearing that one of Ally's sons wanted a rabbit, he arranged for the delivery of a menagerie to Ally's back garden – fish, gerbils, rabbits and hamsters were delivered with cages and food.
>
> I am sure lying in his hospital bed, Gazza will feel that the public are willing him to make a speedy recovery. He may be controversial, but he is a national treasure and anyone who knows him just wants him to be happy.
>
> *Gabby Logan*, The Times, *3 January 2005*

33

THE END OF THE AFFAIR

In the hardback book, I never criticised Shel. I just criticised myself for being a bastard, which I was, beating her up, getting drunk, neglecting the kids. I admitted all that. I'm not proud of how I behaved. I wish I'd never done all that. It meant that I took all the flak, all the stick, so that it looked to everyone else that I was a total, 100 per cent bastard, with no saving graces. I never said a bad word against Shel. Go on, find me a sentence where I was nasty about her. When my family or friends had a go at her, I defended her. I didn't criticise her behaviour for one simple reason – I loved her and loved the kids.

But now, because of what's just happened, I feel I want to talk back, to give my side of our relationship for a change. It's a bit like coming out and saying I was an alcoholic. For years and years I never admitted it. I was just a bloke who drank a lot and got stinking drunk. That was all. Where was the problem? I denied I was an alcoholic, to everyone, most of all to myself. Coming out about my drink problem, admitting it, has helped me to come to terms with it, and move on.

In the same way, if I now tell something about my side of life with Shel, I hope I'll be able to move on. I now realise I've been in denial all these years about her, not admitting the truth that was staring me in the face. I can't see myself ever having a proper relationship again, because I have so little confidence with women, or about myself, unless I try to face up to what happened with Shel. So here's a little of what did happen, from my point of view, as I now see it, looking back over those fifteen years or so since I first met her in 1990.

At that time things were tough for Shel. She had no money, her marriage had finished, her husband was having financial difficulties and she was about to lose her home. As I said before, she had to work hard to support herself and the kids. She was even shoving free newspapers through letterboxes for a few quid.

I helped her out a bit not long after I'd met her, just to keep her in her house, stop her being homeless, then I bought her a car so she could take her kids to school. And then it went on from there, all the time. Yeah, I did shove money at her, indulge every whim, give her daft presents all the time, that's me, how I've always been, too generous for my own good.

I remember one thing about her, even before we were having any arguments. I found some notes that she'd written down. About me and her together. God knows what they were for. I still don't know, even now. I know therapists advise battered wives to keep notes, but this was long before I touched her.

Whatever it all meant, we soon split up, which we did all the time, and got back, and so it went, on then off. I'd behave badly, get drunk, be a pain, which I've told yous all about, then I'd plead with her and she'd have me back. She didn't have to, of course. We weren't married. But she did.

When I went to Italy, I really did beg her to come and live with me. That was all my doing. But it was a mistake. I found myself at twenty-four, having been single all my life, suddenly living with a partner and having to be a father to two children when at the same time I was trying to get to grips with a new culture, new people and a new language. Anyway, that ended in tears and she went back to England.

I got called in one day by Manzini, when I was playing for Lazio, to say she'd been on the phone to the club, wanting to talk to me. I rang her back and found her saying, 'Let's get back again.'

After she's come back to Rome, I was driving her in the car and I slowed down because I wanted to give her a kiss – but she refused, said she didn't want to. We'd just got back together. So that did piss me off. I was really upset. That evening I got blind drunk, smashed up the villa and she got really scared. That was all my fault, really stupid. I admit it. All I'm doing now is telling you the extra little things that were going on, which I didn't mention earlier. I was taking all the blame because I felt so guilty.

When she decided that was it, she was going back for good, I said all right then, I'll give you some help to buy a nice little place back home in Hertfordshire. That will be it, I said, I'm sorry for what's happened. I'm sorry I've been a bastard, but we'll part as friends, and go our independent ways in life from now on. As it turned out, I ended up buying her a much bigger place. But that's down to me being too generous again, I guess.

While in Italy, I was continuing to help her out financially from time to time. I didn't begrudge it at all. I was getting well paid playing for Lazio and I could easily afford it.

It's true that I was not there when Regan was born. I admitted that earlier. But I had arrived the day before to see her, at her house in Hertfordshire, having come down from Scotland where I was playing with Rangers. Regan was born the next day, the Sunday. I wasn't there – because she wouldn't let me in. I stood on the doorstep and she told me to go away. Her mother was there and I asked what should I do. She said it would be best if I did exactly what Shel wanted. So off I went.

There was a double-page spread in a Sunday newspaper the following day, which turned out to be the day Regan was born, revealing that I'd been out on the piss just as Shel was due to give birth, suggesting what a sod I must be, what a lousy father. It was from that story I learned that my son was going to be called Regan. What really was going on behind the scenes? Why would she not let me be there for the birth, even though I arrived the day before?

It's true that for the next two weeks I didn't turn up and was drunk most of the time, but I did want to be there for the birth. And I loved Regan to bits when I saw him for the first time and cuddled him in my arms. We got back together, once again. She got me to do a piece for the *News of the World* saying she was the good one and I was the monster. We split the money. I put £20,000 of my share in Regan's name for when he's twenty-one.

I wanted her to move up to Scotland with Regan. I said we could buy a big house, a proper family house, and be a proper family. She said that would only work if we got married. I so wanted to see my son that I agreed. That's how the subject of marriage first came up. In an article in *Hello!* Shel said that I asked her to marry me and then she found out she was pregnant. But that's not how I remember it happening. I got used to the idea in the end, and fancied getting married, but at the same time I did worry that we were not ready for it. We were still arguing and rowing, splitting up.

When I was in Hong Kong, with the England team, I got this big bunch of flowers one day and a lovely Father's Day card from Regan. Dennis Wise was my room-mate at the time. He can tell you I was so touched I was in tears. So I rang up Shel and before I knew what I was saying, I was asking her to take me back and yes, we would definitely get married. When I got home, I did go down on my knees and propose.

I wasn't talked into it, tricked in any way, though I did worry about selling our wedding to *Hello!* – knowing how often those people who sell themselves end up in divorce.

Shel organised the whole wedding and she looked stunning, she really did. I enjoyed it, the wedding itself. Danny Baker did a funny home video, talking to me when it was all over. He made a joke that we might get divorced. I said no fucking chance. But if we did, Shel wouldn't get a penny.

During the ceremony itself, something serious did upset me. When we were each saying our vows, and it came to my turn to say 'I do', I'm sure I heard this loud whisper, someone saying 'YES!' It was clear to me. They showed the wedding video on that Channel 4 programme about me a couple of years back. The one with all those supposed experts talking bollocks. Paul Merson was on it as well, claiming I was swallowing loads of sleepers. If they show it again, have a look and see if you think

I'm imagining it. What that 'YES!' indicated to me was
that I was trapped. When I heard it, a little tear came
into my eye and my sister Lindsay asked me what was
wrong. I said nothing, pet, nothing's wrong. I didn't tell
her what I'd heard or what had suddenly come into my
head. And that's why the honeymoon was a shambles.
I was still so upset.

I loved our house in Scotland, in Renfrew. Shel
made it really nice, but I never felt positive about our
marriage.

When I beat her up at the Gleneagles hotel, which
was the worst thing I ever did, a photograph of Shel and
her bruises was almost immediately in the papers. I wonder
who told them so quickly, eh? Piers Morgan has now said
in his recent book that he took a call 'from a "friend" of
Sheryl Kyle' (that's Shel, of course), telling him what had
happened. I don't know if that's right, but according to
him this 'friend' said that Shel wouldn't pose for photos,
but if she were caught in a paparazzi-type shot, that would
be okay. And, guess what, that's how it happened. OK, I
was the bastard who did it, no argument there, but I
certainly didn't want it in the papers, did I?

That last time, which I talked about right at the
start of the book, when we gave it one final go, she made

it clear she was being tough with me as a test, to see if I could take it. I could understand that. But I hope the kids have been able to make their own minds up.

I do see Regan. I can have access when I want. I take him to places, give him a good time, then usually arrange with Shel to meet somewhere on the motorway. I then hand him back to her, without us saying anything. Last Christmas, I bought Bianca a car. That's what she asked for. She's now eighteen and left school and got a job in London. For Mason I got lots of bling bling – a diamond watch, a ring, a bracelet, that's what he likes.

After Shel and I got divorced in 1998, as part of the settlement I had to pay her £10,000 a month maintenance, towards the education of the kids. I could manage that when I was still playing in the Premiership, but when that finished in 2002 my income dropped dramatically. The real reason I went to China was for the money. Yes, I said I wanted a challenge, to get away, as I told you at the time, but that was only part of it. I was promised £30,000 a month, more than anybody else was offering me at the time. I took it in order to keep up my monthly payments to Shel. In the end, I only got paid one lot of £30,000 from the Chinese. We're still arguing the toss about it.

When I was in the clinic that first time, and after it she agreed to take me back, I happened to read a story in some newspaper about a young guy saying he'd had an affair with her. When I got back, I asked if it was true, about that bloke. She denied it and I believed her. She said she would sue. Nonetheless, all the time I was with Shel, over all the years, I was always jealous, frightened she would sleep with someone else. My own insecurity.

This last time, when she let me back, she did say she'd been out with someone. I had just got there, been dried out but was on heavy medication, going to a therapist every day, so that was the last thing I needed to hear. That was what was in my mind, driving me mad, when I crashed her Jaguar into the lorry, but I didn't tell you that at the time.

I've since had a couple of anonymous letters from blokes, alleging things, but I don't know whether they are true or not. It is none of my business and she has every right to do what she wants. We are divorced. But I still get upset. When we were married, and when we were back together again, I was always faithful. It was only during one long separation, which lasted seven months, that I had two one-night stands, but they were meaningless. The truth was I always loved Shel. She was the one for me.

I never thought for a moment that Shel and I being together as a couple had anything to do with our lifestyle. I never considered it. She did help me, a lot, and I'll always be grateful, helping me to get into the Priory that first time, helping when I was in a bad way, obsessed and depressed. I know I couldn't have been much fun to be with. But now I am not so sure what she wanted.

That last time, she said I could stay as long as I was sober. I've kept to that, not a drink in over two years. It was arguments about money which finally did it. That's what caused the final split, not me drinking or any bad behaviour. I never touched her, or even physically threatened her, never once, after that scene in Gleneagles in 1996. She's at least admitted that herself.

When I was staying with Shel, she did help me sort out all my papers, which were in a mess, and I was grateful. While I was with her, still on medication, trying to get better, she suddenly started saying, 'Why don't you go out and get a job, why don't you do some work?' Perhaps she was right. As I said earlier, I do need to go out and work now.

Anyway, last year, in January 2004, my Newcastle

lawyer went properly into all my finances and affairs and we went to the High Court in London to try and get the maintenance payments reduced. And we succeeded.

A year later, in February 2005, we went back to court again, because I didn't think the payments I was making were fair when I had no regular income. This time I agreed to a lump sum, so that's it as far as me paying Shel is concerned. We negotiated, and the upshot was that I paid her £235,000. I was able to get that money together because of this book, so thanks to those who bought the hardback version, and I also cashed in a bit of my Channel Islands money. Which I didn't want to do. That's all I have left from my football career and, as I told you earlier, I was advised to put it in US dollars, so I lose money by taking any out at the moment.

I'm still paying for the children but that's been reduced as well. It is now £3,800 a month until Mason and Regan leave full-time education. I don't have to pay for Bianca any more as she's left school.

I've recently found myself lying awake at night, trying to work out how much I've paid to Shel over the last fifteen years. Most of it was my choice of course –

holidays, jewellery, cash to help her out, help with buying a house, presents (including that time-share lodge in Scotland I gave her after we were divorced – crazy or what?), cars, that sort of thing. It made me happy and I loved her. And then the divorce payments I've talked about before. It comes to a pretty big number.

Thinking about all that, it's funny (not really), but when you look at the facts, we were only married for two years – from July 1996 to August 1998 when we got divorced. During those two years, I estimate, because of all the rows and separations, in fact we only lived as a married couple for three and a half months. I know we were on and off together for a few years before that, but it makes you think. And after it all she's ended up today with a house in Hertfordshire worth £1.2 million. Talk about *Footballers' Wives*.

After my book appeared, in which I said nothing personal against her, she gave a big interview to *Hello!*, over ten pages, slagging me off. That's why I now feel justified in pointing out a few things. She said I wasn't the great guy I made myself out to be in my book. Jee-sus. I can't believe she read it. I couldn't have made it clearer what a bad, mad, daft guy I had been, and I dragged no one else into it, blaming only myself. In

Hello!, she also claimed I hit her when she was pregnant, which is totally untrue.

There were also photographs of her posing with the kids, my kids, which is how I have always looked upon them, even though only Regan is my son. I didn't like that, putting our kids on show, dragging them into our row. It's not, of course, the first time she's gone to the press over the years. She'll probably do it again now, but as she's already said all the bad things she can about me, several times, and so have I, I can't think what else remains to be said.

You'll notice she still calls herself Gascoigne. 'Sheryl Gascoigne – ex-wife of Paul Gascoigne', so she gets billed. She loves it. If she hated me so much, for all the bad things I did, why didn't she go back to her maiden name, or her first married name? I did ask her that once, when we'd split yet again. She says it's because of Regan. He's called Gascoigne, so she doesn't want to be different. That's her story. But it's interesting that she's never written an article or sold a story about her first husband. It's always about me.

Everybody always told me she wasn't right for me, but I never believed it. I told people to shut up, even my own family and friends. But it also happened in football. Almost every manager told me to call it a day. I was obsessed by her, but it was doing me harm, and doing her no good either, so they all said. But I ignored them.

At La Manga, when Hoddle chucked me out of the England team, there had just been a nonsense story in the papers about Shel. As usual, that sent me almost insane, as everyone in the squad could see. It might well have been one of the reasons why Hoddle later said 'my head was not right'. He knew I was worrying about her.

When I talk to Regan on the phone at home, she's always in the background, I can hear her. But when he's at school, and she's not around, he talks to me a lot. There are no problems. I've visited his school and I took a spelling class. I asked the teacher and he said fine. The kids came up and I checked their spelling. All the kids loved it. And so did Regan.

I'm sorry to go on about Shel so much. I just don't seem to escape, which is why I decided to talk about her, in a way I have never done before. It's also because I'm still living with the consequences. I haven't had sex for over a year now. I don't miss it, not really. I've got used to it. For the moment.

I forgot to tell you last time about one romantic interlude. It began in 2000, just after I'd joined Everton.

I took Hazy – David Hayes – and another of my old Newcastle friends to Miami for a fishing and drinking holiday.

We were in our hotel one night and I saw this stunning blonde sitting at the bar, on her own. I stared at her for about an hour, without getting any response. I was gutted when this guy appears, obviously her fella.

We then went off to another bar, the Flamingo on South Beach, where I got talking to a girl from Manchester. As I'm talking to her, the stunning blonde I had seen in our hotel suddenly appears – with Hazy's arm round her. I think fucking hell, how has he managed it? I go over and he says he's talked her into coming to see me, because I'd said she was so stunning. I chat to her and then we go back to our hotel, where we're both staying. I have a cigar, she has a cigar, and we both sit there talking in the reception area till about four in the morning.

Then suddenly her bloke appears. He gets out of the lift in his boxer shorts, looking furious. I ask him if he'd like a drink with me and my girlfriend. Just to wind him up. He tells me he's a lawyer, from somewhere like Philadelphia, down in Miami for an important case, and he has to be up early in the morning. I say, 'Oh, a lawyer, I could always do with a good lawyer, can I hire you?'

He grabs the girl by the hand and pulls her into the lift. They disappear.

During our chat, I had found out her name was Lina, she was Russian, and I'd got her mobile phone number. Nothing happened between us. I'd not even kissed her, never mind shag her. A year passed. During that time I'd been thinking of her, remembering how stunning she was, what a good chat we had, so one day I decided to ring her. This was after I'd left Burnley – before I went to China. So some time in the spring of 2002.

'Hi, I'm Paul, we met in Miami', and after a bit she said, 'Oh aye, I remember you. You told me you were a footballer. My friend looked you up and she told me you were a bad person.' I said, 'Ignore all that, it's newspaper stuff. I'm a nice guy really.'

Anyway I talked her into seeing me again. It turned out she was returning to Russia. She'd been living with this rich American lawyer for about four years, but was now going back to Moscow.

When I'd first met her, I'd asked her what she was doing with that fat bastard. She said, 'That's funny, those are the exact words your friend used.' She told me the lawyer was a nice guy, and he looked after her well.

Two days later, I booked a plane to Moscow and went off to see Lina. I did have a few drinks on the plane, and was probably a bit noisy and stupid. When I was going through passport control, these two huge guys grabbed hold of me. I thought I'd been reported for causing some sort of commotion on the plane, but the real reason was that I didn't have a visa for Russia. I hadn't realised you had to have one.

I was put in jail, a proper jail, but it was inside the airport. I was told I was allowed to make one phone call – one only. Should I ring me dad? Over the years, I've usually rung him when I'm in trouble. Or should I ring the British Embassy? See if they can sort out the visa problem. Or should I ring Lina? She was supposed to be meeting me, and she was Russian, could speak to them in their own language.

I was shitting myself, all alone, not knowing what to do. Eventually I decided to ring Lina. I rang her number – and got her mum, who couldn't speak a word of English. Every time I said 'Lina', she said 'Airport'. I realised she was somewhere at the airport, waiting for me, but not knowing I was in jail.

An hour went by, then two, three, then at four in the morning one of the jailers says, 'There's a woman outside for you.' I ask what kind of woman. They say she's blonde and Russian. I says it must be Lina.

Lina explains the whole story to them, that it was ignorance that made me not get the visa. They agreed I could spend twenty-four hours in Moscow, but then I must be deported.

We book into a hotel and have a wonderful night together. In the morning, instead of me going off on my own, I suggested to her that she come with me. We could have a romantic holiday together.

So I ring BA, book flights on my credit card, and we go to Miami. We arrive and book into a hotel. We had ten brilliant days together. Very romantic. I gave her flowers, chocolates, everything. It turned out she had been married, to a Russian, but that the marriage had long since finished.

At the end of the ten days, we parted. She went back to Moscow, in tears. I flew to London. We did ring each other for about four months, then it sort of tailed off. I haven't had any contact with her for over a year now, but I still think about her. She was a stunning girl.

One point about telling you this story is that it was interesting, and upsetting, that she'd looked me up – and found I was a bad lad. When I was in China, I was asked to be the judge for a fashion show. I got the winner's number and later rang her up, saying it would be nice to have a drink with her. She said her friend had looked me up on the web – and found out I was a bad man. Fucking hell. This was Lanzhou, in the back of beyond in China. What chance have I got?

What happens is that I worry that no nice girls will come near me. I'm a bastard, ain't I? I've said so. Now Shel has said so. Must be true. So who wants to get mixed up with someone with my problems who might beat them up? I know I haven't harmed anyone, or done anything bad to anyone for almost ten years, and I know I'll never do so again. But other people don't know that.

So I imagine that any girl who does come along, makes advances and that, will just be a gold digger, who'll turn me over, take my money and sell their story. I do seem to have attracted them, especially when I was drunk, which of course doesn't happen any more. I'm so fucking sober and sensible these days, I've been keeping away from all women, whatever their motives. So I haven't been looking for another relationship.

Now my financial relationship with Shel has been settled, and I don't have to pay her any more, a huge weight is off my shoulders – financially and emotionally. I can now sit down, see where I'm at, look at what I've got left and what I might be earning in the future. This summer I'm planning to buy something, either the flat I've rented in Jesmond or a little house. When I've settled down domestically, I might then be open to meeting some nice lass. I might come across her anywhere, up in Newcastle in the queue at the fish and chip shop back in Dunston, or in Jesmond.

But there's one thing that still worries me. It came to me the other day. I said it to Jimmy – and he couldn't believe it. In fact I'm shitting myself that it might turn out to come true. If Shel were to ring me up tomorrow, when I come out of here, and ask me to come back, you know what, I'd probably say yes. Fucking hell. I'm a daft enough bastard, even now, to be tempted. After all we've put each other through. Let's hope it won't happen.

Right, I'm not talking about Shel again. That's it, for ever. By talking like this, at long last, I've got her out of my system. And I know she's better off without me. So good luck to her.

Here's the doctor to do some tests. All I'm having now is an injection into my neck. They're going to put me under, see if they can relieve the pain in the discs.

I should be out tomorrow. And then off to Newcastle. Perhaps I might strike lucky in the fish queue . . .

> The truth is he wanted my full attention and would have been happy to have me without the children. I don't think it could ever work between us as a couple now. I was always prepared to be his friend but he never wanted that.
>
> *Do you regret having met him?*
>
> No, because regrets are a waste of energy – and most importantly I have Regan. My time with Paul was a part of my life and I am the person I am now because of what happened.
>
> *Sheryl Gascoigne, interviewed in* Hello!, *13 July 2004*

CAREER STATISTICS

PAUL GASCOIGNE

Paul John Gascoigne, born Dunston, Gateshead 27 May 1967.

CAREER

Redheugh Boys' Club, Dunston juniors, trials for Ipswich Town, Middlesbrough, Southampton. Newcastle United schoolboy 1980, apprentice 1983, professional 1985. Transferred to Tottenham Hotspur June 1988 £2.3 million. Transferred to Lazio May 1992 £5.5 million. Transferred to Rangers July 1995 £4.3 million. Transferred to Middlesbrough March 1998 £3.45 million. Free to Everton July 2000. Free to Burnley March 2002. Washington DC (trial) 2002. Free to Gansu Tianma 2003. Wolverhampton Wanderers (reserves) 2003. Non-contract player-coach Boston United July to October 2004.

CLUB RECORD

Season	League		FA Cup S/Cup		Lge Cup/ SL Cup		Other Cups		Champions Lge		UEFA Cup	
	Apps	Goals	Apps	Goals	Apps	Goals	Apps	Goals	Apps	Goals	Apps	Goals
NEWCASTLE U												
1984–85	2	-	-	-	-	-	-	-	-	-	-	-
1985–86	31	9	1	-	3	-	-	-	-	-	-	-
1986–87	24	5	-	-	2	-	1+	-	-	-	-	-
1987–88	35	7	3	3	3	1	2#	-	-	-	-	-
TOTTENHAM H												
1988–89	32	6	-	-	5	1	-	-	-	-	-	-
1989–90	34	6	-	-	4	1	-	-	-	-	-	-
1990–91	26	7	6	6	5	6	-	-	-	-	-	-
1991–92	-	-	-	-	-	-	-	-	-	-	-	-
LAZIO												
1992–93	22	4	4*	-	-	-	-	-	-	-	-	-
1993–94	17	2	-	-	-	-	-	-	-	-	-	-
1994–95	4	-	-	-	-	-	-	-	-	-	-	-
RANGERS												
1995–96	28	14	4	3	3	1	-	-	7	1	-	-
1996–97	26	13	1	-	4	3	-	-	3	1	-	-
1997–98	20	3	3	-	-	-	-	-	3	-	2	-
MIDDLESBROUGH												
1997–98	7	-	-	-	1	-	-	-	-	-	-	-
1998–99	26	3	1	-	2	-	-	-	-	-	-	-
1999–2000	8	1	1	-	2	-	-	-	-	-	-	-
EVERTON												
2000–01	14	-	-	-	1	-	-	-	-	-	-	-
2001–02	18	1	4	-	1	-	-	-	-	-	-	-
BURNLEY												
2001–02	6	-	-	-	-	-	-	-	-	-	-	-
GANSU TIANMA												
2002–03	4	2	-	-	-	-	-	-	-	-	-	-
BOSTON U												
2004–05	4	-	-	-	1	-	-	-	-	-	-	-
Totals	388	83	28	12	37	13	3	0	13	2	2	0

* Italian Cup
+ Full Members Cup
# Simod Cup

ROTHMANS
FOOTBALL YEARBOOK
1986-87

Editor: Peter Dunk

Rothmans

17th YEAR

ENGLAND APPEARANCES

Date	Competition	Opponent	Venue	Result	Scored	Sub in	Subbed
14.9.88	FR	Denmark	Wembley	1–0	-	85	-
16.11.88	FR	Saudi Arabia	Riyadh	1–1	-	80	-
26.4.89	WCQ	Albania	Wembley	5–0	88	67	-
23.5.89	RC	Chile	Wembley	0–0	-	-	-
27.5.89	RC	Scotland	Hampden Park	2–0	-	78	-
6.9.89	WCQ	Sweden	Stockholm	0–0	-	72	-
28.3.90	FR	Brazil	Wembley	1–0	-	78	-
25.4.90	FR	Czechoslovakia	Wembley	4–2	89	-	-
15.5.90	FR	Denmark	Wembley	1–0	-	-	-
22.5.90	FR	Uruguay	Wembley	1–2	-	-	-
2.6.90	FR	Tunisia	Tunis	1–1	-	-	-
11.6.90	WCF	Republic of Ireland	Cagliari	1–1	-	-	-
16.6.90	WCF	Holland	Cagliari	0–0	-	-	-
21.6.90	WCF	Egypt	Cagliari	1–0	-	-	-
26.6.90	WCF	Belgium	Bologna	1–0	-	-	-
1.7.90	WCF	Cameroon	Naples	3–2	-	-	-
4.7.90	WCF	West Germany	Turin	1–1+	-	-	-
12.9.90	FR	Hungary	Wembley	1–0	-	-	-
17.10.90	ECQ	Poland	Wembley	2–0	-	-	-
6.2.91	FR	Cameroon	Wembley	2–0	-	-	67
14.10.92	WCQ	Norway	Wembley	1–1	-	-	-
18.11.92	WCQ	Turkey	Wembley	4–0	16,61	-	-
17.2.93	WCQ	San Marino	Wembley	6–0	-	-	-
31.3.93	WCQ	Turkey	Izmir	2–0	44	-	-
28.4.93	WCQ	Holland	Wembley	2–2	-	-	45
29.5.93	WCQ	Poland	Katowice	1–1	-	-	79
2.6.93	WCQ	Norway	Oslo	0–2	-	-	-
8.9.93	WCQ	Poland	Wembley	3–0	49	-	-
9.3.94	FR	Denmark	Wembley	1–0	-	-	66
3.6.95	UT	Japan	Wembley	2–1	-	69	-
8.6.95	UT	Sweden	Elland Road	3–3	-	64	-
11.6.95	UT	Brazil	Wembley	1–3	-	78	-
6.9.95	FR	Colombia	Wembley	0–0	-	-	75
15.11.95	FR	Switzerland	Wembley	3–1	-	-	-
12.12.95	FR	Portugal	Wembley	1–1	-	-	-
27.3.96	FR	Bulgaria	Wembley	1–0	-	-	76
24.4.96	FR	Croatia	Wembley	0–0	-	-	-
23.5.96	FR	China	Beijing	3–0	64	-	-
8.6.96	ECF	Switzerland	Wembley	1–1	-	-	74

15.6.96	ECF	Scotland	Wembley	2–0	79	-	-
18.6.96	ECF	Holland	Wembley	4–1	-	-	-
22.6.96	ECF	Spain	Wembley	0–0++	-	-	-
26.6.96	ECF	Germany	Wembley	1–1+	-	-	-
1.9.96	WCQ	Moldova	Chisinau	3–0	24	-	80
9.10.96	WCQ	Poland	Wembley	2–0	-	-	-
9.11.96	WCQ	Georgia	Tbilisi	2–0	-	-	-
24.5.97	FR	South Africa	Old Trafford	2–1	-	-	90
31.5.97	WCQ	Poland	Katowice	2–0	-	-	16
4.6.97	T	Italy	Nantes	2–0	-	79	-
7.6.97	T	France	Montpellier	1–0	-	-	-
10.6.97	T	Brazil	Paris	0–1	-	-	-
10.9.97	WCQ	Moldova	Wembley	4–0	80	-	-
11.10.97	WCQ	Italy	Rome	0–0	-	-	87
15.11.97	FR	Cameroon	Wembley	2–0	-	-	72
23.5.98	FR	Saudi Arabia	Wembley	0–0	-	61	-
27.5.98	KH	Morocco	Casablanca	1–0	-	-	-
29.5.98	KH	Belgium	Casablanca	0–0+	-	-	49

FR	Friendly	ECF	European Championship Finals
WCQ	World Cup Qualifier	T	Tournoi
RC	Rous Cup	KH	King Hassan Cup
WCF	World Cup Finals	+	Lost on penalties
ECQ	European Championship Qualifying	++	Won on penalties
UT	Umbro Trophy		

Paul Gascoigne

I might not have made Hoddle's final squad for the 1998 World Cup, but I did make it on to BP's stickers . . .

ENGLAND '98

Paul Gascoigne

Caps: 54
Goals: 10
Date of Birth: 27/5/67
Ht: 5.10 Wt: 11.7

Details correct 28/2/98

Team England Collection

TOTAL ENGLAND RESULTS: 34 wins, 19 draws, 4 defeats

HONOURS

57 full England caps, 10 goals; 13 Under-21, 5 goals; 4 B, 1 goal. BBC Sports Personality of the Year 1990. Young Player of the Year 1988. Scottish Football Writers and Scottish Professional Footballers Player of the Year 1996.

GAZZA ON THE NET

The Internet is full of stuff about me, a lot of it bollocks, some of it funny, and some of it true. Here are 50 stories currently doing the rounds via websites and e-mail. Which do you think are genuine? Having read this book by now (and paid for it, I hope) you will know roughly what stuff is true – but what about the rest? See page 513 for my comments. And for the real me, check out my own website: www.paulgascoigne.biz

1 One hour after playing for England, met 'showbiz pals' Danny Baker and Chris Evans in a Hampstead pub while still wearing his full kit . . . boots included.

2 When asked for his nationality before an operation, told the nurse: 'Church of England'.

3 On a trip to London, jumped out of his car to demand 'a go' on a workman's pneumatic drill. After getting the go-ahead, happily pounded the pavement to the amusement of shoppers.

4 On first meeting with Lazio's president to discus money move to the Italian club, was quick to esteemed gentleman that he reminded him of

5 Organisers of Italia 90 TV coverage had th of augmenting team line-ups with footage

mouthing his own name. Gascoigne's genius led him to subvert the process by, instead, mouthing 'fucking wanker'. Broadcasters across the world had to use it all the way through the tournament.

6   Booked a series of sunbed sessions for then Newcastle team-mate Tony Cunningham. Who, of course, is black.

7   Asked by a Norwegian camera crew if he had a message for England's upcoming opponents, immediately responded with, 'Yes. Fuck off, Norway.' Then ran off laughing.

8   Turned up for England training the morning after then manager Bobby Robson had called him 'daft as a brush' with a brush sticking out of his sock.

9   When asked for a footballing comment while at Lazio, burped enthusiastically into a TV microphone.

10 Decided it would be a great idea to have massive hair extensions. Looked a fool and had them taken out a day later.

11 After paying for ex-wife Sheryl's breast implants, sent flowers to the hospital after the operation addressed to 'Dolly Parton'.

12 Astounded commuters in London by jumping on a double-decker in London's Piccadilly Circus and asking if he could have a drive. The bus driver said yes, and the passengers thoroughly enjoyed Gazza's impromptu appearance.

13 Sent a rose to the Wimbledon dressing room for Vinnie Jones after the infamous ball-squeezing incident. Got a toilet brush in return.

14 Set up best mate Jimmy 'Five Bellies' Gardner with a 'girl' he knew to be a transvestite.

15 Has taken the piss out of refs constantly during his career. On one occasion he sniffed a hapless ref's armpit while he was holding his hand high to signal a free kick.

16 Undeterred by their frosty reactions, Gazza again tried to prove that refs have a sense of humour by yellow-carding the referee after the official had dropped his card during a Rangers v Hibs game. He was booked for his trouble.

17 While attempting to deflect the 'kebab controversy' which spelled the beginning of the end of his England career, assured reporters that his doner-munching antics following Middlesbrough's promotion to the Premiership would in no way affect his fitness before France 98. One reporter asked: 'What do you feel like now?' Back came the inevitable response: 'I feel like a kebab with onions.'

18 As an apprentice desperate to impress then Newcastle boss Jack Charlton, spent a week's money on fishing gear and begged the famous angler to give him a lesson. On arrival at the riverbank, Charlton promptly threw all but the rod out into the briny, then poured a bottle of Newcastle Brown into the water, dipped in the rod and within seconds was pulling out a whopper. Lesson over.

19 As a 'perk' of boot-cleaning duties during his apprenticeship, took Kevin Keegan's Golas home to show his mates. But left them on a Newcastle bus.

20 When playing for England against Belgium in Italia 90, ridiculed Enzo Scifo as he lay on the ground clutching his leg. Gazza thought he was play-acting, so did a mime of his own which involved hopping on one leg with his tongue lolling out.

21 His departure for the World Cup in 1990 was hampered by the fact he'd left his passport at home. An emotion Gazza wept at the check-in desk until a minion w despatched to bring it to the airport.

22 Celebrated his new-found hero status a from Italia 90 by wearing a huge pair boobs and stomach bearing the legend '

23 On meeting the president of Denmark's FA, pretended he could speak Danish. When invited to demonstrate, imitated *The Muppet Show*'s Swedish chef.

24 Conned Five Bellies into eating a mince pie after he'd scraped out the filling and replaced it with cat excrement.

25 Walked into the Middlesbrough canteen wearing nothing but his training socks and ordered lunch.

26 Paid £320 for a Mars bar in a newsagents in his home town of Dunston, then told the shop owner to spend the change on sweets for local kids.

27 While dining in the prestigious Bedford Arms Hotel in Woburn with a few of his Geordie mates, decided to place his erect member on the shoulder of a diner at the next table. Thinking someone had tapped him on the shoulder the gentleman turned his head only to have Gazza's helmet prod him in the cheek.

28 Took a documentary team to a beautiful Scottish cottage which he informed them was his new place, pretended he'd forgotten his key and knocked instead. When the door opened, told the befuddled housewife inside that he was doing a telly advert and wanted to know if she preferred Daz or Persil.

29 Crashed Middlesbrough's team bus at the club's training ground and caused £310,000 worth of damage.

30 While at Rangers, urinated over sleeping team-mate Richard Gough.

31 Handed £1000 over to Jimmy Five Bellies after betting that the burly boozer couldn't withstand a cigarette lighter's heat on the bridge of his nose for five seconds . . . Jimmy could. Twice.

32 After briefly giving up drinking, was advised to find a new interest. Picked bingo.

33 Bought a £1000 robot and programmed it to travel into

Jimmy Five Bellies' room at Gazza Towers and announce: 'Make a cup of tea, fat man.'

34 Was banned in advance from Liverpool's Cream nightclub within days of joining Everton, because the Evertonians who run the place wanted him to avoid temptation and stay fit.

35 Prepared for England matches during a hugely important tournament by playing marathon games of tennis in the scorching midday sun.

36 Thought it would be appropriate to wear a blue fright wig before the 1991 FA Cup final.

37 In his time, has agreed to dress as a Roman centurion, a clown, Oliver Hardy and Braveheart for photo opportunities.

38 While his Italia 90 team-mate was the hero of Hillsborough, marched into a Sheffield barber shop and demanded 'a Waddle cut'.

39 When Gazza signed for Spurs in 1988, he came down to finalise the deal with a bunch of his Geordie mates. They took over the posh hotel in Hadley Wood where Spurs were footing the bill and wreaked havoc. Gazza met then chairman Irving Scholar and began talks by saying, 'We'd like to thank you for the best three days of our lives.'

40 Was asked to leave West Lodge Park hotel in London after guests were treated to the sight of a naked Five Bellies swimming across the fish pond.

41 On his first night in Rome after signing for Lazio, gave his minder the slip, put his shoes by an open window and hid in a cupboard. The minder thought he'd committed suicide.

42 Recorded a video message for a corporate party and signed off with a cheery 'Happy Christmas, you fucking wankers'.

43 Greeted reporters in Rome by standing up, asking for silence, then farting at ear-splitting volume.

44 Told an interviewer that he was so superstitious about the number 13 that he couldn't ever bear to see the numbers 4 and 9 together. Oddly, the combination of 5 and 8 was deemed OK.

45 Shredded England team-mate Dennis Wise's Armani suit 'for a laugh'.

46 While staying at a Scottish hotel, drove across its golf course in his four-wheel drive Jeep.

47 While his reputation preceded him in Italy, the English language did not. Hence, his Lazio debut was marked by a banner which read: 'Gazza's Boys Are Here . . . Shake Women And Drink Beer.'

48 Conversely, rival Italian supporters once hailed him with a banner which stated bluntly: 'Paul Gazza, You Are Fat Poofta.'

49 After being sent off while playing for Lazio, shook hands with virtually every member of the Genoa side.

50 While staying in a New Zealand hotel, was told there was no bacon for breakfast. Replied, 'What, all the sheep in this country and there's no bloody bacon?'

True or False?

Numbers 1–3: True
4: Rubbish
5–10: True
11: Bollocks
12–13: True
14: True – but it was John Brotherton not Jimmy
15–16: True
17. Cobblers
18: Half true – he threw my rods in the river, saying they were
   rubbish
19: True
20: True
21: True – the minion was Jimmy
22: True
23: Total fiction
24: True – but it was even worse. It was my own shit. My other
   friend Cyril Martin ate one as well.
25: True
26: Sounds like me, but not true
27: False
28: True
29: True, but the damage was only £14,000
30: Utter lie
31–33: True
34: Rubbish
35–40: All true
41: Not true, but I did similar things
42: True
43: False
44: True
45–46: Bollocks
47: The banner I saw said 'Shag'
48: True
49: Almost true – I shook hands with the ref and two players
50: Boring story, not at all funny, and total bollocks

THE GAZZA FILE

Everything you wanted to know and couldn't find in
the match-day programme. I used to enjoy those
surveys, when I just started football, the ones in football programmes and comics, about a player's
favourite meal, favourite pop group. I always loved
reading them. I also enjoy filling in forms.
So here goes . . .

1 Basic Facts
Born: 27 May 1967, Gateshead
Father's job: hod-carrier
Siblings: two sisters, Anna and Lindsay; one brother, Carl
Education: two CSE passes
Marriage: to Sheryl, 1996; divorced 1998
Children: son Regan, b. 1996; two stepchildren, Bianca b.
   1986 and Mason b. 1989
Height: 5ft 9in
Weight: normally 11 stone 10lbs, but have been 14 stone
   – don't talk about it

2 Personal
House: none. Lived in hotels or flats since 1998
Car: at present, none. Gave away last one to Dad in 2002
   when drunk, a Mercedes soft-top worth £70,000
Motorbikes: did have nine Harley-Davidsons, now only two
Last holiday: Dubai

Hobbies, interests: golf, tennis, fishing
Newspapers: *News of the World, Mirror, Sun, Star*

Politics: what did you vote at last election?
    Didn't vote, have never voted. I have given my family a
    lot of money and houses, and yet they still voted
    Labour at the last election. That surprised me. I
    thought they would have become Tory, getting all that
    for nothing. I suppose my heart is still Labour.

Do you follow current events?
    No, just the tennis.

Do you do now or have you ever done any housework?
    When I was young, living at home, I did a lot of jobs
    in the house, cos we had to, with me mam trying to
    do four jobs to keep us going. When I was married, I
    did now and again load the dishwasher.

Can you cook?
    I can do toast and switch on a microwave.

*When your son Regan was a baby, did you change his
nappy?*
    About once, for a photograph. In hospital once, when
    he had the shits, I pretended to Shel I'd changed him,
    but it was the nurse.

Religion: were you baptised – if so, what church?
    Church of England, but I never go.

Do you believe in God?
    Yes.

3 Favourite Things

Favourite food
    At age eighteen, steak sandwich; today, nice bit of
    salmon.

Favourite drink
At eighteen, lager; today, Diet Coke or Red Bull.

When did you last have an alcoholic drink?
April 2003. I was in China, depressed, and drank a
bottle of whisky in my hotel room. It was after that I
went to the clinic in Arizona.

Favourite sweets
At eighteen, Galaxy; today, wine gums.

Do you smoke? If so, how many, what kind?
I didn't start till I was twenty-eight, and it was Paul
Ince at Euro 96 that got me going. I still smoke about
twenty a day to calm my nerves. Regal King Size,
they're very popular in Newcastle.

Favourite TV programmes
Any sports, especially tennis. I find it hard to watch
football. I'd rather be playing.

Favourite music, group
Elvis, my all-time favourite. I've got his autograph, which
I swapped with someone for an England shirt. I also like
Phil Collins and Genesis.

Favourite clothes and designer
Armani suits, Armani jeans.

Favourite film stars
Male, Gene Hackman; female, Julia Roberts.

Last film seen
Gladiator. It was brilliant.

Last book read, or books currently by your bedside
Books about anxiety and depression – how many do
you want? They're mainly American. *Anxiety and Panic
Attacks – their cause and cure* by Robert Handley and
Pauline Neff; *Understanding Obsessions and Compulsions*

by Dr Frank Tallis; *Coping with Anxiety and Depression* by Shirley Trickett; *How to Stop Worrying* by Frank Tallis; *How to Heal Depression* by Harold Bloomfield; *Daily Reflections* by Members of Alcoholics Anonymous.

Last time you cried
Two weeks ago.

4 Football

Has football for you been a job, a career, a profession, a way of life? How would you describe it?
It's a profession, because you get paid and thousands pay to watch you. You have to be at your physical peak to play it.

Any pre-match rituals, superstitions?
Too many to list, but if I won, I kept the same shin-pads for the next game. If we lost, I threw them away and got new ones.

In order of importance, which of these elements do you think are necessary for success in football: coaching, confidence, luck, natural talent, perseverance, personality, physical toughness, any others?
I'd put confidence first, followed by luck. Obviously you need natural talent, but all top pros have that, to have got that far. And there's a lot of it around, and much of it goes nowhere. So I'm putting natural talent third in importance. After that I'd list physical toughness, personality, perseverance, coaching.

From your experience in many dressing rooms, at home and abroad, what would you say were the main topics of conversation, apart from football: cars, clothes, current events, family, jokes and stories, last night's TV, manager and staff, money, music, sex and girls?

Girls and sex first, followed by cars, jokes and funny stories, last night's TV, manager and staff, family, money, current events.

In your experience, have you ever come across a gay player – or one assumed to be gay?
No.

Would you say footballers are prejudiced against homosexuals?
No.

Is there any racism in football, in the dressing room?
None, but you hear it from some crowds.

Would you say footballers were clever, smart, streetwise, cunning, simple, naive – or can you not generalise because they come in all types?
I would say almost all footballers are streetwise. After that, they are all different. You do get clever ones. A few are sly and back-stabbing, which is not on your list.

When playing in Italy, and in Scotland, did you feel any prejudice against you, for being English?
None at all.

Do you get as much fun and pleasure out of playing football today as you did, say, at eighteen?
There was more fun when I was younger, without any tension.

Would you like to stay in football?
I'd like to be a coach and then a manager. By now, I must know most of the tricks players try. I did most of them.

If you don't manage a job in football, then what?
Dunno. Might buy a trout farm and run it, or a pub

and let Jimmy manage it. Or I might go to Australia and open some Gazza soccer coaching schools.

If you hadn't been a player, what do you think you would be doing today?
A joiner. I once made me mam a table – and it didn't fall to pieces.

Your career, would you say it has been brilliant/very good/good/OK/could have been better?
Brilliant, no question.

Have you saved enough never to have to work again?
I have saved something, but I now need to invest it properly.

Do you think today's players are overpaid?
If a team like Chelsea has got all this money, and want to offer you a fortune to join them, then good luck to you. But in the lower divisions, players can work just as hard, try as much, and yet get very badly paid. I feel sorry for them.

When and where were you happiest, as a player, as a person?
As a player I loved being at Rangers, everything to do with it. I also loved being at Spurs. As a person, I was happiest between the ages of sixteen and eighteen when football had not yet become a job but was something I did for fun and had no worries.

Which player did you admire as a boy?
Cruyff.

Who were the best players you ever played with or against?
Bryan Robson, then Waddle and Beardsley.

Of all the clubs you played for, which had the best atmosphere?

Rangers, for two reasons. The banter in the dressing room was great, the crowd was always brilliant and supportive. Lazio had a good crowd, very passionate, but the crowd I enjoyed hearing best of all was Newcastle's when I was young and first started.

Which club had the best training facilities?
Middlesbrough, by a long way. It's state of the art, the best facilities I've seen anywhere. The saunas were amazing, the gym top class, the players' restaurant was like something in the West End.

Which managers/coaches have you personally enjoyed most?
Terry Venables, Walter Smith.

Which of your goals still stick in your memory?
The header for Lazio against Roma in the Rome derby. A hat-trick I scored for Rangers. A free kick for Spurs against Arsenal which got us to the FA Cup final.

Of today's younger players, who do you admire?
Beckham, of course, not just his football but how he has handled the media and his commercial work. I buggered up all that. I always seemed to be at war with them.

Which club's results do you look for first?
Newcastle, followed by Rangers, Spurs, Everton.

Which English club do you admire most today?
Manchester United.

Which well-known people, non-footballers, have you enjoyed meeting in your life?
Phil Collins.

What would you say was your best quality, as a person, as a player?

As a person, I like to think I'm easy-going, fun to be with. As a player, I'm a winner. I'd go through a brick wall for the team.

What about your worst qualities?
As a player, making crazy tackles. As a person, being too spontaneous. That's always when I've let myself down.

INDEX

Paul) 40, 69, 82, 90, 94, 112; v
Birmingham City 81; v Boston
United 451; v Derby County 95;
v Everton 79, 366; v Ipswich
Town 71; v Liverpool 78; v
Manchester United 77, 79; v
Middlesbrough 348-9; v Norwich
City 87; v Oxford United 78; v
QPR 72-3; v Southampton 76-7;
v Sunderland 72; v Tottenham
Hotspur 75, 77, 90, 111; v West
Ham United 89-90, 96-7; v
Wimbledon 91-4
News of the World newspaper 218,
484
Noble, David 452-3
Norway 232, 233-4, 508
Norwich City 87
Nottingham Forest 186-8, 347-8
Notts County 174

Observer newspaper 460
Owen, Michael 445
Oxford United 78

Parker, Garry 187
Parker, Paul 138
Parma 206
Paul Gascoigne Promotions 156
Pearce, Stuart 127, 149, 150, 187,
190, 270, 274, 437
Pele 27, 405
Persaud, Raj 388
Petric, Gordan 250
Philip, Prince, Duke of Edinburgh
162
Platini, Michel 206
Platt, David ('Platty') 97, 126, 136,
137, 144-5, 149, 212, 234, 274
Pleat, David 339
Plymouth Argyle 365
Poland 120, 231
Portsmouth 174

Portugal (Under-21) 86
Powell, Jeff 286
Pringle, Alfie 54, 60
Pringle, Gail 54, 58, 60, 75, 108,
120, 140, 179
Priory (hospital) 343-6, 386

QPR (Queens Park Rangers) 72-3
Queens Park Rangers (QPR) 72-3

Ramsey, Alf 445
Rangers (for PG's involvement *see
under* Gascoigne, Paul) 252-3,
286, 298, 299, 408; v Aberdeen
253; v Ajax 281; v Anorthosis
252; v Celtic 252, 295-6; v
Dundee United 298; v Galatasaray
251; v Hearts 253, 286; v Hibs
300; v Juventus 252-3; v Morton
252; v Motherwell 280; v Steaua
Bucharest 251; v Strasbourg 298
Raynor, Paul 450
Redheugh Boys' Club 27, 37, 38
Redknapp, Jamie 268
Reeves, Nancy 457
Regalia, Carlo 191
Reid, Peter 79
Reilly, George 72
Republic of Ireland 129, 133, 231-2
Ricard, Hamilton 306
Rijkaard, Frank 133, 207
Robson, Bobby 38, 456; England
manager 70, 91, 115, 116, 118,
119, 121, 122, 123, 125-7, 128,
129, 134, 135, 136, 140, 141-3,
144, 145-6, 147, 150, 231, 276,
445, 447
Robson, Bryan: Manchester United
79, 96; England (player and staff)
116, 125, 134-6, 265-6, 267, 323,
403; Middlesbrough manager 305,
306, 315, 336, 338, 340, 342-3,
346, 348, 351, 361, 366

PICTURE CREDITS

Credits are listed according to the order the pictures appear on each page, left to right, top to bottom.
'PG' denotes photographs belonging to Paul Gascoigne or his family.

Section 1
Page 1: North News; **page 2**: PG, PG, PG, North News; **page 3**: North News, PG, PG; **page 4**: PG, PG, Hunter Davies, North News; **page 5**: PG, PG, Foto Felici; **page 6**: Rex Features, Hello! Syndication; **page 7**: Hello! Syndication, Hello! Syndication; **page 8**: PG, PG, Gemini Photography.

Section 2
Page 1: mirrorpix.com; **page 2**: PG, Action Images, courtesy of Hunter Davies; **page 3**: Popperfoto, North News;

page 4: Popperfoto, mirrorpix.com, Action Images, Empics;
page 5: mirrorpix.com, PG, Popperfoto, Popperfoto;
page 6: mirrorpix.com, Rex Features, Popperfoto, Popperfoto;
page 7: Empics, Action Images, Action Images; page 8: mirrorpix.com, Popperfoto.

Section 3

Page 1: Getty Images; Page 2: Rex Features, Empics;
Page 3: Hunter Davies, Empics, Rex Features, TopFoto.co.uk;
Pages 4–7: Path to Recovery; Page 8: Marcus Edwards at Pendleton Events, Rex Features, Empics.

Section 4

Page 1: Rex Features; page 2: Action Images,
mirrorpix.com; page 3: mirrorpix.com, mirrorpix.com,
Popperfoto; page 4: mirrorpix.com; page 5: mirrorpix.com;
page 6: Action Images, Empics, mirrorpix.com; page 7:
Popperfoto, Action Images; page 8: Action Images, Empics.

Section 5

Page 1: Action Images; page 2: Rex Features, Julian
Brannigan, Rex Features, mirrorpix.com, Action Images,
Rex Features, Rex Features, Colorsport, Popperfoto; page 3:
Popperfoto, Action Images, Action Images; page 4: PG,
PG, PG, PA Photos; page 5: PG, North News, Action
Images; page 6: Action Images, TopFoto.co.uk,
mirrorpix.com, Action Images; page 7: PG, Rex Features,
mirrorpix.com; page 8: Getty Images, PA Photos, PG.